Study and Critical Thinking Skills in College

THIRD EDITION

Kathleen T. McWhorter
Niagara County Community College

HarperCollinsCollegePublishers

Acquisitions Editor: Ellen Schatz
Developmental Editor: Susan Messer
Project Coordination and Text Design: Ruttle, Shaw & Wetherill, Inc.
Cover Designer: Kay Petronio
Electronic Production Manager: Angel Gonzalez
Manufacturing Manager: Willie Lane
Electronic Page Makeup: Ruttle, Shaw & Wetherill, Inc.
Printer and Binder: RR Donnelly & Sons Company
Cover Printer: The Lehigh Press, Inc.

Study and Critical Thinking Skills in College, Third Edition

Library of Congress Cataloging-in-Publication Data

McWhorter, Kathleen T.
    Study and critical thinking skills in college / Kathleen T.
  McWhorter. —3rd ed.
        p.   cm.
    Rev. ed. of: Study and thinking skills in college. c1992.
    Includes bibliographical references (p.   ) and index.
    ISBN 0-673-99496-1 (student ed.). —ISBN 0-673-99503-8
  (instructor's ed.)
    1. Study skills.   2. Thought and thinking.   3. Critical thinking.
  I. McWhorter, Kathleen T.   Study and thinking skills in college.
  II. Title.
  LB2395.M445   1995   95-3935
  378.1'7028'12—dc20   CIP

    98   9 8 7 6 5

Contents

PART 5

Exams: Thinking Under Pressure   303

PART 6

Writing: A Vehicle for Thinking   355

❑ ❑ ❑ *Preface*

Over the past several decades, educators have become increasingly aware of the need to teach students how to learn and study. Many two- and four-year colleges offer learning and study skills courses, "how to study" manuals are readily available, and even prestigious graduate and professional schools provide instructional or tutorial services in study skills. The field of study skills, once relatively unknown, now enjoys wide acceptance and academic legitimacy.

Another relatively new discipline—the field of critical thinking skills—has begun to experience similar growth and acceptance. Critical thinking skills have become an important part of the college curriculum, and many institutions include critical thinking skills requirements as part of their general education programs. Consequently, instruction in critical thinking skills has become a rapidly expanding frontier within higher education.

Although these two fields, study skills and critical thinking, have evolved independently of each other, they are integrally connected. This text represents a unique endeavor: to integrate study skills and critical reading and to provide a unified instructional sequence for skills development.

GOALS

Study and Critical Thinking Skills in College was written to enable students to become academically competitive. It achieves the following goals:

Active Learning

The primary purpose of the text is to approach study as an active thinking process. For many students, learning is a passive assimilation process, and their goal is to acquire as many facts and as much information as possible. This book encourages students to take an active role in learning by thinking critically about and interacting with text and lecture material. It focuses on sorting, interpreting, synthesizing, and evaluating ideas and information. It provides students with a repertoire of active study and thinking strategies that will enable them to handle college course work confidently and effectively.

Learning How to Learn

A basic assumption of this work is that students can learn how to learn and can be taught to think critically. The second major purpose of this book, then, is to teach specific learning and thinking strategies. Learning is approached as a highly versatile and adaptive process. Students are encouraged to analyze learning tasks and to choose appropriate strategies that suit the nature of the task and their prior knowledge and experience. Critical thinking is presented as an integral part of all learning and study tasks. Students are also encouraged to analyze the level of thinking each learning task requires and to adapt their approaches accordingly.

Attitudes Toward Learning

While a major emphasis is on cognitive skills, skills in the affective and behavioral domains that shape and control learning are also introduced. Developing positive attitudes toward learning, taking charge and accepting responsibility for one's own learning, and using effective organizational and time-management skills are discussed.

Metacognitive Skills

The final purpose of this book is to apply current research findings in the areas of metacognition, schema theory, and writing as learning. Metacognitive strategies are built into specific learning and study techniques. Academic thought patterns, emphasized throughout, function as schema that provide students with overriding concepts or blueprints with which to organize text, research, and lecture material, and to approach assignments, exams, and term papers. Writing as a learning process is also incorporated into various study and review techniques.

CONTENT OVERVIEW

The text presents a unique integration of study and critical thinking skills. Study and learning are approached as cognitive processes that require various levels and types of thinking. Students are taught to become active learners by analyzing tasks, selecting appropriate learning strategies, and monitoring and revising their strategies to suit the nature of the tasks. Metacognition, the learner's awareness and control over his or her cognitive processes, is, then, a central focus here. A secondary focus is the use of academic thought patterns as thinking and organizing strategies, providing students with a thread that can tie together seemingly divergent courses.

Part One provides an introduction to college learning and thinking and establishes the basic premises and principles around which the text is developed. This organization emphasizes active thinking and learning and acceptance of responsibility for one's own learning. Specific strategies for success as well as organizational and time-management skills are presented.

Part Two emphasizes basic learning and critical thinking strategies. It presents a systematic approach to learning and discusses principles of learning and memory and their application to academic tasks. Critical thinking, problem-solving, and decision-making skills are presented, with an emphasis on application within an academic environment.

Part Three presents skills and strategies for mastering course content. The section begins with a chapter on academic patterns of thought, emphasizing their predominance and use across various academic disciplines. The remaining chapters discuss techniques and strategies for lecture notetaking, textbook reading and study, and organization and synthesis of course content, and discuss academic thought patterns as organizing features.

Part Four focuses on the application of skills within various academic disciplines. The importance of learning specialized and technical vocabulary is stressed, and specific learning strategies are described. Techniques for approaching the social sciences, natural sciences, mathematics, arts and humanities, and career fields are discussed.

Part Five is devoted to skills and strategies needed in preparing for and taking exams. Students learn to organize their review, use thematic study, and develop study strategies for specific academic disciplines.

Part Six discusses writing as a vehicle for generating and clarifying thought. Stages of the writing process are discussed, and an approach to analyzing written assignments is described. Various examples of term papers are presented, along with the kinds of thinking required to prepare each; guidelines for writing term papers are given.

These part divisions were designed to give the user of this text the greatest possible flexibility. The opening chapters provide a basic framework and introduction to study and critical thinking; the remaining units and chapters may be rearranged according to instructor preference. This flexible organization allows instructors to maximize their specific course objectives and to accommodate the needs of their students.

SPECIAL FEATURES

The following features significantly enhance the text's effectiveness as a motivational teaching tool:

❏ **Chapter Objectives.** Each chapter begins with a brief list of objectives that establishes its focus and provides students with purposes for reading. The objectives can also serve as a means of checking retention after reading the chapter.

❏ **Thinking Critically . . . About.** These boxed inserts relate critical thinking skills to chapter content and offer practical suggestions and tips for developing critical thinking skills.

❏ **In-Chapter Exercises.** Numerous exercises within each chapter provide students with opportunities to immediately apply and evaluate techniques. While the exercises take a variety of forms, their focus is the practical application of skills in realistic college course situations, and they often require the use of the students' own textbooks or course materials.

❏ **Class Activity.** Each chapter contains an exercise designed for group interaction. Its purpose is to promote collaborative learning, allowing students to view and learn from the thinking processes of other students.

❏ **Further Analysis.** Each chapter contains a practical reading-study problem that is an application of chapter content. Students are directed to analyze the situation and to offer possible solutions.

❏ **Further Reading.** A brief reference list is provided for each chapter. The references provide sources for further exploration of topics presented in the chapter.

❏ **Summary.** Each chapter ends with a summary intended to help the student consolidate and review chapter content.

❏ **Answer Key.** The Answer Key makes the text adaptable to self-instruction and offers immediate feedback to students as they complete practice exercises.

❏ **Instructor's Manual.** An Instructor's Manual provides many suggestions for using the text, including how to structure and organize the course and how to approach each section of the book. The manual contains a ten-item multiple-choice quiz for each chapter of the text.

CHANGES IN THE THIRD EDITION

The revision of *Study and Critical Thinking Skills in College* focused on strengthening the critical thinking component of the text. This was accomplished in two ways:

1. Boxed inserts called "Thinking Critically . . . About" were added to each chapter. Their purpose is to emphasize the connection between study and critical thinking while offering students practical, immediately usable tips.
2. The types of thinking skills discussed in Chapter 1 of the second edition were replaced with levels of thinking based on Bloom's taxonomy:knowledge, comprehension, application, analysis, synthesis, and evaluation. Throughout the book, students are encouraged to think, question, and respond at each of these levels.

Additional changes include updated material on library usage and current technology, expansion of the mapping section in Chapter 10, and updating of the Further Reference sections.

ACKNOWLEDGMENTS

I wish to acknowledge the contributions of my colleagues and reviewers, who provided valuable advice and suggestions:

Nancy Cannon, Cecil Community College
Barbara Smuckler, College of Mount St. Vincent
Helene Stapleton, Cayuga Community College
Deborah Irwin, Onondaga Community College
Jim Roth, Spokane Community College
Jayne Nightengale, Rhode Island College
Sue Burdette, Wichita State University

I am particularly indebted to Susan Messer, my developmental editor, for her patience, advice, and guidance and to Ellen Schatz for her support of this project.

Kathleen T. McWhorter

COLLEGE: A FOCUS ON LEARNING AND THINKING

College: Learning and Thinking

Strategies for Success

Learning the College System

Organizational and Time Management Skills

Problem-Solving and Decision-Making Strategies

1

Learning and Study: Strategies for Success

Learning Objectives

Discover what is expected in college

Take charge of your college career

Identify early warning signals of academic difficulty

Become an active learner

Recognize the importance of thinking skills to college success

---

You are now a college student. Reaching this point may have required years of hard work, preparation, and planning. Now that you are here, you are ready to begin the challenging, exciting tasks that college involves. At this point it is only natural for you to be wondering "How successful will I be?" or "How well will I be able to meet these new challenges?" The answers to these questions depend on how well you can use the major tools you will need throughout college: studying and critical thinking. The degree to which you sharpen and polish these skills will largely determine your success. Therefore, developing and refining your study and critical thinking skills are the primary purposes of this book. Before we consider specific techniques, it is helpful to know what college

3

learning involves. This chapter describes the new demands of college, offers numerous success strategies, teaches you *how* to learn, and shows you *how* to become an active, involved learner. It also introduces you to critical thinking skills and shows their importance to college success.

COPING WITH NEW DEMANDS AND EXPECTATIONS

College is a unique learning experience. Whether you have just completed high school or are returning to college with a variety of work experiences or family responsibilities, you will face new demands and expectations in college. The following section discusses how to cope with these demands.

Set Your Own Operating Rules

College is very different from lower levels of education and from jobs you may have held because it imposes few clear limits, rules, or controls. There are no defined work hours except for classes; your time is your own. Often, you face no threats or penalties for missing classes or failing to complete assignments. You do *what* you want, *when* you want, *if* you want to at all. For many students, the lack of structure requires some adjustment; at first, it is often confusing. Some students feel they should spend all their free time studying; others put off study or never quite find the right time for study.

One of the best ways to handle this flexibility is to establish your own set of operating rules. For example, you might decide to limit yourself to two absences in each course. Here are examples of rules successful students have set for themselves:

- ❏ Study at least three hours each day or evening.
- ❏ Start studying for a major examination at least a week ahead.
- ❏ Complete all homework assignments regardless of whether you get credit for them.
- ❏ Make review a part of each study session.
- ❏ Read all assigned chapters *before* the class in which they will be discussed.

You may feel more committed to the rules you set if you write them down and post them above your desk as a constant reminder.

Take Responsibility for Your Own Learning

In college, learning is completely up to you. Professors function only as guides. They define and explain what is to be learned, but *you* do the learning. Class time is far shorter than in high school; there is not enough time to provide numerous drills, practices, and reviews of factual course content. College class time is used primarily to introduce what is to be learned, to provoke thought, and to discuss ideas. Instructors expect you to learn the material and to be prepared to discuss it in class. When, where, and how you learn are your decisions.

The course textbook is your main source for learning in each subject. Instructors expect you to read the text independently. Often, on the first day of class, instructors distribute a course syllabus, outline, or set of requirements that lists the topics to be covered each week and corresponding textbook chapters.

Develop New Approaches to Learning

College demands new attitudes and approaches toward learning.

Focus on Concepts

Each course you take will seem to have endless facts, statistics, dates, definitions, formulas, rules, and principles to learn. It is easy, then, to become a robot learner—absorbing information from texts and lectures, then spewing it automatically out on exams and quizzes. Actually, factual information is only a starting point, a base from which to approach the real content of a course. Most college instructors expect you to go beyond facts to analysis: to consider what the collection of facts and details *means*. Many students "can't see the forest for the trees." They fail to see the larger, overriding concepts of their courses because they get caught up in specifics. Too concerned with memorizing information, they fail to ask "Why do I need to know this?" "Why is this important?" or "What principle or trend does this illustrate?" Here are a few examples of details from a course in American government and the more important trend, concept, or principle they represent:

❏ ❏ ❏

Topic	Facts	Importance
Voting Rights Act of 1965	Federal registrars were sent to southern states to protect blacks' right to vote.	This was the beginning of equality in voter registration.
Supreme Court case: Roe v. *Wade*	Court ruling forbade state control over abortion in first trimester of pregnancy; permitted states to limit abortions to protect the mother's health in the second trimester; permitted states to protect fetus in the third trimester.	Established policy on abortions; opened questions of "right to privacy" and "right to life."

❏ ❏ ❏

EXERCISE 1-1

Directions:
Choose one of your textbooks and turn to a section of a chapter you have already read. List six consecutive headings that appear in that text. After each heading, explain why each topic is important. In other words, indicate its significance, the concept or principle it illustrates.

Focus on Ideas, Not Right Answers

Through previous schooling, many students have come to expect their answers to be either right or wrong. They assume that learning is limited to a collection of facts and that their mastery of the course is measured by the number of right answers they have learned. When faced with an essay question such as the following, they become distraught:

> Defend or criticize the arguments that are offered in favor of legalized abortion. Refer to any readings you have done.

You can see that there is not *one* right answer; you can either defend the argument or criticize it. Instead, the instructor who asks this question expects you to think and to provide a reasoned, logical, consistent response using information acquired through readings. Here are a few more examples of questions for which there are no single correct answers:

- ❏ Do animals think?
- ❏ Would you be willing to reduce your standard of living by 15 percent if the United States could thereby eliminate poverty? Defend your response.
- ❏ Imagine a society in which everyone has exactly the same income. You are the manager of an industrial plant. What plans, policies, or programs would you implement that would motivate your employees to work?
- ❏ Is the primary purpose of an artist to represent his or her own feelings?

EXERCISE 1-2

Directions:
Compose a list of five questions for which there are no single correct answers. Leaf through a textbook, magazine, or newspaper for ideas.

Think About and React to Course Content

One professor of literature opens every class with the same question: "What is the significance of the short story (or poem, essay) that you read for today?" After asking the question, he says nothing else. He has been known to sit patiently for an entire 50 minutes waiting for someone in the class to respond. If no one responds, he ends the session by saying the next class meeting will open with the same question and assures the class he will be equally patient. This professor expects his students to read, think about, and be prepared to discuss the assignment.

While not all instructors conduct their classes this way, many have the same expectations. They expect and encourage their students to think and react to readings, lectures, and class discussions, as well as to questions posed in class. You will find that many professors focus and direct your learning rather than present a body of knowledge.

Evaluate New Ideas

Throughout college you will continually encounter new ideas; you will agree with some and disagree with others. Don't make the mistake of accepting or rejecting a new idea, however, until you have really explored

❑ ❑ ❑
Thinking Critically . . . About Course Content

To become an active learner, get in the habit of asking critical questions. Critical questions are questions that help you analyze and evaluate what and how you are learning. As you work through this book, you will learn to ask many critical questions. Here are a few to help you get started:

- Why was this material assigned?
- What am I supposed to learn from this assignment?
- How does this assignment relate to today's class lecture?
- What is the best way to learn this information?
- How will I know I have learned the material?
- What levels of thinking does this assignment or exam require?

it and have considered its assumptions and implications. Ask questions such as these:

❏ What evidence is available in support of this idea?
❏ What opposing evidence is available?
❏ How does my personal experience relate to this idea?
❏ What additional information do I need in order to make a decision?

Considerable research has been conducted on readers' comprehension of ideas. Results of these studies indicate that comprehension is lower for ideas with which the reader disagrees. Readers seem to shut off attention or subconsciously block out information that conflicts with their beliefs or values. With this evidence in mind, you may need to devote additional effort to material on controversial issues or on values and beliefs about which you have strong feelings.

TAKING CHARGE

Research studies suggest that people who make plans and decisions are more successful than those who do not. People without definite plans and goals drift through life passively, letting things happen and allowing others to control their lives. Active decision makers, on the other hand, know what they want and plan strategies to obtain it. Here's how to take charge.

Accept Responsibility for Grades

Certainly you have heard comments such as "Dr. Smith only gave me a B on my last paper" or "I got a C on my first lab report." Students often think of grades as rewards that teachers give to students. Thinking this way is avoiding responsibility, blaming the instructor instead of owning up to the fact that a paper or exam failed to meet the standards set by the instructor. Actually, grades are measures of how thoroughly your instructors feel you have read, prepared, and learned. When you receive a grade, analyze how and why you received it, identifying your strengths and weaknesses.

Avoid Shifting the Blame

Be honest; you will not always earn the grades you want and you will not always score as well as you expect to on every exam. Try to avoid making excuses and blaming others. If you fail an exam, it is easy to say that the questions were too detailed, that the exam covered material not emphasized in class, or that you did not study for it because you were upset about a recent argument with a friend. The fact is that you did not *earn* a passing grade. Analyze what you could have done to improve that grade, and put this to work in preparing for the next exam.

Don't Make Excuses

Studying is not easy; it requires time and conscious effort. Although the remainder of this book will show you many valuable shortcuts, studying is often a demanding, challenging task. Try not to make it more difficult than it really is by avoiding it. Some students avoid studying by following a variety of escape routes. Here are a few common ones:

- ❏ I can't study tonight because I promised to drive my sister to the mall.
- ❏ I can't study for my physics test because the dorm is too noisy.
- ❏ I can't finish reading my psychology assignment because the chapter is boring.
- ❏ I didn't finish writing my computer program because I fell asleep.

Do any of these excuses sound familiar? Each is a means of escaping the task at hand.

If you find yourself making excuses to avoid studying, step back and analyze the problem. Consider possible causes and solutions (see Chapter 4: Problem Solving). For example, if the dorm is too noisy to study, could you study at a different time or leave and find a new place? More likely, however, the problem is that you really did not want to study. When you are just not in the mood to study, be honest and admit you don't want to study. Before you quit and go on to something else, make a definite commitment to finish the assignment later; be specific about when and where. Postponing study may be better than avoiding it completely, but bear in mind that it probably will not be much easier after it has been postponed.

EXERCISE 1-3

Directions:

Analyze your past study performance by answering the following two questions honestly.

1. What excuses have you used to avoid study?
2. Whom have you blamed when you could not study or did not earn the grade you expected?

Develop a Positive Academic Self-Image

Most students enter college with a rigid, narrowly defined academic self-image. They make choices and decisions on an image they express with comments like these:

"I'm not good with math."
"I've never done well with writing."
"If I have to speak in front of a group, forget it."

If you think you are weak in math, then majoring in accounting may not be a good idea. However, avoiding all courses that involve mathematics or calculations is not realistic. In almost any job, you will sooner or later need to work with numbers. Potential employers will look for and expect at least minimum competency.

Work on expanding and modifying your academic image by taking courses (elect a Pass/Fail grade, if you are worried about grades) to strengthen your weaknesses and to acquire basic competencies in a variety of areas. Decide to become computer literate, even if it is not required in your curriculum. An elective course in public speaking will boost your confidence in your ability to present yourself effectively. Think of improving your image as building a marketable package of skills that will place you in a competitive position to land that all-important first job after graduation.

EXERCISE 1-4

Directions:
Define your current academic image by identifying your areas of strengths and weaknesses. Chart a course of action to address each weakness.

EARLY WARNING SIGNALS OF ACADEMIC DIFFICULTY

A major part of getting ahead academically and staying there is monitoring your progress in each course and then adjusting your study strategies accordingly. In courses with weekly quizzes or frequent assignments, it is easy to assess how well you are doing. In other courses, knowing how well you are doing is more difficult. Some instructors give only two or three exams per semester; other may require only a term paper and a final exam. Such courses offer no grades during the term for you to determine if you are doing well; instead, you will have to be alert for the early warning signals of academic difficulty.

Questions That Predict Academic Difficulty

Here are some questions that will indicate whether you are on the right track in a course.

Are you falling behind on assignments? Do you put off studying by saying "I'll wait until this weekend to work on calculus; then I'll have enough time to really concentrate on straightening this out"? Meanwhile, you fall further behind as the week goes by. It is human nature to do what is pleasant and rewarding and to avoid what is unpleasant and difficult. If you are behind on assignments, you may be avoiding them because they are difficult and unrewarding. This is a signal that something may be going wrong with the course.

Have you missed several classes recently? Most instructors agree that student attendance is a good predictor of success in a course; students who attend class regularly tend to earn good grades. If you have missed several classes in a course without a legitimate reason for doing so, this may be another form of avoidance. It isn't pleasant to attend a class for which you are not confident and well prepared; cutting class is an avoidance technique.

Do you feel lost or confused in any course?   If you are having trouble making sense of what the instructor is doing day to day or cannot see how various topics and assignments fit together, you may be in academic difficulty. The course may be at the wrong level for your current academic background or you may lack an overview or perspective on the course.

Are you relying heavily on a friend for help in completing assignments?   Depending regularly on a classmate for help suggests that you are not able to handle the course alone. Remember, your friend won't be much help when it comes to the final exam.

Do you feel restless and listless, as if something is wrong but you're not sure what it is?   If you feel anxious and depressed, most likely something is wrong. Look for patterns and discover where and when you feel this way.

Do you feel constantly tired or spent a lot of time sleeping?   Overtiredness may be a reaction to a general feeling of stress and pressure. It, too, may be a signal that something is wrong. Find out what it is.

Are you following one or more "escape routes"?   Escape routes start with the phrase "I can't study because . . . ." They end with such excuses as "My roommate bothers me" or "My job is too tiring." Regardless of the exact reason, this type of reasoning is a way to avoid a difficult or unrewarding situation.

How to Handle Academic Problems

If you are like many college students, discovering and admitting that you are having trouble with a course is difficult and traumatic. The possibility that you may fail a course is a shock and a threat to your self-image. "Could this really be happening to me?" is a very common feeling. Here is some advice to follow if you should have this feeling.

Maintain your self-confidence.   Don't lose your confidence just because you are having trouble with one course. Don't start thinking differently about yourself; you've always been a good student and you still are.

Remember that you are not alone.   The first semester of college is the most difficult one for most students. A review of students' grade point averages throughout their college experience confirms this. The first semester or quarter grades are the lowest; grades gradually rise as students develop skill and acquire experience in handling college courses. Keep on striving and you will improve.

Take immediate action.   As soon as you suspect you are having trouble in a course, take immediate action. Do not let things slide and hope they will improve on their own; they seldom do. In most cases the longer you wait, the farther behind you fall and the more difficult it will be to catch up.

Talk with your instructor.   Before things get too bad, talk with your instructor. Most instructors have office hours each week, times when they are available to talk with students. When you visit your instructor, try to define topics, areas, or skills that are troublesome. Have specific questions in mind. State the steps you have already taken and ask for advice. Your instructor may recommend additional reading to fill in gaps in your background knowledge or suggest a new approach to follow as you read and study.

Explore sources of help.   Many colleges and universities have sources of academic assistance. Find out if there is an Academic Development Center or Learning Center on your campus. Such centers offer brush-up courses and sponsor peer tutoring programs for popular freshman courses. Check to see if the library or media center has videotapes, computer programs, or self-instructional workbooks that deal with the subject matter of your course. For a troublesome course, if free tutoring is not available, consider hiring an upperclass student as a tutor. Ask your instructor to recommend someone. Although this may be expensive, consider what you will lose if you fail and have to retake the course.

Consider withdrawing from the course.   If you and your instructor feel you cannot handle the course or if you have fallen so far behind that it is nearly impossible to catch up, consider withdrawing from the course. (Your college catalog explains policies and deadlines for course withdrawal.) While it is painful to admit that you were not able to handle the course, withdrawal will free your mind from anxiety and enable you to concentrate and do well with the remaining courses.

If you decide to withdraw from a required course and you must reregister for the course in a subsequent semester, consider taking the course from another instructor, whose approach and teaching style may work better for you. Since course withdrawal is an expensive option, use it only as a last resort.

ACTIVE VERSUS PASSIVE LEARNING

A freshman who had always thought of herself as a good student found herself getting low C's or D's on her first quizzes and exams. She was studying harder and spending more time but was not earning the grade she expected. After discussing the problems with her professors, she realized that, although she was studying, she was not studying *in the right way.* She was using the same study methods she had always used: She read and reread her text and notes and conscientiously completed all homework assignments. However, these methods were no longer effective for the kinds of learning expected by her instructors.

Her approach was essentially a passive one. She did what her instructors requested. She read what was assigned, completed assignments as required, and followed instructions carefully. To be more successful, this student needed to develop a more active approach. She should have interacted with the material she read: asked questions, sorted out what is important to learn, and decided how to learn it. Table 1-1 lists characteristics of the two types of learners. As you read through the list, determine which type you are.

Why Become an Active Learner?

Becoming an active learner is the key to getting the most from your college experience as well as the key to advancement in many careers and professions. For responsible positions, employers are interested in someone who can think and act without being told precisely what to do, and they are willing to pay for such self-direction. As preparation for an active career that you control, start now to develop skills that will be an asset to you throughout college and later in your career.

Think about the many types of learning you have experienced. How did you learn to ride a bike, make pizza, or play tennis? In each case, you

Table 1-1
CHARACTERISTICS OF PASSIVE AND ACTIVE LEARNERS

	Passive learners	*Active learners*
Class lectures	Write down what the instructor says	Decide what is important to write down
Textbook assignments	Read	Read, think, ask questions, try to connect ideas
Studying	Reread	Make outlines and study sheets, predict exam questions, look for trends and patterns.
Writing class assignments	Carefully follow the professor's instructions	Try to discover the significance of the assignment; look for the principles and concepts it illustrates
Writing term papers	Do what is expected to get a good grade	Try to expand your knowledge and experience with a topic and connect it to the course objective or content

learned by doing, by active participation. While much of what you will learn in college is not as physical as riding a bike or playing tennis, it still can be learned best through active participation. Studying and thinking are forms of participation, as are making notes, speaking up in class discussion, or reviewing chapters with a friend. Active involvement, then, is a key to effective learning. Throughout the text, you will learn strategies to promote active learning. Assess your active learning strategies by completing the questionnaire shown in Figure 1.1

Become a More Active Learner

When you study, you should be thinking and reacting to the material in front of you. Here is how to make it happen:

- **Ask questions about what you are reading**. You will find that this helps to focus your attention and improve your concentration.
- **Discover the purpose behind assignments**. Why might a sociology assignment require you to spend an hour at the monkey house of the local zoo, for example?
- **Try to see how each assignment fits with the rest of the course**. For instance, why does a section titled "Consumer Behavior" belong in a retailing textbook chapter titled "External Retail Restraints"?
- **Relate what you are learning to what you already know**. Use your background knowledge and personal experience. Connect a law in physics with how your car brakes work, for example.

EXERCISE 1-5

Directions:
Consider each of the following learning situations. Suggest ways to make each an active learning task.

1. Revising a paper for an English composition class
2. Reading an assignment in a current newsmagazine
3. Studying a diagram in a data processing textbook chapter
4. Preparing a review schedule for an upcoming major exam
5. Looking up synonyms in a thesaurus for a word for your sociology term paper
6. Reading the procedures in your chemistry lab manual for your next laboratory session

Figure 1-1
Rate Your Active Learning Strategies

Directions:

Respond to each of the following statements by checking "Always," "Sometimes," or "Never."

	Always	Sometimes	Never
1. I usually try to figure out *why* an assignment was given.	☐	☑	☐
2. While reading I am sorting important information.	☐	☑	☐
3. I think of questions as I read.	☐	☐	☑
4. I try to make connections between reading assignments and class lectures.	☐	☑	☐
5. I attempt to see how a newly assigned chapter in my text relates to the previously assigned one.	☐	☑	☐
6. I usually try to see how my instructor's class lectures fit together (relate to one another).	☐	☑	☐
7. I think about how the information I am reading can be used or applied.	☐	☑	☐
8. After writing a paper or completing an assignment, I think about what I learned from doing it.	☐	☑	☐
9. I review a returned exam to discover what types of questions I missed.	☐	☑	☐
10. I react to and evaluate what I am reading.	☐	☑	☐

THINKING: THE KEY TO COLLEGE SUCCESS

To be a successful student, you must be able to think about, reason with, and apply the information you have learned. Knowing a large number of facts and ideas is not as important as knowing how to use them—how to interpret, evaluate, and apply them to solve problems, create new ideas, or approach ideas in unique ways.

Thinking is an essential part of many academic activities. Common learning activities should involve a variety of thinking skills.

❏ ❏ ❏

Activity	Thinking Skills
Taking lecture notes	Identifying what is important, organizing information, working with various lecture styles, anticipating the speaker's thought patterns
Reviewing for an exam	Classifying and synthesizing information, making generalizations
Writing papers	Using thought patterns to organize ideas supporting a thesis, judging the relevance and importance of ideas

❏ ❏ ❏

The ability to think is a key ingredient of college success. Thinking is also a key ingredient of success in career and professional life. The ability to think clearly is a marketable, desirable quality sought by many employers. By polishing your thinking skills, you will be preparing not only for a successful college experience but also for success in the career you choose.

Levels of Thinking

To provide you with a better understanding of the variety of thinking skills involved in academic learning, a model is shown in Table 1-2. The model describes a hierarchy or progression of thinking skills. The model was developed by Benjamin Bloom in 1956, and it is still widely used among educators in many academic disciplines. You will notice that the levels move from basic literal understanding to more complex interpretive skills.

[handwritten: Taxonomy - x classification, where your naming the different levels of skill]

Table 1-2
LEVELS OF THINKING

Level	Description	Examples
Knowledge *(Recall)*	Recalling information; repeating information with no changes	Recalling dates; memorizing definitions
Comprehension *[handwritten: Interpretation]*	Understanding ideas; using rules and following directions	Explaining a law; recognizing what is important
Application	Applying knowledge to a new situation	Using knowledge of formulas to solve a new physics problem
Analysis	Seeing relationships; breaking information into parts; analyzing how things work	Comparing two poems by the same author
Synthesis	Putting ideas and information together in a unique way; creating something new	Designing a new computer program
Evaluation	Making judgments; assessing the value or worth of information	Evaluating the effectiveness of an argument opposing the death penalty

[handwritten: Translation - is taking info and letting it out, into your own words, by taking the ideas of someone else.]

Table 1-3
TEST ITEMS AND LEVELS OF THINKING

Test Item	Level of Thinking Required
Define "stereotype"	Knowledge
Explain how a stereotype can negatively affect a person	Comprehension
Give an example of a stereotype that is commonly held for a particular age group	Application
Study the two attached interviews. Which of the interviewers reveals a stereotypic attitude?	Analysis
Construct a set of guidelines that might be used to identify a stereotypic attitude	Synthesis
Evaluate the film shown in class, discussing how a stereotypic attitude was revealed and approached	Evaluation

When they write exams, most college instructors assume that you can operate at each of these levels. Table 1-3 shows a few items from an exam for a sociology course. Notice how the items demand different levels of thinking.

EXERCISE 1-6

Directions:

Here is an opportunity for you to operate at each level of thinking. Read the following excerpt from an interpersonal communication textbook and then answer the questions that follow. Use each level of thinking to understand and evaluate the excerpt.

Forms of Nonverbal Communication

Nonverbal elements, as already noted, sometimes work separately from verbal communication; that is, we may receive a nonverbal message without any words whatsoever. But usually the nonverbal domain provides a framework for the words we use. If we think of nonverbal communication as including all forms of message transmission *not* represented by word symbols, we can divide it into five broad categories: emblems, illustrators, affect displays, regulators, and adaptors.

In their early work in this area, Jurgen Ruesch and Weldon Kees outlined just three categories: sign, action, and object language. Sign language *includes gestures used in the place of words, numbers, or punctuation.* When an athlete raises his index finger to show his team is "Number One," he is using sign language. Action language *includes all those nonverbal movements not intended as signs.* Your way of walking, sitting, or eating may serve your personal needs, but they also make statements to those who see them. Object language *includes both the intentional and unintentional display of material things.* Your hairstyle, glasses, and jewelry reveal things about you, as do the books you carry, the car you drive, or the clothes you wear.[1]

1. *Knowledge*	What is the definition of *"object language"*?
2. *Comprehension*	What does object language include?
3. *Application*	Give an example of object language.
4. *Analysis*	Analyze and describe the object language used by a friend.

| 5. *Synthesis* | What objects are important means of communication among your group of friends? Rank them in order of importance. |
| 6. *Evaluation* | Do you agree or disagree with Ruesch and Kees's categorization of nonverbal communication? Explain your answer. |

The various categories of thinking are not distinct or mutually exclusive; they overlap. For example, notetaking during a lecture class involves comprehension, but it also involves analysis, synthesis, and evaluation. Taking an essay exam may involve, at one point or another, all six levels.

Throughout this book you will learn strategies for improving each level of thinking.

EXERCISE 1-7

Directions:

For each activity or situation described below, indicate the levels of thinking that are primarily involved.

1. Answering the following short answer test question: Give an example of defensive behavior
2. Solving a math problem
3. Taking notes on a college lecture
4. Translating into English a poem written in Spanish
5. Studying a famous painting for an art history course
6. Selecting a topic for a term paper in a criminal justice class
7. Revising a composition to make its thesis clearer and to improve its organization
8. Completing a biology lab in which you dissect an insect
9. Writing a computer program for a class assignment in a data processing course
10. Answering the following essay exam question: Most people would probably be outraged if someone sprayed them with poisonous air or fed them dangerous chemicals. In effect, this is what industrial polluters and many of their products are doing. Why, then, are people not outraged?[2]

SUMMARY

1. College is a unique learning experience with new demands and expectations.
2. Successful students

   - ❏ set their own operating rules
   - ❏ accept responsibility for their own learning
   - ❏ develop new approaches to learning
   - ❏ take charge of their college career
   - ❏ develop positive academic self-images
   - ❏ are alert for warning signals of academic problems
   - ❏ know how to take immediate action to handle academic problems

3. A key to college success is active learning, in which the student becomes involved and interacts with course content.
4. Thinking skills are essential ingredients of college success. The levels of thinking skills in many college courses are

   - ❏ knowledge
   - ❏ comprehension
   - ❏ application
   - ❏ analysis
   - ❏ synthesis
   - ❏ evaluation

CLASS ACTIVITY

Directions:
Form small groups (three or four students) and complete the following steps:

1. Using course descriptions listed in the college catalog as a reference, as well as group members' knowledge of courses they are taking, each group should discuss and list courses that
   a. require new approaches to learning
   b. focus on ideas and concepts
   c. focus on logical thinking
   d. require reaction and discussion
   e. require evaluation of new ideas
   f. involve creative thinking
   g. require problem solving

2. Each group should present its lists to the class; then the class should compare the lists in each category.

FURTHER ANALYSIS

Directions:
Analyze the situation described below and answer the questions that follow:

A political science professor has just returned graded midterm exams to her class. One student looks at the grade on the first page, flips through the remaining pages while commenting to a friend that the exam was "too picky," and files it in her notebook. A second student reviews his exam for grading errors and notices one error. Immediately, he raises his hand and asks for an adjustment in his grade. The instructor seems annoyed and tells the student she will not use class time to dispute individual grades. A third student reviews her exam bluebook to identify a pattern of error; on the cover of the bluebook she notes topics and areas in which she is weak.

1. Compare the three students' responses to the situation.
2. What does each student's response reveal about his or her approach to learning?
3. Analyze the student's response to the instructor's error in grading. What alternatives might have been more appropriate?

DISCUSSION

1. To what extent do you feel your performance as a student is shaped by what you think of yourself as a student?
2. Describe your current profile as a student; include both strengths and weaknesses.
3. Discuss the following hypothetical situation by answering the questions that follow.

A student completed four years of study and received a bachelor's degree in accounting from a prestigious major university. After several months of searching for a job, he was finally hired by a small accounting firm. After six months on the job, he was fired for incompetence. The student sued the university for accepting his tuition but failing to provide him with the knowledge and skills to handle the job of accountant.

a. Do you think the student's claim is legitimate?

b. How does this situation draw upon the distinction between teaching and learning?

c. What questions does this hypothetical situation raise?

4. Which type of thinking is most important for college success? Might your answer vary depending on your major?

5. List five careers or professions you have considered and identify the thinking skills essential to each.

6. Explain why you agree or disagree with each of the following statements:

a. Getting good grades depends on spending enough time studying.

b. The amount of material you learn makes the biggest difference in the grade you get.

c. Academic success is guaranteed if you are able to memorize enough information.

d. Your instructor is responsible for what you learn.

e. Learning from college lectures is simply a matter of focusing your attention.

FURTHER READING

Gardner, John N., and A. Jerome Jewler. *College Is Only the Beginning: A Student Guide to Higher Education.* Belmont, CA: Wadsworth, 1989.

Mayfield, Marlys. *Thinking for Yourself,* 2nd ed. Belmont, CA: Wadsworth, 1991.

Risko, Victoria J., Marino C. Alvarez, and Marilyn M. Fairbanks. "Internal Factors That Influence Study." In *Teaching Reading and Study Strategies.* Edited by Rona R. Flippo and David C. Caverly, 236–293. Newark, DE: International Reading Association, 1991.

Ruggiero, Vincent R. *The Art of Thinking: A Guide to Critical and Creative Thought.* New York: Harper, 1987.

The College System:
An Orientation

Learning Objectives

Identify information sources

Discover college services

Understand course organization

Understand the grading system

Use classroom success tips

College is very different from any other place you have worked or studied. It has its own way of operating, its own set of rules and regulations, and its own procedures. To function effectively within any new environment, you have to learn how it works and how to make it work to your advantage. For example, when you started a new part-time job, it may have felt strange at first; you weren't sure who was in charge, what was expected of you, and how best to get tasks accomplished. Then, once you learned how the business operated, who was who, and what was expected of you, the job became routine and comfortable. College, too, may seem strange and uncomfortable until you learn how it works and how to function within it.

Most colleges invite new students to attend college orientation sessions in which campus services, academic policies, financial aid, and campus life are discussed. Some students mistakenly choose not to attend; some attend but do not realize the importance of such sessions until it is too late. Others feel overwhelmed and confused by the barrage of information. The purpose of this chapter is to provide a general orientation to college—one you can refer to as needed and reread whenever you like. This chapter cannot, however, provide detailed information about your particular college. You, to be an active learner ready to take charge of your college career, will need to follow the advice suggested in this chapter to learn the specifics of your campus.

Before continuing with the chapter, assess your knowledge of your college by completing the questionnaire shown in Figure 2-1.

INFORMATION SOURCES

Important official information sources include the college catalog, one's academic advisor, the student newspaper. An important part of learning the college system is knowing where to find needed information, as you can see from the following situation.

A student is considering dropping his psychology class because he realizes he was overly ambitious in registering for 18 credit hours for his first college semester. Unsure of how and when to drop a course, the student consults a friend in his math class who tells him not to worry about it until after midterm week. Later, this student learns that the deadline was the fifth week of classes. This student, mistakenly, relied solely on a friend for information and failed to check official or authoritative sources.

Using the College Catalog

You probably read portions of the college catalog when you were choosing a college. Now that you are enrolled, you should read it with a different purpose, searching for certain types of information. It is your responsibility to know and work within the college's regulations, policies, and requirements to obtain a degree. Although faculty advisors are available to provide guidance and advice, you must be certain that you are registering for the right courses in the right sequence to fulfill requirements to obtain your degree. The college catalog, then, is your primary source of information for staying in and graduating from college.

Figure 2-1
Rate Your Knowledge of Your College

Directions:
Answer each of the following questions about your college.

	Yes	No
1. Do you know the hours of the college library?	❏	❏
2. Do you know the last date by which you can withdraw from a class without penalty?	❏	❏
3. Do you know where to go or whom to see to change from one major (or curriculum) to another?	❏	❏
4. Do you know how your grade point average (GPA) is computed?	❏	❏
5. Do you know where the student health office is located?	❏	❏
6. Do you know who your advisor is and where he or she is located on campus?	❏	❏
7. Do you know whether your colege uses pluses and/or minuses as part of the letter grading system?	❏	❏
8. Do you know the location(s) of computers available for student use?	❏	❏
9. Do you know how to contact each of your instructors if it should be necessary?	❏	❏
10. Do you know what assistance is available in locating part-time jobs on campus?	❏	❏

❏ ❏ ❏

Be sure to obtain a current edition. Furthermore, be sure to obtain a complete catalog, not a preadmissions publicity brochure. A complete catalog usually provides several types of information.

Academic rules and regulations	Course registration policies, grading system, class attendance policies, academic dismissal policies
Degree programs and requirements	Degrees offered and outlines of degree requirements for each major
Course descriptions	A brief description of each course, the number of credits, and course prerequisites (Note: Not all courses listed are offered each semester)
Student activities and special services	Student organizations, clubs and sports, student governance system, and special services

---

❏ ❏ ❏

EXERCISE 2-1

Directions:

Use your college catalog to answer the following questions.

1. Does the college allow you to take courses on a Pass/Fail or Satisfactory/Unsatisfactory basis? If so, what restrictions or limitations apply?
2. What is the last date on which you can withdraw from a course without academic penalty?
3. On what basis are students academically dismissed from the college? What criteria apply to readmission?
4. What is the institution's policy on transfer credit?
5. What rules and regulations apply to motor vehicles on campus?
6. List five extracurricular programs or activities the college sponsors.
7. Describe the health services the college provides.
8. What foreign languages are offered?
9. Is a course in computer literacy offered?
10. What courses are required in your major or curriculum?

Your Academic Advisor

In most colleges, each student is assigned an academic advisor. In some schools, the person may be a faculty member who is given a certain number of students to advise; in others, your advisor may be a full-time advisor or counselor who does not teach. Meet with your advisor early in the semester and get to know him or her. Your advisor's primary function is to help you select appropriate courses and make certain that you meet all requirements for your degree. Be sure to consult with your advisor before adding or dropping courses or making other important academic decisions. Your advisor can also give valuable advice, put you in touch with sources of assistance, and help you learn the college system. Sometimes he or she can help you resolve a problem by "cutting through the red tape" or knowing whom to call. Your advisor is an important source for a letter or recommendation, which you may need for college transfer, graduate school, or job applications, so it is important to develop and maintain a positive relationship with him or her.

Student Newspaper

The student newspaper is another useful source of information. It provides a student perspective on issues, problems, and concerns on campus. It may also contain important announcements and list upcoming events. The advertising will help you to learn what is available in the surrounding community.

COLLEGE SERVICES

A large portion of your tuition is spent to provide a wide range of academic, social, recreational, and health services. Since you are paying for these services, you should take advantage of them. Table 2-1 lists the most common services offered on college campuses. Check to see exactly what services are offered on your campus.

Table 2-1
COLLEGE SERVICES

Office	*Services offered*
Student Health Office	Handles illnesses and injuries; may dispense over-the-counter drugs
Student Activities Office or Student Center	Offers a range of recreational activities; sponsors social events; houses offices for student organizations
Counseling and Test Center	Provides personal and career counseling and testing
Financial Aid Office	Offers assistance with loans, grants, and scholarships

Table 2-1 *(continued)*

Office	*Services offered*
Placement Office	Lists job openings (full time and part time); establishes a placement file that records student references and transcripts
Library	Lends books, records, and films; provides listening, typing, and study rooms; has photocopy machines; offers assistance in locating reference material; obtains books and research materials from other libraries through interlibrary loans
Learning Lab	Offers brush-up courses; individualized instruction or tutoring in study skills; reading, writing, math, and/or common freshman courses

EXERCISE 2-2

Directions:
Answer the following questions about college services on your campus.

1. What services does the student health office offer?
2. List five student organizations sponsored by the college.
3. Where is the counseling center located?
4. Where would you go to find out if tutoring is available for mathematics courses?
5. In what intercollegiate sports does the college participate?
6. List five services offered by your college library.

COURSE ORGANIZATION

No two college courses are conducted in exactly the same manner. Each course is tailored by the instructor to best express his or her approach to the subject matter, teaching style, and educational objectives. Two sections of the same course offered the same semester may be structured entirely differently from one another. One instructor may require a text; the other may assign readings. One instructor may lecture; the other may conduct class discussions. One instructor may give exams; the other may assign papers. The key to success in college courses, then, is to understand and work within the instructor's course organization. Many instructors distribute materials the first day of class that explain their organization and approach. Often, this material is called a *syllabus*. These, too, vary according to instructor, but they usually list the following:

- ❏ the required text
- ❏ the attendance policy
- ❏ the grading system
- ❏ the course objectives
- ❏ weekly assignments or readings
- ❏ dates of exams or due dates for papers

An excerpt from a syllabus for a human anatomy and physiology course is shown in Figure 2-2. One of the most important parts of the syllabus is the course objectives. Objectives state, in general terms, what the instructors intend to accomplish and what they expect you to learn through the course. Objectives can provide valuable clues about what the instructor feels is important and how he or she views the subject matter. Since objectives state what you are to learn, exams, then, are built to measure if and how well you have learned it. For example, in the sample syllabus shown in Figure 2-2, objective 2 states "demonstrate familiarity with the terminology." Consequently, you can anticipate exams that contain questions measuring your mastery of definitions and terminology.

Figure 2-2
A Sample Course Syllabus Excerpt

DEPARTMENT OF LIFE SCIENCES

BIO 131: HUMAN ANATOMY & PHYSIOLOGY 1

INSTRUCTOR: Dr. Paul Eberhardt

COURSE DESCRIPTION
This course is the first semester of a two-semester study of the topics involved in Human Anatomy and Physiology. The major emphasis in the course is bodily structure and function. A molec-ular-cellular approach will be used in the course.

COURSE OBJECTIVES
Upon completion of this course, students will
1. demonstrate an understanding of bodily structure and func-tion.
2. demonstrate familiarity with the terminology used to describe bodily structure and function.
3. perform laboratory activities for collection analysis of experi-mental data.

EXERCISE 2-3

Directions:

Study the syllabus for one of your courses and answer as many of the following questions as possible.

1. Summarize the grading system.
2. What types of thinking are emphasized? (Refer to Chapter 1.)
3. How is the subject matter of the course divided?
4. Predict three topics that might be asked in a final exam consisting entirely of essay questions.

GRADES AND THE GRADING SYSTEM

Most colleges use a letter grade system in awarding final grades. Each college has its own variations, special policies, and unique designations, so be sure to read the section in your college catalog on grading policies. Specifically, find out about the following:

Pass/Fail Options

Some colleges allow you to take certain courses on a Pass/Fail basis. You earn the credit but receive only a Pass or Fail grade on your record. The grade is not figured into your overall average (see section below on grade point average). The Pass/Fail option, if available, allows you to take courses without competing for a letter grade. You might consider electing a Pass/Fail option for a difficult course. If, for example, you are required to take one math course and math has always been difficult for you, then consider taking that course on a Pass/Fail basis. Be sure to check you college catalog and with your advisor to be certain that required courses can be taken on a Pass/Fail basis and how to initiate the process. The instructor's permission may be required. Also, there may be a restriction on the number or types of courses that may be elected using this option.

The Pass/Fail option also provides an opportunity to take interesting elective courses without worrying about grades. Suppose you are interested in taking a History of Modern Music course but know that it is a difficult course taken mostly by students majoring in the arts. A Pass/Fail option would allow you to enjoy the course without competing for a letter grade.

Course Withdrawal

Most colleges have a provision by which you can withdraw from a course up to a given deadline in the semester without academic penalty. Be sure to check the college catalog for the deadline for course withdrawal. If you withdraw, you receive neither credit nor a grade. A letter code such as "W" may appear on your transcript following the course number. If you know you are doing poorly in a course, discuss the possibility of course withdrawal with your instructor. Some students who think they are in danger of failing learn otherwise by speaking with their instructor. Also, consult your advisor and the financial aid office to learn what, if any, impact course withdrawal will have on your academic and financial aid status.

Incomplete Grades

Many grading systems have a provision for students who are unable to complete a course for which they are registered. This grade, often called an "Incomplete," is awarded at the discretion of the instructor when he or she feels the student has a legitimate reason for being unable to complete the course. Instructors may award an Incomplete if you were injured during the last week of classes or if a death of a close relative prevents you from taking the final, for example. Be sure to contact your instructor as soon as possible; offer to provide the instructor with verification. Many colleges have a deadline by which an Incomplete must be converted to a grade. This means you must arrange with your instructor to complete whatever course requirements he or she specifies by a given date. Be sure it is clear what assignments must be done, how to do them, and when they must be completed.

Grade Point Average (GPA)

Each semester an average is computed using the individual grades you received that semester. This average is computed by assigning numerical value to letter grades. An A may be assigned 4 points, a B 3 points, a C 2 points, a D 1 point, and a F 0 points, for example. Consult your college catalog to discover what numerical values are used at your school and specifically how they are calculated. Find out if pluses and minuses are considered.

A cumulative GPA is computed over successive semesters by averaging all the grades you have received since you began attending college.

Many colleges require a specific cumulative GPA for admission to an academic department and for graduation. Grade point average may also influence financial aid eligibility and your academic status. Check your college catalog to learn about academic dismissal policies.

EXERCISE 2-4

Directions:

Answer each of the following questions about the grading system at your college.

1. What is the deadline for course withdrawal?
2. Is the Pass/Fail grading option available? If so, is there a limit for the number of courses you may elect using this option?
3. Is there a time limit by which the work for Incomplete grades must be completed?
4. Are pluses and minuses considered part of your grading system?
5. What is the point value of D grades in your college's grading system?

❏ ❏ ❏
Thinking Critically . . . About Grades

Grading is an important part of most college courses. Successful students learn to use the grading system to their advantage. Here are a few tips:

1. Use the grading system to help you organize your study. For example, if biweekly quizzes on textbook chapters constitute 50 percent of your grade, weekly chapter review is important.
2. Use the grading system to help you decide what is important to learn. For instance, if 40 percent of your grade is based on weekly summaries and critiques of films shown in class, you should be sure to take careful notes during and immediately after each film.
3. Use the grading system to help you make choices. You might, for example, have the choice of taking a final exam or writing a paper. Weigh your choices carefully, considering your strengths and weaknesses as a student as well as your time commitments. (If you already have three finals scheduled, for example, consider writing a paper, which you could complete before the semester ends.)

CLASSROOM SUCCESS TIPS

The following suggestions are intended to help you be successful in each of your courses.

Attend Classes

Even if class attendance is optional or not strictly monitored by your instructor, make it a rule to attend *all* classes. For most students, class time totals 12 to 15 hours per week, except for laboratory and studio courses. This amounts to less than 10 percent of your time each week! If you say you don't have enough time to attend all classes, you are not being honest with yourself. Remember, class instruction is a major part of what your tuition is paying for. You are cheating yourself if you don't take advantage of it. Seldom is a class taught in which you do not learn something new or gain a new perspective on already familiar ideas.

Get Acquainted with Faculty

Try to get to know your professors; you will find your classes more meaningful and interesting, and you will learn more. Challenging and stimulating conversations often result, and you can gain new insights into and perspectives on the subject matter that you might never obtain by merely attending class. Don't hesitate to talk with your professor or ask questions. Talking with your instructors is an opportunity to apply and connect the course with your academic interests, goals, and points of view. Getting to know your instructor can also be to your advantage at final grade time. If you have established yourself as a conscientious and interested student, an instructor may be more willing to reread an essay to find an extra point or two to boost your average than if you are a name-with-no-face on the class roster.

Keep Up with Assignments

It is tempting to let projects and assignments wait until you feel like doing them or until you have an exam or quiz on them. This approach is a mistake and can lead to a failing semester. Students who procrastinate end up with an impossible amount of reading to do within a short time. As a result, they don't do the reading at all or read the assignments passively and hurriedly.

Project a Positive Image

Be sure to approach each class positively and demonstrate that you are a serious student. Unfortunately, some students do act thoughtlessly or rudely in class. The unspoken message they send is that the class is unimportant and uninteresting, and instructors are quick to perceive this. Work on establishing a positive image by

- ❏ arriving at class promptly
- ❏ participating in class discussions
- ❏ asking or answering questions
- ❏ sitting in the front of the room
- ❏ maintaining eye contact with the instructor
- ❏ completing assignments on time
- ❏ reading assigned material before class
- ❏ saying "hello" when you meet your instructor on campus

Take Action If You Are in the Wrong Class

You may find yourself in a class that is either too easy or too difficult. Courses in which this most often occurs are mathematics, foreign languages, the sciences, and skills courses such as typing or athletics. If you suspect you are in the wrong course, talk with your instructor immediately. If he or she confirms that you are misplaced, ask for advice. Also consult with your advisor. Generally, it is inadvisable to continue in a course that is too difficult; dropping the course, if possible, is a reasonable alternative. Be certain, however, that dropping the course does not reduce your course load to below the minimum if you are a full-time student.

Purchase Recommended Materials

While most instructors require a textbook, some make the purchase of other materials optional. These materials include review books, workbooks, dictionaries, or other reference books, manuals, or style sheets. Your instructor would not recommend the materials unless he or she felt they would be helpful. Therefore, make sure you purchase these optional materials. Often you will find that these materials make review easier and/or are helpful in completing required assignments or papers.

Take Action When You Miss an Important Exam or Deadline

Hopefully you will never have to miss an important exam or deadline for a paper. However, if you should wake up with the flu on the morning of a midterm exam, for example, you may have to miss the exam. Be sure to contact your instructor *before* the exam. Leave a phone message in the department office if you are unable to contact him or her directly. Explaining the situation ahead of time is preferable to making excuses later. If a paper is due and you are ill, ask a friend or fellow student to deliver it for you.

Get Involved with College Life

Academic course work is, of course, the primary reason for attending college. However, if all you are doing on campus is taking courses and studying, you are missing an important part of college life. College is more than textbooks, exams, and lectures. The academic environment is a world of ideas, a place where thought, concepts, and values are of primary importance. It is a place where you can discuss and exchange ideas, explore new approaches to life, and reevaluate old ones. College also provides an opportunity for you to decide who you are (or who you want to be) and how you would like to spend the rest of your life. There are people to meet with diverse backgrounds and experiences who will broaden your knowledge and view of life.

Considerable research indicates that students who become involved with college activities tend to be more successful in college than those who do not. Activities provide an opportunity for you to get involved and to feel part of a group with similar interests. On large campuses, where it is easy to feel lost, involvement is especially important. If you are preparing for a career, getting involved with college life is important. Most employers are interested in hiring well-spoken, interesting people who are aware of the world around them and can interact with it effectively. College can help you become well rounded, if you take advantage of it.

To get involved with college life, find out about activities and issues on campus. Many interesting lectures, debates, films, and concerts are sponsored weekly. Make it a point to meet someone in each of your classes; you will feel better about going to class, and a worthwhile friendship may develop. Find out if there is a student group that shares your interests, and join it. You may meet interesting people in the ski club, chorus, nursing students' association, or black students' union, for example.

If You Plan to Transfer

If you are attending a two-year college and plan to transfer to a four-year school after completing your associate's degree, plan accordingly. Do not assume that any course you take at one institution will be accepted for a degree at another. Each college and each academic department has its own policies and guidelines for the acceptance of transfer credit.

To insure that most or all your credits will transfer, be sure to do the following:

❏ Obtain the college catalog of the institution to which you intend to transfer and read about degree requirements and transfer credit policies and procedures.
❏ Contact an admissions counselor to answer any questions.
❏ Make your current academic advisor aware of your plans. He or she can assist you in determining and selecting appropriate courses for transfer.

SUMMARY

1. College is a unique educational setting with its own rules, procedures, and policies.
2. Information sources that are helpful in learning the college system are

   ❏ college catalog
   ❏ academic advisor
   ❏ student newspaper

3. Colleges offer a wide range of academic, social, and recreational services.
4. Course organization is unique and determined by the individual instructors.
5. Syllabi are useful in discovering course organization and identifying what to learn.
6. The grading system involves numerous grading options:

   ❏ Pass/Fail
   ❏ course withdrawal
   ❏ incomplete grades

7. Semester grades are computed using a numerical weighting system known as *grade point average* (GPA).

CLASS ACTIVITY

Directions:
Form groups of two or three students and compile a list of additional success tips (not included in this chapter) that could be included on a tip sheet

to be distributed to first-year students. Include advice on things you've learned so far this semester. (Hints: registration, parking, dorms, food service, bookstore, add-drop procedures.)

FURTHER ANALYSIS

Directions:

Analyze the following situation and answer the questions below.

A private four-year college does not award grades to first semester first-year students. Instead, all grades are given on a Pass/Fail basis. The college implemented this policy to reduce stress and pressure on beginning students. It was intended to deemphasize grades and competition and to place greater emphasis on learning.

1. Discuss the advantages and disadvantages of this grading policy.
2. Do you feel the policy encourages students to learn? If so, how?

DISCUSSION

1. What should a student do if he or she finds the academic advisor frequently unavailable or not helpful?
2. What additional college services do you feel should be offered on your campus?
3. Should the student newspaper be able to print articles critical of the college, of its faculty, or of its administration?

FURTHER READING

Jewler, A. Jerome, and John A. Gardner, *Step by Step to College Success*. Belmont, CA: Wadsworth, 1987.

Leitch, Andrew. "Staying in Control." *Canadian Living* 120 (1994): 62.

Higgins, Ruby. *The Black Student's Guide to College Success*. Westport, CT: Greenwood Press, 1995.

3

Organizational and Time Management Skills

Learning Objectives

Use organizational skills to become more efficient

Develop time management skills

Monitor your concentration

Manage stress

Being a college student is difficult an demanding, but it need not overwhelm you. Certainly, a great deal is expected of you, and at times you will wonder if you can handle the workload. Assignments, papers, and exams seem to keep coming, and just when you feel as if you've got things under control, another assignment or examination is announced. But you can learn to cope with the tremendous workload of college if you develop two essential skills: organization and management.

Management and organization are two highly marketable skills in career and professional fields as well. Handling the pressures of the workload of a responsible, fulfilling job also requires organizational and management skills. If you develop and apply these skills to college life, you will be able to make an easy transition to career or professional life.

[*Organization* is a skill that enables you to get things done in the least time and ensures that you are able to accomplish what you intend.] This chapter presents numerous suggestions for organizing your approach to college learning and study. [*Management* is the skill of taking charge or control.] Just as the manager of a store makes certain that the store operates efficiently, effectively, and profitably, so you must manage the various facets of your life in order to become a productive, successful student. Management involves planning, conserving time and resources, maintaining peak efficiency, and controlling stress. In this chapter you will learn how to manage your college career. You will see how to get your work done effectively and efficiently and have time left to enjoy college life. Before beginning this chapter, rate your present level of organization and time management skills by completing the questionnaire shown in Figure 3-1.

ORGANIZATIONAL SKILLS

Organize a Place to Study

A first step in taking control of your life is to assess your living arrangements, determine if they are conducive to study, and, if necessary, make changes. If you live on a floor of a dorm where parties occur frequently, then you are going to have difficulty studying. If you share an apartment or live at home, you may find studying at busy times nearly impossible. If you find your situation intolerable (your dorm roommate is entertaining friends in your room every evening, for example), then make a change as soon as possible. In the meantime, make temporary adjustments; alter the time or place of study. Consider alternatives such as the library, student lounge, or designated campus study areas.

It is usually beneficial to study in the same place each day, where all the materials you need (pens, calculator, paper) are readily at hand. There is a psychological advantage to studying in the same place each day: You build a mental association between an activity and the place where it occurs. If you become accustomed to studying at a particular desk, you will build up an association between the place (your desk) and the activity (reading and studying). Eventually, when you sit down at the desk, you expect to read or study, and the expectation makes getting started much easier. Be sure not to select a place you already associate with a different activity. Don't try to study in your TV chair or stretched out across your bed; you already have built associations with your chair and bed as places to relax or sleep.

Figure 3-1
Rate Your Organizational and Time Management Skills

Directions:
Respond to each of the following statements by checking "Always," "Sometimes," or "Never."

	Always	Sometimes	Never
1. Do you use a pocket calendar or assignment notebook to record due dates of assignments and exams?	☐	☑	☐
2. Do you study at your peak periods of concentration?	☐	☑	☐
3. Do you study difficult subjects first?	☐	☐	☑
4. Do you avoid studying in front of the TV?	☐	☐	☑
5. Do you use lists to keep organized?	☑	☐	☐
6. Do you assign priorities to your assignments?	☐	☑	☐
7. Do you give yourself deadlines or establish time limits by which assignments should be completed?	☐	☑	☐
8. Do you know when you are losing concentration and recognize when your attention span is weakening?	☐	☑	☐
9. Do you plan out what needs to be done each week?	☐	☑	☐
10. Do you plan to study at least two hours outside of class for every hour spent in class?	☐	☑	☐

Organize Each Course

For each course you are taking, some preliminary organizational strategies are helpful.

Become familiar with each textbook. Even though the lines in the bookstore may be long, purchase your textbooks as soon as possible in each new term. Be certain to buy new rather than used texts. Used textbooks that are already marked or underlined are distracting and make learning more difficult. You may not have an assignment right away, so spend time becoming familiar with each of your texts. Find out how each is organized and identify what learning aids it contains.

- ❏ Read the preface or introduction and study the table of contents.
- ❏ Choose a chapter at random and examine its format. What special features does it contain? How does the author emphasize what is important to learn? Does it contain review questions and vocabulary lists?
- ❏ Check the end of the book. Does it have an index, glossary (minidictionary of important words), bibliography, or appendix? If so, check to see what each contains. (The appendix often contains useful tables, charts, documents, or reference material to which you may frequently need to refer when using the text.

Previewing a text in this way will give you a working knowledge of it, and when the first assignment is made, you will be able to put your texts to work for you immediately.

Buy any additional material your professor recommends. Professors often recommend, but do not require, useful aids that will make the course easier to handle or save you time. Such aids might include handbooks, study guides, review books, or special equipment such as a calculator, drawing pencil, and so forth.

Organize a notebook for each class. Decide what type of notebook best suits each of your courses. For lecture classes with few or no supplementary materials, a spiral notebook works well. A looseleaf notebook works best for courses in which numerous handouts, outlines, and supplementary materials are distributed. Date and organize these day-to-day class handouts, and place them next to the lecture notes with which they correspond. Handouts are important when studying and reviewing for an exam. Include all class homework assignments and returned quizzes, exams, and written assignments.

Use a pocket calendar. College professors frequently give long-term assignments and announce dates for papers, assignments, and exams far in advance. Many do not feel that it is their responsibility to remind students as the dates approach. Consequently, you will need to organize a system for keeping track of what assignments need to be done and when each is due.

Many students keep pocket diaries or calendar notebooks in which they record all their assignments as they are given, as shown in Figure 3-2. These allow you to see at a glance what assignments, tests, and quizzes are coming up. Most useful are the monthly calendars that display a full month on one page. These allow you to anticipate work requirements easily without flipping pages.

Organize Your Part-Time Job to Work for You

Many students hold part-time jobs while attending college; others work full time and attend college part time. A job can be either a refreshing break from the routine of studying or a source of additional stress, depending upon how you organize and approach it. If you are a full-time student, here are a few suggestions for managing your part-time job.

Keep work hours to a minimum. The number of hours you work should be moderate and should not take needed time away from study. If you are unsure of how much time you will need for study, underestimate rather than overestimate the number of hours you can spend on the job. Many college-sponsored work-study programs limit students to a maximum 15 hours per week; use this number as a guide.

Figure 3-2
A Week in a Calendar Notebook

March

Sun	Mon	Tue	Wed	Thu	Fri	Sat
2	3	4	5	6	7	8
	English comp due *Math H.W.*	*Speech– draft*	*Math H.W.*	*Speech– give* *edit computer program*	*Topic for term paper due* ——— *Math H.W.*	

Choose a job with a regular work schedule. Unless you know in advance when and how long you will work each week, the job may turn your life into a nightmare of confused commitments, missed classes, and uncompleted assignments.

Make sure your employer understands your college commitments. If an employer or supervisor knows you are working toward a degree, he or she is often helpful and supportive.

Choose a job that provides a break or diversion from the task of studying. A job that is physically active or involves working with people may be refreshing.

Organize Your Finances

Unless you are fortunate enough to have access to unlimited funds, organizing your finances, often for the first time in your life, is a unique experience. Worrying about money can be a major source of distraction and can interfere with your ability to concentrate on your coursework. Budgeting, then, is essential; be sure to allow a "cushion" for hidden and unexpected expenses. These costs, especially if you are living away from home, may include local transportation, laundry and dry cleaning, phone tolls, toiletries, and higher clothing costs in small college towns. Check with the college's financial aid office to be sure you are taking advantage of all sources of aid.

EXERCISE 3-1

Directions:
Assess your organizational skills by answering each of the following questions.

1. When an instructor makes an assignment during class, where do you record it? In your pocket calander
2. Do you have a specific place to keep returned quizzes, completed homework, and graded papers for each course? Yes
   a. Have you previewed each of your texts to learn if each contains a glossary, appendix, and answer key? Yes
   b. Have you read the preface or introduction in each and studied the table of contents? Yes
   c. Have you reviewed a random chapter in each text and become familiar with its format? No
3. What is the average cost of books per semester or quarter at
$55.00 - 65.00

your college? (Estimates often appears in college financial aid brochures.)

4. Have you chosen and organized a place to study? If you do not *Yes* live on campus, have you found a place on campus to study during free hours?

5. Do you have a filing system (envelopes, folders) for keeping both college paperwork (transcripts, financial aid agreements) and everyday documents (car insurance, registrations, licenses, checking account statements)? *Yes*

ESTABLISHING PRIORITIES AND GOALS

As you proceed through each academic term, keep a focus and perspective on why you are in college and what your goals are when you finish. Two dangers lie ahead: (1) Once you learn the college system and function comfortably and successfully within it, you may become complacent, stop questioning, and no longer see the need to develop new strategies, approaches, and methods of evaluating your performance. It is easy to slip into a comfortable, nonthinking mode, as if you put your mind on automatic pilot. (2) Rather than becoming complacent, you might begin to take yourself and your work too seriously. Grades become all important, pressure and anxiety heighten, and before long, you feel overworked and burned out.

The way to avoid either of these pitfalls is to establish your priorities. This involves deciding what you want out of college, how badly you want it, and how hard you are willing to work to achieve it. Establishing priorities involves sorting out what is more important and what is less important in your life. It also involves deciding what you are willing to sacrifice in order to obtain other things of higher priority. Here are a few questions you will have to answer:

Is attending college the most important thing I'm doing now? If not, *Yes* what is more important?
How does my job fit in? *Entirely second*
Where does my family fit in? *Second*
What other responsibilities do I have? *None*
Are my courses the most important part of college? *Yes*
Are sports, friends, and social or cultural activities important, too? *No*

In answering these questions, be honest with yourself. Your answers are an important preliminary to setting you long-term goals and determining the context from which you will be approaching college study.

Many of us have trouble setting priorities. It is difficult to step back from one's own life, look at it objectively, and sort out what is important. The following exercise explains a technique that may give you that needed perspective.

EXERCISE 3-2

Directions:
Try the following technique to order your priorities.

1. Obtain 10 to 15 index cards (or small sheets of paper). On each write the following: "I am a(an)_____ ."
2. Now fill in the blank on each card. Work rapidly. Write what ever comes to mind. Be completely honest; there are no right or wrong answers. Answers such as video game addict, basketball player, attractive woman, parent, religious person, and serious student are all acceptable. Use only as many cards as needed; add cards if necessary.
3. Arrange the cards in order of importance and number each.
4. Take a few minutes to look over and think about the cards. Decide what they tell you about yourself. Do they reflect the priorities in your life?

Once you have identified your priorities, the next step is to establish a set of specific long-term goals. Think of goals as targets you want to hit at some point in your life. Working toward specific goals prevents you from getting caught up with daily activities and losing sight of more important directions. Goal setting also makes you more productive and efficient. You will find that decisions are easier to make and some problems easier to solve once you have defined your goals.

To be most effective, goals must have three qualities.

They must be specific. In order to work well, a goal must describe particular events or situations in a detailed manner. For example, to be specific, the goal "Do well in engineering drawing" should be translated to "Earn a B (or A) in engineering drawing."

They must include a time frame. The goal "Earn a bachelor's degree in accounting" should include a date, for example.

They must be flexible and open to change. When your priorities change, you may need to revise your goals.

With the remainder of your college career ahead, you still have time to establish both short- and long-term goals. Short-term goals usually refer to those that can be accomplished in a year or less; long-term goals extend beyond.

Begin by identifying your long-term goals. Once these are defined, your short-term goals are often smaller things you need to do in order to accomplish a more important long-term goal. Here are a few examples of long-term goals:

❏ Earn dual degrees in English and business within eight semesters.
❏ Be accepted into law school after earning my B.A. degree.
❏ Become a pediatric nurse and obtain a job in a private health care center by (date).

Next, identify specific things you want to accomplish within the next year. It is important to write these goals, rather than just think about them. Writing will make them concrete and help you shape and define them. Here are a few examples of short-term goals:

❏ Complete all math requirements by next June.
❏ Complete a public speaking course in the next term.
❏ Move to a dorm or apartment more conducive to study by the beginning of next semester.
❏ Get a summer job this year that pays more than minimum wage.

MANAGING YOUR TIME

Time is one of our most valuable resources, yet few people use it wisely. Many large companies pay consultants generous fees to conduct time management seminars to encourage their executives to make better use of their time. These seminars show executives how to manage their time more effectively and how to accomplish more. Time management is a skill few people have but one that most people need.

Effective time management can make the difference between being a mediocre student and being an excellent one. It can also determine whether you feel as if you should spend every waking moment studying or whether you are confident about your courses and know you can afford time for fun and relaxation.

ANALYZE YOUR TIME COMMITMENTS

A second step in managing your time more effectively is to analyze your commitments and determine the time each requires. In time management seminars, business executives are first asked to identify required tasks and responsibilities—travel time, weekly meetings, reading and responding to memoranda, supervising subordinates, and so forth—and then to estimate the time each involves. You can profit from doing the same. To determine how much of your time is already committed, estimate the amount of time various activities require per week. In estimating study time, use the "2-for-1" rule.

Most colleges and professors assume the 2-for-1 rule of student time management: Students should spent 2 hours studying outside of class for every hour spent in class. If you spend 12 hours per week attending classes, you should spend 24 hours outside class reading text assignments, doing research or experiments, studying for exams, or writing papers. This explains why carrying 12 credit hours is usually considered full-time study.

Depending on your familiarity with the expertise in a given discipline, adjust the 2-for-1 rule. If you are an excellent math student, you may need less than 2 hours on math courses. On the other hand, if mathematics is a weak area, you may need to spend 3 or $3\frac{1}{2}$ hours.

Many students find it motivating to set their sights on a particular grade and to work toward earning it. Allot more time for study for higher grades. The 2-for-1 rule estimates the time the typical college student will need to earn an average passing grade (a C).

Consider each of your courses, its workload, your expertise in the field, and the grade toward which you are working, to estimate the amount of time per week each will require. Then consider your other time commitments and complete the chart below.

❏ ❏ ❏

Activity	Hours per week
Classes and labs	_____
Study	_____
Sleep	_____
Breakfast, lunch, dinner	_____
Part-time job	_____
Transportation (driving, walking to class)	_____
Personal care (showering, dressing)	_____
Other	_____
Total	_____

❏ ❏ ❏

After you have totaled your time commitments, subtract that total from 168, the number of hours in a week. The remainder represents the number of hours of uncommitted time you have available for having fun and relaxing. If you find you have very little uncommitted time, you have several choices. You may need to revise your goals to settle for a B instead of an A in English composition, for example. Or you may need to reduce the number of hours you work at your part-time job. You can become more efficient and spend less time completing required tasks by applying the principles of effective time management described in the following sections.

Analyze Your Efficiency

Another feature of time management seminars is the time study. An observer spends a day with the executive analyzing and recording how he or she actually spends the workday. Wasted time, inefficient use of time, and duplication of effort are noted. Since you do not have a consultant to observe you, you must function as your own observer. As you go through the day, record how, when, and where you spend your time. You will be surprised to see where your time actually goes and how much of it is used up by nonessential tasks. In particular, try to identify times of the day when you seemed least efficient and activities on which you seemed to waste the most time. Be aware of the common time traps for college students. Specifically,

❏ Avoid spending time making small decisions (what to wear, what to study, where to order pizza).
❏ Don't let friends and classmates direct your time. Innocent invitations like the following can be time traps: "Let's go for coffee," "Let's stop in and visit Sam," "Let's study together."
❏ Don't waste time worrying or feeling guilty about not studying.
❏ Handle details of living in efficient ways. For example, return books to the library when you are passing by; avoid making a special trip. Go to the cafeteria at off-peak times so you won't have to wait in line.

Apply Principles of Time Management

The next step in your time analysis is to determine if you get the most from the time you do spend studying. The following section lists 11 principles of effective time management.

Use peak periods of concentration. Everyone has high and low periods of concentration and attention. First, determine when these occur for you; then reserve peak times for intensive study and use less efficient times for more routine tasks such as recopying an assignment or collecting information in the library. Use the lowest concentration times for errands, laundry, phone calls, and so forth.

Study difficult subjects first. While it is tempting to get easy tasks and short little assignments out of the way first, do not give in to this approach. When you start studying, your mind is fresh and alert and you are at your peak of concentration. This is the time you are best equipped to handle difficult subjects. Thinking through complicated problems or studying complex ideas requires all the brain power you have, and you are able to think most clearly at the beginning of a study session.

Include time for review of previously learned material. Learning something once is no guarantee that you will remember it. In fact, unless you review learned material periodically, you are likely to forget it. Be sure to organize a system to provide for periodic review of previously assigned chapters and of lectures. (See Chapter 8 for more complete discussion of review strategies.)

Schedule study for a particular course close to the time when you attend class. Plan to study the evening before the class meets and soon after the class meeting. If a class meets on Tuesday morning, plan to study Monday evening and Tuesday afternoon or evening. By studying close to class time, you will find it easier to relate class lectures and discussions to what you are reading and studying, to see connections, and to reinforce your learning.

Include short breaks in your study time. Take a break before you begin studying each new subject. Your mind needs time to refocus—to switch from one set of facts, problems, and issues to another. Short breaks should also be included when you are working on just one assignment, but for a long period of time. A 10-minute break after 50 to 60 minutes of study is reasonable.

Use distributed learning and practice. Learning occurs more effectively if it is divided and spaced over time, rather than done all at once. Distributed practice means that you should spread out your study sessions. For example, try to study a subject for an hour each of three nights rather than three hours one evening. Distributed practice is effective for several reasons.

Research evidence suggests that although you may stop studying, learning seems to continue for a brief time. In a sense, your mind continues to work on or mull over the material after you have stopped studying. Most likely, a type of sorting or organizational processing is occurring. If, then, you study over several blocks of time, this aftereffect occurs several times rather than once, as illustrated below.

Distributed learning   *Single session learning*

1 hour study	1 hour study	1 hour study	3 hours study

Distributed practice prevents mental fatigue and keeps you working at peak efficiency. Distributing the material to learn over several sessions allows you to approach the task in reasonable pieces that can be mastered more easily.

Study when your surroundings are conducive. If your dorm or household is busy and noisy during late afternoon, for example, don't attempt intensive study then. Work at more routine task at that time.

Be generous when estimating needed time. It is better to overestimate than underestimate how much time you need to complete an assignment or prepare for an exam. If you overestimate, the free time left will function as a reward for hard work; however, if you underestimate you will feel pressured, rushed, and dissatisfied.

Plan carefully to eliminate worry and frustration. Many students spend a great deal of time and energy worrying about their coursework. In fact, some are unable to relax and enjoy themselves because even when they are supposed to be having fun, they find themselves thinking about their coursework. However, if you plan and manage your study time carefully, you will feel confident and in control, and you will be able to have fun and relax.

Leave room for fun and relaxation. There is more to college than attending classes; the social and recreational aspects of college life are important as well. If you plan carefully and work efficiently you can have time to study and have fun too.

Don't shortchange yourself on sleep or healthful and relaxing meals. While you can get by with four hours' sleep once in a while and can afford to skip or rush through a meal occasionally, don't try to maintain such a pace all semester. If you find yourself regularly skipping meals or not getting enough sleep, you need to reevaluate your priorities and make some changes.

EXERCISE 3-3

Directions:
Review each of the above time management principles, and mark those that you do not use regularly. Refer to these principles as you build your semester plan as described in the next section.

Build a Semester Plan

You have already estimated your total study hours per week and identified other weekly time commitments. The next step in successful time management is to combine these commitments into a semester plan, using the principles of effective time management. Begin by blocking out class time and scheduled work hours. Next, identify time blocks during the week that you'll devote to study. Schedule specific times that you will devote to each course. Use the blank weekly schedule in Figure 3-3 as a worksheet.

A computer science major designed the semester plan using the worksheet shown in Figure 3-4. (Vertical entries indicate study sessions; horizontal ones indicate classes.) Since calculus was this student's most difficult course, he planned to devote nine hours a week to it. The class met Monday, Wednesday, and Friday; he decided to study the day before each class since the instructor spent most of the class reviewing difficult problems previously assigned as homework. He also planned to work on Saturday and Sunday afternoons, reviewing the previous week's assignment and reading new material. Because English was his strongest subject, he scheduled five hours weekly and six hours each for business communications and computer programming logic.

The best time to develop your semester plan is during the second week of the semester. By this time, your professors will have detailed course requirements and given the first assignment; you should have a fairly realistic view of the workload and difficulty of each course. After you have worked with the schedule for a week or so, evaluate its effectiveness and make necessary changes. Keep this schedule in a prominent place above or on your desk. It will serve as a reminder to follow the schedule.

Develop a Weekly To-Do List

Once you have constructed a semester plan, the next step is to use the plan as a basis for developing a more specific, detailed weekly schedule. Before each week begins, preferably on Saturday or Sunday, review upcoming assignments, papers, and examinations. For each course, identify what needs to be done or reviewed; list specific chapters and pages along with assignments to complete.

Once you have constructed your weekly list, tentatively identify which study sessions you will use to accomplish each task, and make any adjustments necessary in your semester plan. If a midterm exam in coming up in chemistry, for example, you may decide to add two 2-hour blocks of study time. Or, if you learn that a Friday English class has been

Figure 3-3
A Semester Plan Worksheet

	Sunday	Monday	Tuesday	Wednesday	Thursday	Friday	Saturday
7:00							
8:00							
9:00							
10:00							
11:00							
12:00							
1:00							
2:00							
3:00							
4:00							
5:00							
6:00							
7:00							
8:00							
9:00							
10:00							
11:00							

Figure 3-4
Sample Worksheet

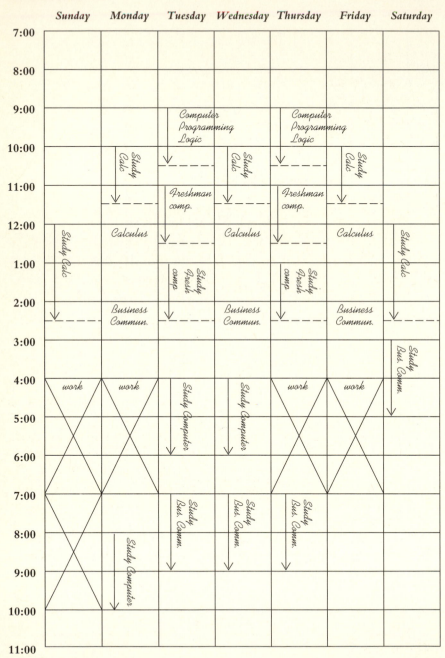

Figure 3-5
A Weekly To-Do List

Oct. 2

To do

Revise English comp. — Tues
Revise Eng comp. — Wed
Review Ch. 6 Calc problems — Sun
Write computer program — Assign. #3 — Tues
Read short story — Thurs
Revise computer program #2 — Mon eve
Calc homework — Ch. 7 — Mon
Study for Bus. Comm. exam — Tues, Thurs
Read Ch. 8 calc — Wed, Sat
Read Ch. 4 — Bus Comm. — Tues

canceled, reschedule use of that hour. A sample weekly list is shown in Figure 3-5.

Planning Long-Term Assignments

When a term paper or semester project is assigned, draft a timetable for its completion. Since assignments such as these usually constitute a major portion of your final grade, you want to be certain to meet each deadline.

EXERCISE 3-4

Directions:
Build a semester study plan, using the guidelines given above. Work with the plan for a week and then analyze its effectiveness. Revise it so it becomes more effective.

EXERCISE 3-5

Directions:
For each of the next several weeks, prepare a weekly to-do list. After each week, stop and analyze whether the list helped to improve your efficiency.

TIMESAVING TIPS

Here are a few suggestions that will help you to make the best use of your time. If you are an older student with family responsibilities or if you are trying to work and attend college, you will find these suggestions especially valuable.

Use the telephone.   When you need information or need to make an appointment, phone rather than visit the office. For example, to find out if a book you have requested at the library has come in, phone the circulation desk.

Assign priorities to your work.   There may be days or weeks when you cannot get every assignment done. Many students just start working and work until they are exhausted, often leaving remaining assignments unfinished. A better approach is to decide what is most important to complete immediately and which assignments could, if necessary, be completed later.

Use spare moments.   Think of all the time that you spend waiting. You wait for a class to begin, for a ride, for a friend to call, for a take-out order to be ready. Instead of wasting this time, use it to review a set of lecture notes, work on review questions at the end of a chapter, or review a set of problems. Always carry with you something you can work on in empty moments.

Learn to combine activities.   Most people think it is impossible to do two things at once, but busy students soon learn that they can combine some daily living chores with some more routine class assignments. Some students, for example, are able to outline a history chapter while waiting for their wash to finish at the laundromat. Others work on routine assignments during coffee breaks at work. Still others mentally review formulas for math and science courses or review vocabulary cards for a foreign language course while walking to class.

Use lists to keep yourself organized and to save time.   A daily reminder list is helpful in keeping track of daily living and household tasks and errands as well as course assignments that need to be done. As you think of things to be done; jot them down. Then, each morning look over the list and try to find the best way to get everything done. You may find, for instance, that you can stop at the post office on the way to the bookstore, thus saving yourself a trip.

Don't be afraid to admit you are trying to do too much.   If you find your life is becoming too hectic or unmanageable or that you are facing pressures beyond your ability to handle them, consider dropping a course. Don't be too concerned that dropping a course will put you behind schedule for graduation; more than half of all college students take longer than the traditional time expected to earn their degrees. Besides, you may be able to pick up the course during a summer session or carry a heavier load another semester. Time pressures such as these are often a basic cause of failure in college. Unless you relieve some of the pressure, your performance in all of your courses may be affected.

CONCENTRATION TIPS

Regardless of how effectively you plan your time, if you are not able to concentrate when you *do* study, you are not using your time efficiently. Spending time studying is not sufficient; time must be spent productively. Results are what counts. The key to concentration is monitoring—always keeping aware of your concentration level. Just as pilots constantly monitor their airplanes' performance, so must you continually check to make certain that you are operating at peak efficiency. You can do so by focusing your attention and monitoring your concentration.

❏ ❏ ❏
Thinking Critically . . . About Procrastination

Procrastination is the tendency to postpone tasks that need to be done. If you know you should review your biology notes but decide to do something else instead, you are procrastinating. Many people tend to put off tasks that are difficult, dull, or unpleasant. Procrastination can serve as an early warning signal that something is going wrong in a course. For example, frequently putting off assigned math problems is a signal that you are having or will have trouble with your math course.

If you find yourself procrastinating in a particular course, take immediate action:

1. Make a list of all tasks you have avoided.
2. Think honestly about *why* you have avoided them.
3. If you have avoided these tasks because they are dull, divide each task into manageable pieces and set up a schedule in which you do a small part each day. Dividing the task will make it seem less formidable.
4. If you have avoided the tasks because they are difficult, you should seek further information or assistance. You might

   • consult a classmate
   • talk with your instructor
   • get a tutor
   • visit the academic skills center
   • obtain a more basic text

Focus Your Attention

Concentration is focusing attention on the task at hand while shutting out external distractions such as noises, conversations, and interruptions.

Vary your activities. Avoid working on one type of activity for a long period of time; instead, alternate between several types of study. For example, you might plan your study schedule so that you read sociology for a while, then work on math problems, and finally switch to writing an English paper. This plan would be much more effective than doing all reading activities in the same study session, say reading sociology, then reading chemistry, then reading an essay for English. The change from one skill or mental process to another will be refreshing and will make concentration easier.

Write and underline as you read. It is easy to let your mind wander while reading. Have you ever read an entire page and then not remembered anything you had read? One way to solve this problem is to write or underline. After reading a section, write or underline what is important to remember. This activity forces you to think: to identify what is important, too see how ideas are related, and to evaluate their worth and importance.

Approach assignments critically. Keep active as you read. Instead of trying to take in large amounts of information, read critically, looking for ideas you question or disagree with. Look for points of view, opinions, and statements that are not supported. Try to predict how the author's train of thought will develop. Make connections with what you have already learned about the subject, with what you have read previously in the course, and with what the instructor has said in class. If you are able to maintain an active, critical point of view, you will find distraction will be minimal or nonexistent.

Challenge yourself with deadlines. If you have difficulty maintaining concentration, try setting deadlines for completion of various tasks. Give yourself $1\frac{1}{2}$ hours maximum to draft a one-page English composition; allow only 2 hours for working on your computer program. Establishing a deadline will force you to stick with the assignment. You also will be motivating and conditioning yourself to work within time limits on exams.

End on a positive note. When you stop working on a project or long-term assignment for an evening, stop at a point at which it will be easy to pick up again. If you end on a positive note, then you will be starting with that same positive note when you return to it.

Techniques for Self-Monitoring

An important part of strengthening your concentration is increasing your own awareness of your levels of concentration. Once you are aware of your concentration level and can recognize when your focus is beginning to blur, then you can take action to control and improve the situation. Here is some advice on how to monitor, or assess and control, your concentration.

Check your own concentration. Keep track, for a half hour or so during a particular study session, of how many times you are distracted. Make a tally, or count, of distractions as they occur. Each time you think about something other than what you are studying, make a mark on the paper. Total up your marks at the end of the specified time. You probably will be surprised to see how many times your concentration was broken. Work on decreasing the tally. Do not keep this tally every time you read or study anything. Instead, use it once a week or so as a check on your concentration.

Learn to read your symptoms of distractibility. When you find that your concentration is broken, stop and analyze the situation. Why did you lose your concentration? Was it an external distraction? Did an idea in the text trigger your memory of something else? Look for patterns in loss of concentration: At what time of day are you most easily distracted? Where are you studying when distractions occur? What are you studying? Use this information to adjust your semester study plan.

Keep a list of distractions. Often, as you reading or studying, you will think of something you should remember to do. If, for example, you are trying to remember a dental appointment you have scheduled for the next afternoon, you will find that a remainder occasionally flashes through your mind. To prevent these mental reminders from flashing through your mind as you study, keep a distractions list. Have a separate sheet of paper nearby as you read or study. Each time one of these mental reminders occurs, jot it down. You will find that by writing it down on paper, you will temporarily eliminate it from your memory. Use the same paper to record other ideas and problems that distract you. A list of distractions might look like this:

> *dentist — Tues. 2 p.m.*
> *call Sam*
> *Buy Mother's Day card*
> *Return library books*

MANAGING STRESS

Do you often feel worried and upset about your classes? If so, you are probably feeling pressured or are under stress. Stress often results when you face new or difficult situations. Stress is a common problem for college students because college represents a dramatic change in lifestyle—socially, economically, or academically—and changes in lifestyle may affect you psychologically, emotionally, and even physically. Many college students feel pressure to perform well and to earn good grades. This pressure also contributes to stress.

Although limited amounts of stress keep us active and alert, too much stress is harmful and produces negative psychological and physical effects. Stress can also interfere with concentration and often affects academic performance. If you are worried about getting good grades, you may feel stress when taking quizzes and exams and, as a result, may not score as well as you normally would.

Symptoms of Stress

Here are some common symptoms of stress:

headaches	feeling rushed
worn-out feeling, fatigue	difficulty concentrating
short-temperedness	queasiness, indigestion
listlessness	weight loss or gain

Stress can manifest itself in irrational thinking; small problems seem overwhelming; minor annoyances are exaggerated into serious confrontations. A disagreement with a friend may become a major conflict or argument, or receiving a stale doughnut from the snack bar seems more important than it is.

How to Reduce Stress

How you manage your life can reduce or prevent stress. Here are a few suggestions:

Avoid simultaneous life changes. College is a major change in lifestyle and is stressful in itself. Therefore, try to avoid additional major changes, such as marriage, initiating a conflict about religion with parents, or starting a new job.

Eliminate stressors. Once you've identified a source of stress, eliminate it if possible. If, for instance, a part-time job is stressful, quit it or find another that is less stressful. If a roommate is causing stress, attempt to rearrange your living conditions. If a math course is creating stress, take action: Go to the learning lab or math lab for assistance or inquire about tutoring.

Establish a daily routine. To eliminate hassles and make tasks as simple as possible, establish a daily routine. A routine eliminates the need to make numerous daily small decisions and, thereby, gives you a sense of smooth sailing.

Accentuate your accomplishments. When you feel pressured, stop and review what you have already accomplished that day and that week. This review will give you confidence that you can handle the workload. A positive attitude goes a long way overcoming stress.

Avoid added stress. When you are already under stress, it is easy to become disorganized and to use your time ineffectively. Actually, poor time management creates *more* stress, because you are able to accomplish less than you normally are able to do. When you find yourself under stress, it is helpful to follow a tighter, stricter time schedule then usual.

Get involved with campus activities. Some students become so involved with their course work that they do little else but study or worry about studying. In fact, they feel guilty or stressed when they are not studying. Be sure to allow some time in each day to relax and have fun. Campus activities provide a valuable means of releasing tension and taking your mind off your work.

Seek knowledgeable advice. If stress becomes an insurmountable problem, seek assistance from the student counseling center. The office may offer workshops in stress reduction techniques such as relaxation or biofeedback training.

Get physical exercise. Exercise often releases tension, promotes a general feeling of wellness, and improve self-concept. Many students report that as little as 30 minutes of exercise produces immediate relaxation and helps them to place daily events into perspective.

Get adequate amounts of sleep. Sleep allows the body time to replenish energy and to recover from the daily demands placed upon it. The amount of sleep one needs is highly individual. Discover how much you need by noticing patterns. For several weeks, analyze how well your day went and consider how much sleep you had the night before. Soon you will recognize patterns: You may notice irritability or bad days when you are short on sleep, or you might find you have caught a cold after a hectic weekend with little sleep. Try to respond to body signals rather than let work load or the expectations of others control your schedule.

Eat nutritious meals. Strength and endurance are affected by diet. When you feel rushed, eating available snacks rather than taking time to buy or prepare lunch or dinner or going to the dining hall may be tempting. Consuming large amounts of snacks food may produce fluctuations in your blood sugar level, which can cause headaches or queasiness. During rushed, stressful time, such as exam days, nutritious food can help you keep calm and think more clearly. In general, try to eat fruits, vegetables, and protein; avoid refined sugar, large amounts of caffeine, and high-calorie, low-nutrient snacks.

Use visualization. Create a mental picture of yourself calmly and systematically handling problems and new situations. Think of a real problem or create a hypothetical one and imagine yourself solving it carefully and systematically.

EXERCISE 3-6

1. List any symptoms of stress you have recently noticed.
2. Identify possible sources of stress by completing the following statements:
   a. What worries me most is _____.
   b. I get upset when _____.
   c. The problem I think about most is _____.
   d. The situation I would most like to changes is _____.
   e. I wish I could (had) _____.

SUMMARY

1. Time management and organization are two essential skills for college success. This chapter presents numerous suggestions for

   ❏ organizing your place of study
   ❏ approaching each course
   ❏ completing assignments and course requirements
   ❏ managing part-time jobs and finances

2. Effective time management can make the difference between mediocre academic performance and excellence. It involves

   ❏ establishing priorities
   ❏ analyzing time commitments
   ❏ building a semester plan
   ❏ using timesaving tips

3. Stress can affect your academic performance, health, and ability to concentrate. Symptoms of stress are described and stress reduction methods presented.

4. Concentration is essential for productive use of your time.

5. Strategies for focusing your attention and monitoring techniques are presented.

CLASS ACTIVITY

Directions:

Each student should prepare a semester plan. Working in pairs, students should analyze the efficiency of each other's plan and offer suggestions for increasing its efficiency.

FURTHER ANALYSIS

Directions:

Analyze the following situation and answer the questions below.

A freshman business student is returning to college after eight years working full time and is taking the following courses: writing, mathematics, economics, and introduction to business management. She has recently started her own business, a manicure shop which she opens two evenings a week and weekends. She is the single parent of a six-year-old son who has just begun kindergarten. This student is frustrated with college and feels constantly under stress. When she is working in her shop, she worries about her classes. When she studies, she finds herself thinking about how to get more clients for her shop. She feels guilty about not spending enough time with her son.

1. Analyze this student's source(s) of stress.
2. Is her return to college well timed?
3. What time management strategies would you suggest she use?
4. How can she reduce the stress she feels?

DISCUSSION

1. Students who must work 20 to 30 hours per week in order to afford college often experience academic difficulty. They face a Catch-22 situation: If they reduce their work hours, they cannot pay their tuition, and if they reduce their course load, they lose their financial aid. What alternatives might these students explore?
2. What advice would you give to a student who says he cannot work productively because his concentration is frequently broken by thoughts of problems with his two girlfriends, one from his hometown and another on campus?

3. Analyze the following situation: A student is failing his 8:00 A.M. western civilization class. He misses, on the average, one class per week. He says he just cannot wake up that early. What advice would you offer?
4. Identify additional time traps besides those mentioned in the chapter.
5. What timesaving tips, not mentioned here, have you found help to increase your efficiency?

FURTHER READING

Covey, Stephen R. *The Seven Habits of Highly Effective People.* New York: Simon, 1989.

Lakein, Alan. *How to Get Control of Your Time and Your Life.* New York: Signet Books, 1989.

Mancini, Marc. *Time Management.* Boston: Irwin, 1994.

4

Problem-Solving and Decision-Making Strategies

Learning Objectives

Develop a systematic approach to problem solving

Solve problems effectively and creatively

Develop decision-making strategies

Each day as a college student you are faced with numerous problems and decisions. Some are more serious than others, and some are more difficult to solve than others. Some of the problems and decisions you face are academic—how to solve math problems, how to conclude an English composition, or which of two essay questions to answer. You also face nonacademic problems and decisions in day-to-day living—how to get to class if your car won't start, whether to buy a compact disk player, or how to get that attractive person across the room to notice you. While these two types of problems and decisions seem quite different, the strategies for resolving them are very similar.

While we have all solved hundreds of problems and made thousands of decisions in our lifetimes, we may not have resolved them in the *best* possible ways. Nearly everyone can recall saying "Why didn't I think of . . . ?" or "If only I had thought of . . . !" after the fact. The purpose of this chapter is to present systematic approaches to problem solving and decision making.

PROBLEM-SOLVING STRATEGIES

Problem solving is a skill, like reading, writing, driving a car, or playing tennis. While some people may have a natural aptitude for it, problem solving is a skill that you can and should develop. This means you must be willing to give up the comfort of such defenses or excuses as "I'm not good at problem solving" or "I'm not creative." It also means that you have to be willing to think in new ways, to break old habits and develop new approaches to solving problems.

The ability to solve problems is a valuable asset. It can make a substantial difference in your success in academic courses, your future career, and in life. Many employers regard it as a necessary skill for holding positions of responsibility. Problem solving is a skill frequently assessed during a job interview. Questions that begin with "What would you do if . . . ?" or "Suppose you arrive at your desk one morning and you learn . . . " are designed to evaluate your problem-solving abilities.

A Model for Problem Solving

Put simply, a problem occurs when "what is" is not "what is desired." A problem exists when your grade in chemistry is not what you want it to be. A problem exists when you haven't finished your drawing for engineering, which is due tomorrow.

Let's call the "what is" your *present state* and the "what is desired" the *goal state*. Usually there are a number of ways to solve a problem, some more desirable than others. These various ways to solve a problem are called *solution paths*. A model for problem solving is shown in Figure 4-1.

This model, when used as a basis for problem solving, forces you to identify existing circumstances, the desired goal, and the various ways to

Figure 4-1
Problem-Solving Model

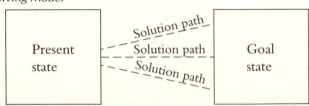

achieve it. Here's an everyday situation that fits the problem-solving model:

❏ ❏ ❏

Present State:	You have earned B- and C+ grades on your presentations for your public speaking course.
Desired State:	Solid B or A grades.
Solution Paths:	1. Practice your presentations with friends and ask them to critique your performance.
	2. Ask your instructor for advice.
	3. Spend more time organizing your presentations.

❏ ❏ ❏

EXERCISE 4-1

Directions:

For each of the following situations, identify the present state, the goal state, and suggest several solution paths.

1. You are scheduled to address your speech communication class when you suddenly realize you left your note cards on the desk in your room. The class begins in 10 minutes.
2. Your political science instructor has asked you to declare a topic for your term paper by Friday. When you go to the library to select a topic, you discover that all the sources you want to consult have been checked out by other students.
3. You find your assigned lab partner in biology to be irresponsible and careless, more intent on finishing and leaving early than on following procedures and discovering principles.

Problem-Solving Processes

The best way to improve your problem-solving abilities is to develop a systematic approach and to use it consistently with all types of problems. While some problems are solved easily with a burst of insight, most require deliberate, step-by-step analysis. It is easy to panic and let your mind run wild, jumping rapidly from one possible solution to another. However, this random approach to problem solving may create more problems than it solves; some solutions may be partially evaluated, and the long-range consequences of others ignored. Here's a step-by-step approach to problem solving.

Step 1: Specify the Problem

A first step to solving a problem is to identify it as specifically as possible. It involves evaluating the present state and determining how it differs from the goal state. For example, instead of saying, "My problem is my mass media course," try to pinpoint the problem: "My problem is the low grades I'm getting on the reaction papers," or "I don't understand what my professor is talking about in her lectures." Use the following suggestions to pinpoint a problem:

State the problem. The more specific you can be, the more likely it is that you will be able to identify workable solution paths.

Express the problem verbally or in writing. This process often helps to define and clarify the situation by eliminating extraneous information, focusing your attention, and triggering alternative perspectives.

Focus on language. Often language further clarifies the problem. For instance, if you approach a professor to change a grade, is your problem how to *argue* for a higher grade, to *persuade* him or her, or to *request* a reevaluation of your paper? The more specifically you can state the problem, the more likely it is that you will be able to identify workable solution paths.

Step 2: Analyze the Problem

Once you have specified the problem, the next step is to analyze it. Let us suppose you identified low grades on papers in mass media as your main problem with the course. Analyzing the problem involves learning as much as you can about it. You might begin by rereading each paper you have submitted and studying the professor's comments. Other possibilities include (1) arranging the papers from low to highest grade and analyzing the differences, (2) reading and comparing a friend's high-grade papers with yours, (3) asking a friend to criticize yours, or (4) discussing the papers with your professor.

On occasion, in analyzing a problem, you may need to look beyond the obvious, surface situation, to stretch your imagination and reach for more creative options. For example, a nursing student was having difficulty establishing a trusting rapport with patients. She and her clinical supervisor discussed various communication breakdowns, but none seemed to pinpoint the problem. Finally, after thinking about and discussing her problem with a lifelong friend, she understood her problem. She was working in a geriatrics ward, and both her elderly grandparents, to whom she had been very close, had recently died. She realized she was emotionally blocking the establishment of any rapport with an elderly person. She discussed the problem with her supervisor and then identified several solution paths.

In analyzing a problem, use the following suggestions:

Seek other perspectives: Discuss problems with professors, parents, or friends.

Be flexible in your analysis. Do not eliminate possibilities because they do not "sound like you" or seem likely.

Consider various strands of impact. Although a problem may seem economic (for example, how to afford a car for transportation), don't ignore social or emotional aspects (have you failed to consider public transportation because your friends do not use it?).

Brainstorm about all possibilities and implications. Spend three to five minutes listing anything you think of that remotely relates to your problem. Sort through the list later, preferably the next day. Most likely you will discover seeds of new ideas or new ways of looking at the problem.

Research problems for which you lack complete information. Libraries contain a wealth of information, and reading in related areas can trigger your mind and lead you to a solution. For example, a student having problems arranging for the care of her infant son discovered a book titled *Get Help*, which outlined procedures for locating and hiring babysitters. She learned that she needed to actively seek and advertise—rather than to passively follow up advertisements and references from friends.

EXERCISE 4-2

Directions:

Identify, as specifically as possible, the problem involved in each of the following situations, and suggest analyses.

1. A friend says she plans to drop out of school for the year—she has morning classes and now she realizes that her seven-year-old son needs supervision while walking to school: He fights with his peers and is picked on by older children.
2. A two-year college student is enrolled in a data processing curriculum. He did not realize that the curriculum is programming oriented and involves higher mathematics and technical skills. He wants to change his curriculum but doesn't know what area to transfer to.

Step 3: Formulate Possible Solution Paths

Once you have identified and analyzed the problem, you are ready to formulate possible solution paths. At this stage, your goal is to identify a wide range of possible solutions. Returning to the mass media problem, let's suppose that in analyzing your reaction papers you determined that your writing style and weak organization were causing low grades. Your ideas seemed adequate, but were not expressing them in a manner acceptable to your professor. The next step is to identify all possible ways to correct the problem. You consider: (1) getting help from a classmate, (2) getting a tutor from the learning lab, (3) asking the mass media instructor for help, (4) visiting the writing lab on campus for tutoring, (5) having a friend who has superior English skills edit and proofread your papers, and (6) asking your English instructor to recommend a book on writing style.

When formulating possible solutions, use the following tips:

Try to think of all possible solutions. For complicated problems, write down all possible solutions. At this stage, try not to evaluate a solution as you think of it. Just jot it down and continue thinking of others. Then reread your list; often it will help you think of alternative solutions.

Be creative. Don't be afraid to think of crazy or outlandish solutions. Often, while wild solutions may in themselves be unacceptable, some aspect is workable or may trigger a solution that is.

Consider similar problems and how you have solved them.

EXERCISE 4-3

Directions:

For each of the problems described in Exercise 4-2, identify as many solution paths as possible.

Step 4: Evaluate Possible Solution Paths

Once you have identified all possible solution paths, the next step is to weigh the advantages and disadvantages of each. To do so, you will need to think through each solution path in detail, considering how, when, and where you could accomplish each. For example, if you decided to get a tutor to help you write papers for the mass media course, you would need to consider practical details such as these:

Do I have time to meet with a tutor?
How will I feel working with a tutor?

What will I do if I don't like my tutor?
What if my tutor does not or cannot help me?

Consider both immediate and long-term results of each solution. For instance, for the mass media problem, having a friend edit and proofread your paper may be a workable solution to correct the immediate problem. In the long term, however, it may not be the best solution because you will not have improved your writing style and organizational skills.

For complex problems with numerous solution paths, the technique of *mapping* is often useful. Mapping is simply drawing a picture that connects details for each solution path.

For example, suppose you are majoring in business and your advisor is encouraging you to consider a double major. He has suggested English, communications, or psychology, but you cannot decide which to choose. To evaluate each, you might draw a chart such as the one shown in Table 4-1.

By studying the chart, you can more easily see the advantages of each and make comparisons. While a map usually clarifies the situation, it seldom identifies clearly the best solution. (If the best solution were that obvious, you wouldn't need to make the map.) Instead, the map enables you to evaluate each alternative logically and systematically.

In solving some problems, you may realize that you need more information before you can evaluate various solution paths. For the mass media course problem considered throughout this chapter, you may need to know whether tutoring can be arranged conveniently before you can evaluate it as an alternative. Or, in choosing a double major, you may find

Table 4-1
EVALUATING SOLUTION PATHS

	English	*Communications*	*Psychology*
Required credit hours outside major	0–16	24	0
Number of electives	24–48	35–45	64–74
Total credit hours in major	57	36	31
Graduation requirement	Thesis	No	Senior seminar
Foreign language requirement	Yes	No	No
Additional semester needed	Yes	No	No

that you want more information than is provided in the college catalog. You might talk with your advisor or meet with the department chairperson or research information on job opportunities in your career guidance and placement center or library.

<hr>

EXERCISE 4-4

Directions:
Working in small groups, evaluating each of the solution paths you devised for the problems listed in Exercise 4-2.

<hr>

Step 5: Choose a Solution

The last step in problem solving is the selection of one solution path. In weighing the various solution paths, there are three factors to consider. **Compatibility with your priorities.** In choosing a solution, you must match the solution with your priorities—what you have identified as most important to you. In the case of the mass media course papers, if an immediate improvement in grades is more important than improving your writing skills, some solutions are better than others. In evaluating majors, for example, you will need to decide how convenient spending an additional semester is, whether it fits within your short-term and long-term goals.

Amount of risk. Some solutions involve more risk than others. For instance, working with a tutor from the learning lab may be a more reliable, controlled, and organized solution (and therefore less risky) than depending on the good nature of a classmate to help. The amount of risk you are willing to take depends on the seriousness of the problem and the consequences if the solution fails.

Practicality. The most logical of solutions won't work if it is not practical. Regardless of how good a solution may seem, if you cannot carry it through, it is worthless. For instance, getting a tutor may seem the best solution to the reaction paper problem. However, if the tutor is only available at 8:00 in the morning and you know you'll have trouble keeping appointments at that time, then the solution is not practical.

KEYS TO PROBLEM SOLVING

Here are a few tips to make the problem-solving process work for you. Use them in conjunction with the problem-solving model just described.

Think aloud. Problem solving is a cognitive, mental process. For complicated problems, many people find it useful to think aloud or talk to themselves as they work through the problem-solving steps. Hearing yourself think, so to speak, seems to facilitate the process. Sometimes, especially when solving academic problems, by thinking aloud you catch yourself using the wrong rule or formula, or saying something that is contradictory to what you have read.

Allow time for incubation. Archimedes, an ancient Greek, is said to have run naked through the streets shouting "Eureka!" He was announcing that he had, while taking a bath, discovered the solution to a problem he had been studying for years, which is known today as Archimedes's principle. How and why was Archimedes able to arrive at a solution at a time when he wasn't even thinking about it? You may have had similar experiences when all of a sudden during an exam you know an answer you couldn't think of ten minutes ago, or a new solution to a problem you have been wrestling with for days flashes in your mind without warning.

What happened to Archimedes and what happens to you when you get sudden flashes of insight illustrates a principle known as *incubation.* Just a chicken eggs are nurtured in the warmth and humidity of an incubator until ready to hatch, ideas, too, need incubation, until they are ready to hatch or come together to solve a problem. Even though you may not be consciously thinking about a problem, it is still there, in the back of your mind.

Time away from the problem allows ideas to gel or consolidate. It also provides a psychological distance and new perspective on the problem. The best advice, then, for when you cannot solve a problem is to wait. Give yourself time for the various solution paths to settle in. Distance from a problem also clears your mind, lessens its importance, and may provide a fresh outlook.

Talk about the problem. If you describe the problem to someone else and talk about it, the problem often crystallizes, becoming clearer and more defined so that new solution paths sometimes surface. Talking to someone else externalizes the problem (takes it outside of you) and provides a measure of psychological distance.

EXERCISE 4-5

Directions:

Study the two problems listed below and apply the five-step problem-solving approach to each. Keep a written record of the process. Generate as many solutions as possible, and then state which solution you would select. Justify your choice.

1. A major change has occurred recently in your family's financial situation, and you are not sure whether you will be able to af-

ford to attend college next semester. Because it is near the end of the spring semester, you have heard that all financial aid funds have already been distributed for the next academic year.

2. It is the sixth week of a 15-week semester, and you have been hospitalized for complications resulting from bronchial pneumonia. Your doctor estimates you can return to classes in two to three weeks. You have already missed one week of classes.

DECISION-MAKING STRATEGIES

Decision making is a process of making choices. Each of us makes numerous choices each day: what to wear, which way to walk to class, which assignment to work on first, which essay question to answer. Many are relatively unimportant—what to order for lunch, for example. Others, however, are of critical importance with far-reaching impact—what major to choose, for instance.

The purpose of this section is to present strategies for effective decision making, to enable you to make those important choices in a reasoned, deliberate manner.

Types of Decisions

Let us consider several situations and analyze the type of decision making involved in each.

❑ ❑ ❑

Situation 1	You order a pizza with cheese, pepperoni, and mushrooms.
Situation 2	On a spring afternoon you and a group of friends, at the last minute, decide to cut class and take a ride to the lake.
Situation 3	You decided to register for child psychology next semester because you've just finished Introductory Psychology and it is required in your major.

❑ ❑ ❑

While each of the situations involved choice, each involved very different types of thinking. In ordering a pizza, you made a *routine decision* involving little or not thought; you usually or always order it that way. The trip to the lake was a last-minute *impulsive decision*. The decision to register for child psychology was a *reasoned decision* based on evidence.

Routine decisions are usually safe, habitual choices that make your life run smoothly and eliminate the need to constantly make choices. Impulsive decisions on social occasions, for example when everyone decides to go bowling at midnight, can be fun and interesting. However, in other situations, since they are not well thought out, they can cause or lead to problems. Suppose, for example, that the day you impulsively decide to cut class, the instructor gives an unannounced quiz.

In new or important situations, the best type of decision to make is a reasoned one, in which alternatives are identified and weighed and outcomes are predicted.

Making Reasoned Decisions

Decision making has much in common with problem solving. In problem solving you identify and evaluate solution paths; in decision making you make a similar discovery and evaluation of alternatives. The crux of decision making, then, is the careful identification and evaluation of alternatives, as shown in the following example.

Suppose your criminal justice instructor allows each student to elect, at the end of the third week of class, one of four grading options: (1) half the grade from your quiz average and half from the term paper (2) half from the quizzes and half from the final exam, (3) half from the term paper and half from the final exam, (4) only the final exam. In analyzing the situation, you realize you must choose the option that best suits your learning style and will enable you to earn the best possible grade. Since your instructor already identified all alternatives, your next step is to

---

❏ ❏ ❏
Thinking Critically . . . About Alternatives

An important step in decision making is weighing alternatives and selecting the one that is best for you. As you weigh alternatives, use the following suggestions:

- Consider the outcome each is likely to produce, in both the short term and the long term.
- Compare alternatives based on how easily you can accomplish each.
- Evaluate possible negative side effects each may produce.
- Consider the risk, if any, involved in each.
- Be creative and original; don't eliminate alternatives because you have not heard about or used them before.

weigh and compare them. Factors you must consider include how well you perform on quizzes and exams, how easily and how well you can write a term paper, and so forth. Then, in making a decision, you must consider risks and predict future outcomes.

An important part of decision making is to predict both short-term and long-term outcomes for each alternative. You may find that while an alternative seems most desirable in the present, it may pose problems or complications over a longer time period. For example, in choosing courses for next semester, suppose you decide against taking a public speaking course. You reason that it is not required, only recommended, and a mass media course would be more interesting. Your decision is acceptable for the short term. However, if you are considering a career in teaching, you may later find that a public speaking course would have been beneficial and that your decision was not effective in the long term.

EXERCISE 4-6

Directions:
For each of the following situations, identify several alternatives and then list factors that you would weigh in making a decision.

1. Decide whether to attend summer session this year.
2. Decide what to do about a roommate who frequently interrupts you and distracts you from studying.
3. Decide which campus organizations or social groups to join.

SUMMARY

1. Problem solving and decision making each require a systematic approach.
2. A problem exists when what is (the present state) differs from what is desired (the goal state).
3. Problem solving involves five steps:

   ❏ specifying the problem
   ❏ analyzing the problem
   ❏ formulating possible solution paths
   ❏ evaluating solution paths
   ❏ choosing a solution

4. Three strategies for solving problems effectively are

❏ thinking aloud
❏ allowing time for incubation
❏ verbalizing the problem

5. Decision making is a process of identifying and evaluating choices. Routine, impulsive, and reasoned are the three types of decisions.

CLASS ACTIVITY

Directions:

Working in groups of four or five students, discuss the following situation and answer the questions below:

Suppose you have just read an article in the campus newspaper that a faculty committee at your four-year college is discussing a proposal to eliminate letter grades for each student's first two semesters of study. Proponents argue that the proposed scheme will eliminate grade pressure and competition and allow students to focus on learning.

1. Identify the present state, goal state, and solution path in this situation.
2. Identify the problems this proposal, if approved, might create for particular types of students.
3. Identify alternative solution paths and evaluate each.
4. Assume a member of your group is student representative on the committee and the group must direct this member as to how to respond to this proposal at the next committee meeting. What process would you use to come to a decision? What factors would you weigh in making this decision? Justify your decision. Choose a group spokesperson who will describe your decision-making process to the class. The class should then evaluate various decision-making strategies.

FURTHER ANALYSIS

Directions:

Analyze the following situation and answer the questions below:

A student has completed his freshman year at a community college. When advance registering for his third semester classes, he realizes that a normal course load would put him within six credit hours of graduation. He is considering registering for a six-hour overload and graduating a semester early. As an accounting major, he has consistently earned high C and B grades. Upon graduation, he intends to get a full-time job and pursue a four-year degree part time. His goal is to become a Certified Public Accountant. He works part time to earn living expenses.

1. What is the real problem this student faces? What solution paths are available?
2. List the advantages and disadvantages of each solution path.
3. What factors should he consider in evaluating various solution paths?
4. Project several different final outcomes.

DISCUSSION

1. Consider your college and its surrounding campus. Identify current problems it faces. (Local or campus newspapers may serve as a reference point for the discussion.)
2. What problems and decisions do you feel college students typically face? Do they differ according to age? What other factors control the level and type of problems students encounter?
3. Describe an instance in which incubation occurred in problem solving.
4. How do you decide how much risk to take in making a decision?
5. In what situation, if any, do you feel routine, habitual decision making can limit or restrict your opportunities?
6. Describe an instance of ineffective problem solving you have recently observed or read about.

FURTHER READING

Hayes, John R. *The Complete Problem-Solver*. Philadelphia: Franklin, 1989.

Janis, Irving L. *A Practical Guide for Making Decisions*. New York: Free, 1980.

Rubinstein, Moshe, and Kenneth Pfeiffer. *Concepts in Problem Solving*. Englewood Cliffs, NJ: Prentice, 1980.

PART

□ □ □

2

LEARNING AND THINKING STRATEGIES

5

□ □ □ ▬▬▬▬▬▬▬▬▬▬▬▬▬▬

Learning and Memory

Learning Objectives

Discover how learning and memory processes work

Learn how to store and retrieve information more efficiently

L et's assume you have just finished reading a chapter in a data processing text; you read carefully and underlined important ideas. How much of that chapter are you likely to remember tomorrow? How much will you recall next week? The answers are surprising! Research evidence suggests that within one day, you will have forgotten more than half of what you read, and within a week, your recall will have dropped to less than 30 percent. These statistics have serious implications for you as a learner as well as later in your career. Despite all seriousness of purpose and good intentions, the rate of forgetting is rapid and dramatic *unless* you take specific steps to prevent it. This chapter briefly describes how learning and memory work. Once you become familiar with the learning process, you will learn numerous strategies for improving storage and retrieval of information and for overcoming forgetting.

HOW LEARNING AND MEMORY WORK

A popular but incorrect notion of memory is that it is a vast storage tank or a huge repository where information is deposited and retained. Rather, memory is a three-stage process involving encoding, storage, and retrieval. *Encoding* (or acquisition) is a process of acquiring information. Suppose you are unable to answer the question on a business exam, "Define a capital account." If you never heard of a capital account, your memory broke down at the encoding stage; that is, you never acquired the information. The next stage of memory, *storage,* occurs when information is stored, briefly or permanently. A change in your nervous system occurs that allows storage to occur. This change is described as a neural or memory trace. If you once knew the term "capital account" and now cannot recall it, the memory trace may have faded or decayed. *Retrieval* is the process of getting at and using information held in storage. Another reason for your inability to remember the definition of capital account is retrieval failure. Although the information is stored, you are unable to retrieve it. Figure 5-1 is a visual model of verbal learning and memory processes. Refer to it frequently as you read the sections that explain each stage.

Figure 5-1
A Model of Memory

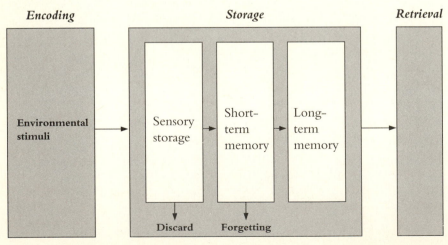

Stage 1: Encoding

Every waking moment your mind is bombarded with information and impressions of what is going on around you. Your five senses—hearing, sight, touch, taste, and small—provide information about the world around you and your interaction with it. Think for a moment of all the signals your brain receives at a given moment. If you are reading, your eyes transmit not only the visual patterns of the words, but also information about the size and color of the print. You may hear a door slamming, a clock ticking, a dog barking. Your sense of smell may detect perfume or cigarette smoke; your sense of touch and feeling may signal that a pen you are using to underline will soon run out of ink or that the room is chilly. When you listen to a classroom lecture, you are constantly receiving stimuli—from the professor, from the lecture hall, from students around you. All these environmental stimuli are transmitted to your brain for a very brief *sensory storage* and interpretation.

Stage 2: Storage

Sensory Storage

Information received from your sense organs is transmitted through the nervous system to the brain, which accepts and interprets it. The information lingers briefly in the nervous system for your brain to interpret it. This lingering is known as *sensory storage.*

How does your mind handle this barrage of information from the senses? Thanks to *selective attention,* or *selective perception,* your brain automatically sorts out the more important signals from the trivial ones. Trivial signals, such as insignificant noises around you, are ignored or discarded. Through skills of concentration and attention, you can train yourself to ignore or discard other, more distracting signals, such as a dog barking or people talking in the background.

Although your sensory storage accepts all information, data are kept there only briefly, unless less than a few seconds. Then the information either decays or is replaced with incoming new stimuli. The function, then, of sensory storage is to retain information long enough for you to selectively attend to it and transmit it to your short-term memory.

Short-Term Memory

Short-term memory holds the information acquired from your sensory storage system. It is used to store information you wish to retain for only a few seconds. A telephone number, for example, is stored in your short-term memory until you dial it. A lecturer's words are retained until you can record them in your notes. Most researchers agree that short-term memory lasts much less than one minute, perhaps 20 seconds or less. Information can be kept or maintained longer if you practice or rehearse the information (repeating a phone number, for example). When you are introduced to someone, then, unless you repeat or rehearse his or her name at the time of introduction, you will not be able to remember it. New incoming information will force it out of your short-term memory.

Your short-term memory is limited in capacity as well as in time span. Research conducted by George Miller, a psychologist who studied memory, suggests that we have room in our short-term memory to store from five to nine bits (or pieces) of information at a time, or on the average, seven.[1] Known as the Number Seven Theory, this finding has direct implications in both daily and academic situations. When you read a textbook chapter or listen to a lecture, for example, your short-term memory is unable to retain each piece of information you are receiving. To retain information beyond the limitations of short-term memory, it must be transferred to your long-term memory for more permanent storage.

EXERCISE 5-1

Directions:
Answer the following items using your knowledge of the memory process.

1. Observe and analyze the area in which you are sitting. What sensory impressions (sights, sounds, touch sensations) have you been ignoring due to selective attention?
2. Can you remember what you ate for lunch last Tuesday? If not, why not?
3. Why are dashes placed in your social security number after the third and fifth numbers?
4. Explain why two people are able to carry on a deep conversation at a crowded, noisy party.
5. Explain why someone who looked up a phone number and then walked into another room to dial it forgot the number.

Learning: The Transfer from Short- to Long-Term Memory

To retain information beyond the brief moment you acquire it, you must transfer it to long-term memory for permanent storage. Several processes can help you store information in long-term memory: rote learning, rehearsal, and recoding.

Rote learning. Rote learning involves repetition of information in the form in which it was acquired in sensory storage. Learning the spelling of a word, memorizing the exact definition of a word, or repeating a formula until you can remember it are examples. Material learned through this means is often learned in a fixed order. Rote learning is usually an inefficient means to store information because, as you will see later, it is difficult to retrieve.

Elaborative rehearsal. Rehearsal, used at this stage, involves much more than simple repetition or practice. Elaborative rehearsal is a thinking process. It involves connecting new material with already learned material, asking questions, and making associations. It is a process of making the information meaningful and fitting it into an established category or relating it to existing memory stores. This form of rehearsal is discussed in more detail later.

Recoding. Recoding is a process of rearranging, changing, or grouping information so that it becomes more meaningful and easier to recall. For example, you could recode the following shopping list into three easier to remember groups:

> eggs, carrots, bleach, oranges, laundry soap, milk, onions, yogurt, detergent, cheese, plums, ammonia

❏ ❏ ❏

Dairy	*Produce*	*Cleaning supplies*
Eggs, milk, cheese, yogurt	Carrots, onions, oranges, plums	Laundry soap, ammonia, bleach

❏ ❏ ❏

You could recode information from a reading assignment by outlining it. Taking notes from lectures is also a form of recoding.

Rehearsal and recoding are the underlying principles on which many learning strategies presented later in this book are based. Chapter 10, for example, discusses textbook underlining and marking. Underlining is, however, actually a form of elaborative rehearsal. When you decide which information to underline, you are reviewing the information and sorting the important from the unimportant. When you make marginal notes, you are recoding the information by classifying, organizing, labeling, or summarizing it.

EXERCISE 5-2

Directions:

Answer the following questions using your knowledge of the memory process.

1. On many campuses, weekly recitations or discussions are scheduled for small groups to review material presented in large lecture classes. What learning function do these recitation sections provide?
2. A literature instructor showed her class a film based on a short story that she had assigned. What learning function(s) did the film provide?
3. Why might a text that contains pictures and diagrams be easier to learn from that one without them?
4. Two groups of students read the same textbook chapter. One group underlined key ideas on each page. The second group paraphrased and recorded the important ideas from each page. Explain why the second group received higher scores on a test based on the chapter than did the first group.

Long-Term Memory

Long-term memory is your permanent store of information. Unlike short-term memory, your long-term memory is nearly unlimited in both span and capacity. It contains hundreds of thousands of facts, details, impressions, and experiences that you have accumulated throughout your life.

Information is stored in long-term memory in three types of codes: (1) linguistic (language), (2) imaginal (mental or visual images), and (3) motor (physical). The linguistic code, which deals with verbal information, is the most important in academic learning. Ideas, concepts, and facts are encoded and often stored using language. Activities such as taking lecture notes, underlining texts, and writing outlines are forms of linguistic coding. Imaginal coding involves creation of mental or visual images. If, for example, you drew a diagram of a process or sketched the human ear in order to learn its parts, you would be using imaginal, or visual, coding. The third form of coding, motor, refers primarily to physical activities such as riding a bicycle, driving a car, or hitting a baseball. Significant research evidence suggests that dual coding—using more than one type of coding to store information—produces better recall than if only one code is used.

Stage 3: Retrieval

Think of retrieval as pulling stored information from your memory. Academic tasks requiring you to retrieve knowledge include math or science problems, quizzes and exams, and papers. Retrieval is integrally tied to storage. The manner in which information is stored in your memory affects its availability and the ease with which you can retrieve it. For example, suppose you have studied a topic but find that on an exam you are unable to remember much about it. There are several possible explanations: (1) you never completely learned (stored) the information at all, (2) you did not study (store) the information in the right way, (3) you are not asking the right questions or using the right means to retrieve it, or (4) you have forgotten it. Later this chapter suggests strategies for improving the effectiveness of both storage and retrieval.

EXERCISE 5-3

Directions:

Use the principles of memory discussed so far in this chapter to explain each of the following situations.

1. A student does well on multiple choice items on a test, but has difficulty with easy questions. What does this indicate about how he stored the information?
2. A student spends more time than anyone else in the class preparing for the midterm exam, yet she cannot remember important definitions and concepts at the time of the exam. Offer several possibilities that may explain her dilemma.
3. What form(s) of coding does each of the following situations involve?
   a. Replacing a ribbon in your printer or typewriter
   b. Drawing a blood sample from a patient's arm
   c. Plotting a graph to include in a term paper that shows the relationships between median income, sex, and educational level
   d. Interpreting a map
   e. Solving a problem in business math

4. You cannot state the sixth number of your social security number without repeating the first five.

EXERCISE 5-4

Directions:
Identify the encoding, storage, and retrieval stages in each of the following tasks.

1. Learning to read a patient's chart
2. Learning the lyrics to a popular song
3. Learning to balance a ledger in accounting
4. Learning to operate a computer

Forgetting

Despite the vast capacity of human long-term memory, not all information remains there indefinitely. Forgetting does occur, and for newly learned material, it can occur at a dramatic rate. Table 5-1 summarizes the results of a research study[2] designed to measure the rate at which subjects forget previously learned verbal material.

These data have serious implications for you as a learner. They indicate that you will quickly forget a large portion of information you have learned *unless you take action to prevent it.*

Numerous theories have been offered to explain why forgetting occurs. One argues that the learned information fades from disuse. Fading may occur when the neural trace established when new learning occurs weakens from disuse, much as handwriting on a piece of paper fades over

Table 5-1
RATE OF FORGETTING

Time Lapse from Initial Learning	Amount of Material Remembered
1 day	54%
7 days	35%
14 days	21%
21 days	18%
28 days	19%
63 days	17%

Figure 5-2
Types of Interference

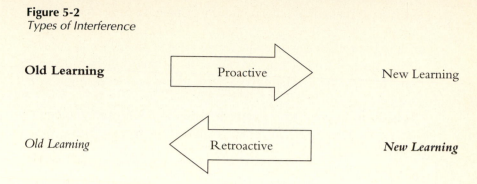

time. Another more popular theory suggests that interference with competing information causes forgetting. Two types of interference have been identified, as shown in Figure 5-2.

Proactive Interference

This situation occurs when old knowledge interferes with the recall of new, recently acquired knowledge. For example, you may have difficulty remembering a new formula in math if it is very similar to one you had learned last week. To combat this type of interference, make a conscious effort to examine similarities and differences between old and new learning.

Retroactive Interference

New learning sometimes interferes with the recall of old learning. You may be unable to recall a lecture of two weeks ago because the content of this week's lecture is blocking it. To overcome this type of interference, be certain to review often previously learned material as well as to keep current with new material.

EXERCISE 5-5

Directions:
Answer the following questions using your knowledge of memory and forgetting.

1. Someone who memorized a phone number before he left a party is unable to recall it the next evening. Why?
2. A victim of a robbery is unable to give a detailed, accurate description of the criminal to a police artist the morning after the

robbery. What could the victim have done to improve his or her recall?

3. A student is taking an introductory course in Spanish and, at the same time, is completing several years of study of Hebrew as part of his religious training. What learning problems might he expect?

4. What learning problems would you expect if you were taking a British literature and an American literature course during the same semester?

STRATEGIES FOR IMPROVING ENCODING, STORAGE, AND RETRIEVAL

Now that you have a notion of how memory works, you are ready to learn strategies that will both increase the effectiveness of your memory processes and retard forgetting.

Strategies for Improving Encoding

Use the following suggestions to improve encoding, which is the process of taking in information.

Exclude competing stimuli. Consciously exclude everything that does not relate to what you want to encode. For instance, if you are reading, do not sit where there are other competing visual stimuli, such as television.

Use various sensory modes. Use as many senses as possible to take in information. When listening to a lecture, for example, pay attention to visual clues the lecturer provides as well as to what he or she says.

Carefully and specifically define your purpose. As you filter incoming information, know clearly and specifically what types of information you need. If you are reading reference material for a research paper, you may need to pay attention to facts and statistics. If you are reading material to prepare for a class discussion, however, you might focus on controversial issues.

Use previewing. Since encoding involves accepting an incoming message, it is helpful to anticipate both the content and structure of that message. Previewing, discussed in Chapter 6, provides this preliminary information.

Strategies for Improving Storage

Use the following suggestions to improve how efficiently you store information.

Use immediate review. After working on a chapter for several hours (with frequent breaks) it is tempting, when you finish, to close the book and move on to something else. To quit, however, without taking five to ten minutes to review what you have read is a serious mistake. Since you have already invested several hours of time and effort, it is worthwhile to spend a few more minutes insuring that investment. Review *immediately* following reading is an effective way of storing information and facilitating retrieval. Review of your notes immediately following a lecture is also effective.

Immediate review is effective because it consolidates new knowledge. Material that is meaningful and related to existing learning is more easily stored. As you read, you encounter a great deal of information that is not organized or focused. The relative importance of ideas is not completely clear until you establish the connections among ideas. Immediate review allows you to begin to see the big picture, to discover how individual portions of the chapter fit together and how they relate to prior learning.

To review a chapter you have just read, follow these seven steps:

1. Begin as soon as you have finished reading the chapter.
2. Go back to the beginning of the chapter and review all the boldface headings.
3. For each heading, form a question. If a heading is "Causes of Hormonal Imbalance," asks "What are the causes of hormonal imbalance?" For the heading "Treating Hormonal Imbalance," ask "What are the treatments?"
4. Then look away from the page, or cover it up with a sheet of paper, and try to answer each question. Try to recall the causes of hormonal imbalance and its treatment. You can answer mentally, aloud, or on paper.
5. Check to see if you have answered the question completely by referring back to the text. If you could not answer your question or only partially recalled information, check to see what you have missed and then retest your recall.
6. Continue through the chapter in this manner, heading by heading.
7. When you have finished, stop and think. Try to recall how the chapter was organized and how it progressed from idea to idea. Try to identify five to ten key points it discussed. Reread the chapter summary, if available, to verify these points.

Substantial research evidence supports the value of immediate review. Students who use immediate review consistently experience higher retention than those who do not review.

Use numerous sensory channels to store information. Many students regard reading and studying as only a visual means of processing and reviewing information. Learning can be enhanced, however, by using sight, sound, and touch, as well. If you can incorporate writing, listening, drawing or diagramming, and recitation or discussion into your study habits, storage will be more effective. Think of this technique as a means of reducing the burden on your linguistic processing systems by transferring some of the load to other forms of processing. Evidence suggests that each form of coding is distinct and that each creates its own path or trace. Using several forms of coding, then, creates several paths through which information can be retrieved.

Organize or recode information to be stored. Remembering a large number of individual facts or pieces of information is often a difficult, frustrating task. *Recoding* is a primary means of storing information in your long-term memory. Recoding involves organizing or reducing information into groups or chunks. Instead of overloading your memory with numerous individual facts, you are inputting an organized, meaningful set of information that is stored as one chunk rather than numerous individual facts. Retrieval, then, is easier, too, because a chunk is retrieved as one piece and related information stays together. For example, a physics student used the chunking strategy to organize and connect the topic of speed, velocity, and acceleration into one topic, motion. A business student studying the differences among consumer markets used chunking to group the differences into three categories: geographic, demographic, and income differences.

To organize information, keep the following suggestions in mind:

❏ Discover how the material you are studying is connected. Search for some organizing principle.
❏ Look for similarities and differences.
❏ Look for sequences and for obvious divisions or breaking points within the sequences.

EXERCISE 5-6

Directions:
Decide how you could organize or recode each of the following types of information for most effective storage.

1. The problems two-career families face

2. The causes of the Vietnam War
3. The importance of Third World countries
4. Ecological problems of the future

Use elaboration. Mere repetition of material is seldom an effective storage strategy. Studying a chapter by rereading it, for instance, would not be effective. Instead you must think about, or *elaborate,* upon the material—ask questions, make associations and inferences, think of practical applications, and create mental images. Elaboration makes the new material meaningful and easier to store. For example, a mechanical engineering student was studying the first law of thermodynamics: Whenever heat is added to a system, it transforms to an equal amount of some other form of energy. The student began by being certain she understood the law, so she expressed it in writing using her own words. She wrote: "Heat added = increase in internal energy and/or external work done by the system." Then she began to think of situations in which she had observed the law, a steam engine's operation, for instance. Then she asked herself: What happens in the atmosphere when a body of air is heated? What external work is done?

<hr>

EXERCISE 5-7

Directions:
Discuss techniques that might improve storage of the following tasks.

1. Learning to identify and distinguish various types of figurative language used in literature
2. Learning various bacterial forms and characteristics
3. Learning the environmental factors that effect entry of a product into a foreign market for a business marketing course
4. Learning the process of federal budget preparation for an American government course

<hr>

Connect new learning with previous learning. Isolated, unrelated pieces of information are difficult to store and also difficult to retrieve. If, however, you can link new learning to already stored information, it will be easier to store and retrieve since you have an established memory slot in which to hold it. For example, an economics student associated the factors influencing the supply and demand curves with practical instances from his family's retail florist business.

Strategies for Improving Retrieval

Your ability to retrieve information is the true test of how accurately and completely you have stored it. The following strategies will improve your ability to retrieve information.

Use visualization. As you read, study, and learn a body of information, try to visualize, or create a mental picture of it. Your picture or image should be sufficiently detailed to include as much related information as possible. A student of anatomy and physiology found visualizations an effective way to learn the parts of the skeletal system. She would first draw it on paper and then visualize, or mentally draw, the system.

❏ ❏ ❏
Thinking Critically . . . About Learning Strategies

In this chapter you encountered many learning strategies. Some will work better for you than others; a few may not work for you at all. Some may work for one course but not for another. The key to making information in this chapter work for you is to try to *critically evaluate* each strategy.

Begin by selecting two or three strategies that appeal to you. Decide which ones you will use for which course. Use them for a week. At the end of the week, do a preliminary evaluation. Rate the strategy as "very useful," "somewhat useful," or "not useful," and record your evaluation in the chart shown opposite.

Use the following questions to help you in rating each strategy:

1. Did the strategy seem to make a difference in how easily I was able to learn? (You may be able to answer this question more accurately after you take an exam or quiz.)
2. Was it easy to use?
3. Was it time consuming?
4. Did it help me see the information in a new way?
5. Did it improve my understanding of the material?

The next week, choose two or three more strategies to concentrate on and evaluate.

A word of caution: Some strategies may take a little time to get used to. If a strategy seems to have potential but does not work right away, stick with it for a longer period of time.

Visualization, a type of imaginal coding, makes retrieval easier because the information is stored in one unified piece, and, if you can recall any part of the mental picture, then you will be able to retrieve the whole picture.

Develop retrieval clues. Think of your memory as having slots or compartments in which information is stored. If you can name or label what is in the slot, you will know where to look to find information that fits that slot. Think of memory slots as similar to the way kitchen cupboards are often organized, with specific items in specific places. If you need a knife to cut a pizza, you look in the silverware and utensils drawer. Similarly, if

SKILL	*RATING*		
	Very Useful	*Somewhat Useful*	*Not Useful*
Encoding			
Exclude competing stimuli	☐	☐	☐
Use various sensory modes	☐	☐	☐
Define your purpose	☐	☐	☐
Use previewing	☐	☐	☐
Storage			
Use immediate review	☐	☐	☐
Use numerous sensory channels	☐	☐	☐
Recode information	☐	☐	☐
Use elaboration	☐	☐	☐
Connect new to previous learning	☐	☐	☐
Retrieval			
Use visualization	☐	☐	☐
Develop retrieval clues	☐	☐	☐
Simulate rehearsal tasks	☐	☐	☐
Learn beyond mastery	☐	☐	☐

you have a memory slot labeled "environmental problems" in which you store information related to pollution, its problems, causes, and solutions, you can retrieve information on air pollution by calling the appropriate retrieval clue. Developing retrieval clues involves selecting a word or phrase that summarizes or categorizes several pieces of information. For example, you might use the phrase "motivation theories" to organize information for a psychology course on instinct, drive, cognitive, arousal, and opponent-process theories and the major proponents of each.

Simulate rehearsal tasks. Practice retrieving learned information by simulating test conditions. If you are studying for a math exam, prepare by solving problems. If you know your exam in a law enforcement course will consist of three essay questions, then prepare by anticipating possible essay questions and drafting and answer to each. The form and process of practice, then, must be patterned after and modeled upon the event for which you are preparing.

Learn beyond mastery. It is tempting to stop studying as soon as you feel you have learned a given body of information. However, to ensure complete, thorough learning, it is best to conduct a few more reviews. When you learned to drive a car, you did not stop practicing parallel parking after the first time you accomplished it correctly. Similarly, for a botany course you should not stop reviewing the process of photosynthesis and its place within the carbon cycle at the moment you feel you have mastered it. Instead, use additional review to make the material stick and to prevent interference from subsequent learning.

EXERCISE 5-8

Directions:

What strategies would you use to learn (encode, store, and retrieve) each of the following types of information most efficiently?

1. Vocabulary words for a Spanish I course
2. The process of leaf development in plants for a botany course
3. A comparison between the Bill of Rights at the time it was written and in today's political and social climate
4. Types of nonverbal communication and their uses in communicating with an audience

SUMMARY

1. Memory involves a three-stage process;

   ❏ encoding
   ❏ storage
   ❏ retrieval

2. You are constantly bombarded with information from each of your five senses. *Encoding* is a process of receiving or acquiring information from your senses.

3. There are three levels of storage:

   ❏ sensory storage
   ❏ short-term memory
   ❏ long-term memory

4. Information received from your senses lingers briefly in sensory storage. Through selective attention, your brain filters out the unimportant and transmits the more important from sensory storage to short-term memory in the brain.

5. Since short-term memory is limited in both span and capacity, information can be held there only briefly.

6. Information you wish to retain permanently must be transferred to your long-term or permanent memory.

7. Information can be transferred from short-term to long-term memory through

   ❏ rote learning
   ❏ elaborative rehearsal
   ❏ recoding

   Retrieval refers to pulling information out of long-term memory.

8. Forgetting occurs at a dramatic rate unless it is prevented through various encoding, storage, and retrieval strategies.

9. Encoding strategies include

   ❏ controlling competing stimuli
   ❏ using various sensory modes
   ❏ defining purpose
   ❏ previewing

10. Techniques for improving storage include

   ❏ immediate review
   ❏ sensory channels

❏ recoding
❏ elaboration
❏ previous learning

11. Retrieval can be improved by use of

❏ visualization
❏ retrieval clues
❏ simulation
❏ learning beyond mastery

CLASS ACTIVITY

Directions:

Form groups of four or five students and discuss causes of and solutions to each of the following situations:

1. A student frequently misplaces his car keys and wastes valuable time looking for them.
2. A friend has difficulty remembering names of new people he meets at a party.
3. A student's parents own an Apple computer, and he learned to use Appleworks, a word processing program, to type his papers. Now that he lives on campus and must use the IBM computers, he is trying to learn to use a new software program, WordPerfect. He is having difficulty because he frequently confuses commands.

FURTHER ANALYSIS

Directions:

Analyze the following situation and answer the questions that follow.

You are taking a course in mass media and you are studying techniques and effects of advertising. Your instructor has given the following assignment:

What principles of learning and memory do advertisers take advantage of when preparing and running an advertisement for television?

1. What do you think the instructor's purpose was in giving the assignment?
2. Outline a response to the question, discussing encoding, storage, and retrieval.

DISCUSSION

1. A drafting student said she felt that the storage and retrieval strategies presented in this chapter were of little use to her because her course required little factual learning. The focus of her course is labs, drawing assignments, and exams that require drawings. Do you agree with this student's assessment?
2. In what everyday situations do you use visualization?
3. Give several examples of situations where you have over-learned, or learned beyond mastery.
4. List the courses you are taking. Then review this chapter and indicate which storage and retrieval strategies would be useful for each.
5. Some researchers have proposed that human memory is structured and functions like a computer. Discover as many similarities and differences as possible.

FURTHER READING

Highbee, Kenneth L. *Your Memory: How It Works and How to Improve It.* Englewood Cliffs, NJ: Prentice, 1988.

Lucas, Jerry, and Harry Lorayne. *The Memory Book.* New York: Ballantine, 1989.

George Miller. "The Magic Number Seven Plus or Minus Two; Some Limits on our Capacity for Processing Information." *Psychological Review,* 1956:81-97.

6

A Systematic Approach to Learning

Learning Objectives

Analyze how you learn

Develop previewing techniques

Analyze a learning task

Select appropriate strategies

Revise and modify your strategies

Let's suppose you have decided to learn to play racquetball. You first need an overview of the sport: how it is played, how it is similar to and different from other racquet sports, and what general rules govern it. With this knowledge you can draw on your previous experience with similar sports such as tennis or badminton.

Once you have identified aspects of the game that you need to learn, such as serving, you would choose appropriate strategies to learn them, such as instruction and practice. Finally, as you play, you monitor your game, noticing good plays, weak areas, and where further practice is needed. Through a systematic approach you learn effectively and continue to improve your game.

A systematic approach is also important in academic situations. Unfortunately, many students who learn daily tasks systematically fail to use the same approach in academic situations.

Academic learning involves five essential steps:

1. Analyzing how you learn.
2. Previewing. Get an overview of the task to determine what is involved and what is expected.
3. Analyzing the learning task. What do I already know? What do I need to know? What should I learn? How should I learn it?
4. Selecting appropriate reading and study strategies.
5. Revising and modifying learning strategies.

ANALYZING YOUR LEARNING STYLE

An important first step in learning how to study is analyzing how you learn. In the previous chapter, you learned how learning and memory work and about the processes of encoding, storage, and retrieval. Now you need to know how to make these processes work for you. Specifically, you need to know: What are the best ways for you to encode (take in) information? What means of storage are most effective for you? How can you best retrieve information? To answer these questions, you need to analyze your learning style. There are individual variations in how people learn and process information. These variations are known as *learning styles.*

Have you found some types of learning tasks easier than others? Perhaps writing a term paper is easier than solving calculus problems; taking lecture notes may be easier than reading and marking textbook chapters. Essay exams may be more difficult than objective exams. Or perhaps you have found one instructor easier to learn from than another. Have you also noticed that tasks that may be easy for you may be difficult for others? Each person has his or her own approach to and mode of encoding, processing, storing, and retrieving information. For example, some students learn best visually, seeing charts, diagrams, or models. Others are auditory learners; they learn best by listening. Such students would learn more quickly from an instructor's lecture than from a textbook chapter on the same topic.

The following questionnaire is designed to assist you in analyzing your learning style. Complete and score the questionnaire now before continuing with the chapter.

Learning Style Questionnaire

Directions: Each item presents two alternatives. Select the alternative that best describes you. In cases in which neither choice suits you, select the one that is closer to your preference. Write the letter of your choice in the blank to the left of each item.

Part One

_____1. For a grade in biology lab, I would prefer to
   a. work with a lab partner.
   b work alone.

_____2. When faced with a difficult personal problem, I prefer to
   a. discuss it with others.
   b. resolve it myself.

_____3. Many instructors could improve their classes by
   a. including more discussion and group activities.
   b. allowing students to work on their own more frequently.

_____4. When listening to a lecture or speaker, I respond more to
   a. the person presenting the ideas.
   b. the ideas themselves.

_____5. When on a team project, I prefer to
   a. work with several team members.
   b. divide up tasks and complete those assigned to me.

_____6. I prefer to shop and do errands
   a. with friends.
   b. by myself.

_____7. A job in a busy office is
   a. more appealing than working alone.
   b. less appealing than working alone.

Part Two

_____1. To solve a math problem, I would prefer to
   a. draw or visualize the problem.
   b. study a sample problem and use it as a model.

_____2. To remember things best, I
   a. create a mental picture.
   b. write it down.

_____3. Assembling a bicycle from a diagram would be
   a. easy.
   b. challenging.

_____4. I prefer classes in which I
   a. handle equipment or work with models.
   b. participate in a class discussion.

_____5. To understand and remember how a machine works, I would
   a. draw a diagram.
   b. write notes.

_____6. I enjoy
   a. drawing or working with my hands.
   b. speaking, writing, and listening.

_____7. If you were trying to locate an office on an unfamiliar university campus, would you prefer a student to
   a. draw you a map.
   b. a set of written directions.

Part Three

_____1. I prefer to
   a. learn facts and details.
   b. construct theories and ideas.

_____2. I would prefer a job involving
   a. following specific instructions.
   b. reading, writing, and analyzing.

_____3. I prefer to
   a. solve math problems using a formula.
   b. discover why the formula works.

_____4. I would prefer to write a term paper explaining
   a. how a process works.
   b. a theory.

_____5. I prefer tasks that require me to follow
   a. careful, detailed instructions.
   b. reasoning and critical analysis.

_____6. For a criminal justice course I would prefer to
   a. discover how and when a law can be used.
   b. learn how and why it became law.

_____7. To learn more about the operation of a high-speed computer printer, I would prefer to

a. work with several types of printers.
b. understand the principles on which they operate.

Part Four

_____1. I would prefer to follow a set of
    a. oral directions.
    b. written directions.

_____2. I would prefer to
    a. attend a lecture given by a famous psychologist.
    b. read an article written by the psychologist.

_____3. I am better at remembering
    a. names.
    b. faces.

_____4. It is easier to learn new information using
    a. language (words).
    b. images (pictures).

_____5. I prefer classes in which the instructor
    a. lectures and answers questions.
    b. uses films and videos.

_____6. To obtain information about current events, I would prefer to
    a. listen to news on the radio.
    b. read the newspaper.

_____7. To learn how to operate a fax machine, I would
    a. listen to a friend's explanation.
    b. watch a demonstration.

Part Five

_____1. To make decisions I rely on
    a. my experiences and "gut" feelings.
    b. facts and objective data.

_____2. To complete a task, I
    a. can use whatever is available to get the job done.
    b. must have everything I need at hand.

_____3. I prefer to express my ideas and feelings through
    a. music, song, or poetry.
    b. direct, concise language.

_____4. I prefer instructors who
   a. allow students to be guided by their own interests.
   b. make their expectations clear and explicit.

_____5. I tend to
   a. challenge and question what I hear and read.
   b. accept what I hear and read.

_____6. I prefer
   a. essay exams.
   b. objective exams.

_____7. In completing an assignment I prefer to
   a. figure out my own approach.
   b. be told exactly what to do.

To score your questionnaire, record the total number of choice *a*'s and the total number of choice *b*'s you chose for each part of the questionnaire. Record your totals in the scoring grid provided below.

Now, circle your higher score for each part of the questionnaire. The word below the score you circled indicates an aspect of your learning style. The next section explains how to interpret your scores and describes these aspects.

Interpreting Your Scores

The questionnaire was divided into five parts; each part identifies one aspect of your learning style. Each of these five aspects is explained below.

Part One—Social or Independent Learners

This score reveals your preferred level of interaction with other people in the learning process. If you are a social learner, you prefer to work with others—both peers and instructors—closely and directly. Social learners tend to be people oriented and enjoy personal interaction. If you are an independent learner, you prefer to work and study alone. You tend to be self-directed or self-motivated, and often goal oriented.

Part Two—Spatial or Verbal Learners

This score reveals your ability to work with spatial relationships. Spatial learners are able to visualize or mentally see how things work or how they are positioned in space. Their strengths may include drawing, assembling things, or repairing. Verbal learners lack skills in positioning things in space. Instead they tend to rely on verbal or language skills.

❑ ❑ ❑

Scoring Grid

Parts	Total Number of Choice A	Total Number of Choice B
Part One	_____ Social	_____ Independent
Part Two	_____ Spatial	_____ Verbal
Part Three	_____ Applied	_____ Conceptual
Part Four	_____ Auditory	_____ Visual
Part Five	_____ Creative	_____ Pragmatic

❑ ❑ ❑

Part Three—Applied or Conceptual Learners

This score describes the types of learning tasks and learning situations you prefer and find easiest to handle. If you are an applied learner, you prefer tasks that involve real objects and situations. Practical, real-life learning situations are ideal for you. If you are a conceptual learner, you prefer to work with language and ideas; practical applications are not necessary for understanding.

Part Four—Auditory or Visual Learners

This score indicates through which sensory mode you prefer to process information. Auditory learners tend to learn more effectively through listening, while visual learners process information by seeing it in print or other visual modes including film, picture, or diagram. If you have a higher score on auditory than visual, you tend to be an auditory learner. That is, you tend to learn more easily by hearing than by reading. A higher score in visual suggests strengths with visual modes of learning.

Part Five—Creative or Pragmatic Learners

This score describes the approach you prefer to take toward learning tasks. Creative learners are imaginative and innovative. They prefer to learn through discovery or experimentation. They are comfortable taking risks and following hunches. Pragmatic learners are practical, logical, and systematic. They seek order and are comfortable following rules.

Evaluating Your Results

Hopefully, through activities in this section and the questionnaire, you have discovered more about yourself as a learner. However, several words of caution are in order.

❏ The questionnaire is an informal indicator of your learning style. Other more formal and more accurate measures of learning style are available. These include *Kolb's Learning Style Inventory* and *Myers-Briggs Type Indicator*. These tests may be available through your college's counseling, testing, or academic skills center.

❏ Learning style has many more aspects than those identified through the questionnaire in this chapter. To learn more about other factors, one or both of the tests listed above would be useful.

❏ Learning style is *not* a fixed, unchanging quality. Just as personalities can change and develop, so can learning styles change and develop through exposure, instruction, or practice. For example, as you experience more college lectures, your skill as an auditory learner may be strengthened.

❏ People are not necessarily clearly strong or weak in each aspect. Some students, for example, may be able to learn equally well spatially or verbally. If there was very little difference between your two scores on one or more parts of the questionnaire, then you may have strengths in both areas.

❏ When most students discover the features of their learning style, they recognize themselves. A frequent comment is "Yep, that's me." If, for some reason, you feel the description of yourself as a learner is incorrect, then do not make changes in your learning strategies based on the information. Instead, discuss your style with your instructor, or consider taking one of the tests listed above.

EXERCISE 6-1

Directions:

Evaluate the results of the learning style questionnaire by answering the following questions.

1. How accurately do you think the results describe you? Identify aspects that you agree and disagree with. Explain why you disagree.

2. Evaluate your current study methods in light of the question-naire's results. What are you doing that is effective? What changes are needed?

EXERCISE 6-2

Directions:

Discuss what learning strategies might be effective for each of the following students for each of the following situations.

Student A: strong visual spatial learning style

Student B: strong social, applied learning style

Student C: strong auditory, conceptual learning style

Situation 1: Attending a city court trial as an assignment for a criminal justice class

Situation 2: Reading a supplementary reading chapter assignment in a book titled *The Intelligence Controversy* for a psychology course. The instructor plans a class discussion of the assignment

Situation 3: Reading an assigned research report on North-South wage differences in the *American Economics Review* for which the student must write a synopsis

Situation 4: Watching a class demonstration in psychology designed to explain various forms of conditioning

Figure 6-1
Differing Learning Strategies

Course:	Anatomy and Physiology	
Type of Exam:	Multiple Choice	
	Student A	**Student B**
Learning Style:	Social, spatial, applied	Independent, nonspatial, conceptual
Learning Strategies:	1. study with classmate(s)	1. study alone
	2. draw diagrams, sketches	2. prepare index cards
	3. prepare charts	3. use summary sheets
	4. associate with practical situations	4. reorganize the information

Now that you are aware of some of the characteristics of your learning style, you can use that information in deciding how best to study. Because your learning style is unique, you may need to approach a task differently from others in your class. In fact, two students with differing learning styles may study for the same exam in the same class in very different ways, as shown in Figure 6-1.

Figure 6-2 provides examples of learning strategies that are compatible with various aspects of learning style discussed earlier in this chapter.

Figure 6-2
Examples of Learning Strategies for Various Learning Styles

Applied	*Conceptual*
1. Associate ideas with their application	1. Use outlining
2. Take courses with lab or practicum	2. Focus on thought patterns (see Chapter 7)
3. Think of practical situations to which learning applies	3. Organize materials that lack order
4. Use case studies, examples, and applications to cue your learning	

Auditory	*Visual*
1. Tape review notes	1. Use mapping (see Chapter 10)
2. Discuss/study with friends	2. Use visualization
3. Talk aloud when studying	3. Use computer-assisted instructions if available
4. Tape lectures	4. Use films, videos when available
	5. Draw diagrams, charts, maps

Social	*Independent*
1. Interact with instructor	1. Use computer-assisted instructions if available
2. Find a study partner	2. Enroll in courses using traditional lecture-exam format
3. Form a study group	3. Consider independent study courses
4. Take courses involving class discussion	4. Purchase review books, study guides, if available
5. Work with a tutor	

Spatial
1. Draw diagrams, make charts and sketches
2. Use outlining
3. Use visualization
4. Use mapping (see Chapter 10)

Nonspatial
1. Record steps, processes, procedures in words
2. Write summaries
3. Translate diagrams and drawings into language
4. Write your interpretation next to textbook drawings, maps, graphics

Creative
1. Take courses that involve exploration, experimentation, or discussion
2. Use annotation to record impressions and reactions
3. Ask questions about chapter content and answer them

Pragmatic
1. Write lists of steps, processes procedures
2. Write summaries and outlines
3. Use structured study environment
4. Focus on problem-solving, logical sequence

PREVIEWING TECHNIQUES  → important

Familiarity with a task enhances your ability to perform it effectively. If you are familiar with a large city, driving to a destination there is relatively simple. Similarly, if you are familiar with a reading or class assignment before you begin, you will find that you can read or complete it more easily and retain more information. *Previewing* provides a means of familiarizing yourself quickly with the content and organization of an assignment before you begin.

How to Preview Textbook Reading Assignments

Think of previewing as getting a sneak preview of what a chapter will be about. Use the following steps:

1. Read the title and subtitle. The title provides the overall topic of the article or chapter, the subtitle suggests the specific focus, aspect, or approach toward the overall topic.

2. Read the introduction or the first paragraph. The introduction or first paragraph serves as a lead-in to the chapter, establishing the overall subject and suggesting how it will be developed.

3. Read each boldface (dark print) heading. Headings label the contents of each section, announcing the major topic of the section.

4. Read the first sentence under each heading. The first sentence often states the central thought of the section. If the first sentence seems introductory, read the last sentence; often this sentence states or restates the central thought.

5. Note any typographical aids. Italics are used to emphasize important terminology and definitions by using slanted (*italic*) type to distinguish from the rest of the passage. Notice any material that is numbered 1, 2, 3, lettered a, b, c, or presented in list form.

6. Note any graphic aids. Graphs, charts, photographs, and tables often suggest what is important in the chapter. Be sure to read the captions for photographs and the legends on graphs, charts, or tables.

7. Read the last paragraph or summary. This provides a condensed view of the chapter, often outlining the key points in the chapter.

8. Read quickly any end-of-article or end-of-chapter material. This might include references, study questions, discussion questions, chapter outlines, or vocabulary lists. If there are study questions, read them through quickly since they will indicate what is important to remember in the chapter. If a vocabulary list is included, rapidly skim through it to identify terms that you will need to learn as you read.

Figure 6-3 illustrates how previewing is done. A section of a business communications textbook chapter discussing job application letters is reprinted there; the portions to focus on when previewing are shaded. Read only those portions. After you have finished, test the effectiveness of your previewing by answering the questions in Exercise 6-3.

Figure 6-3
Demonstration of Previewing

The Unsolicited Letter

Ambitious job seekers don't limit their search to advertised openings. The unsolicited, or "prospecting" letter is a good way of uncovering other possibilities. Such letters have advantages and disadvantages.

Disadvantages. The unsolicited approach does have two drawbacks: (1) You may waste time writing letters to organizations that simply have no openings. (2) Because you don't know what the opening is (if there is one), you can't tailor your letter to specific requirements as James Calvin did in his solicited letter.

Advantages. This cold-canvassing approach does have one important advantage: for an advertised opening, you will compete with legions of qualified applicants, whereas your unsolicited letter might arrive just when an opening has materialized. If it does, your application will receive immediate attention, and you just might get the job. Even when there is no immediate opening, companies usually file an impressive application until an opening does occur. Or the application may be passed along to a company that has an opening. Therefore, unsolicited letters generally are a sound investment if your targets are well chosen and your expectations realistic.

The Aggressive Approach to Unsolicited Letters. If you've thoroughly researched a company and its needs, you might find that your specific qualifications can benefit a company. (For further discussion on how to research a company, see the following chapter. "Interviews".) Your unsolicited letter then becomes the means to achieve your end – getting a particular job with a particular company. Thorough research is the key, for, in effect, you ideally create your own position by showing a personnel director or executive how your particular qualifications, skills, and aptitudes match that company's needs. Even if you don't convince them that they need you for the position you want, they may consider you for another – or refer you to another company looking for a person such as yourself. After all, you have demonstrated your initiative and desire to accept responsibility. Employers actively seek candidates with such qualities.

Reader Interest. Because your unsolicited letter is unexpected, attract your reader's attention early and make him or her want to read further. Don't begin: "I am writing to inquire about the possibility of obtaining a position with your company." By now, your reader is asleep. If you can't establish a direct connection through a mutual acquaintance, use an interesting opening, such as:

```
Does your hotel chain have a place for a junior man-
ager with a college degree in hospitality manage-
ment, a proven commitment to quality service, and
customer-relations experience that extends beyond
textbooks? If so, please consider my application for
a position.
```

Unlike the usual, time-worn, and cliched opening, this approach gets through to your read-

The Prototype

Most of your letters, whether solicited or unsolicited, can be versions of your one model, the prototype. Thus, your prototype must represent you and your goals in the best possible light. As you approach your job search, give yourself plenty of time to compose a model letter and résumé. Employers will regard the quality of your application as an indication of the quality of your work.

Above all, your letter and résumé must be visually appealing and free of errors. One or two spelling or grammatical errors might seem minor. But look at these documents from the employer's point of view. An employer expects you to present yourself in the most favorable way. A candidate who doesn't take the time to proofread carefully doesn't project the qualities employers want. After all, if you aren't conscientious about such important documents as your own application letter and résumé, how conscientious will you be with the employer's documents? Businesses incur a good deal of expense projecting favorable images. The image you project must measure up to their standards.

(continued)

Figure 6-3 (continued)

> **Your Dossier**
>
> **Your dossier is a folder containing your credentials, college transcripts, letters of recommendation, and any other items (such as a notice of scholarship award or letter of commendation) that testify to your accomplishments.** In your letter and résumé, you talk about yourself; in your dossier, others talk about you. An employer impressed by what you've said will want to read what others think about you and will request a copy of your dossier.
>
> If your college has a placement office, it will keep your dossier on file and send copies to employers who request them. In any case, keep your own copy on file. Then, if an employer writes to request your dossier, you can make a photocopy and mail it, advising your reader that the placement office copy is on the way. This isn't needless repetition! Most employers establish a specific timetable for (1) advertising an opening, (2) reading letters and résumés, (3) requesting and reviewing dossiers, (4) holding interviews, and (5) making job offers. Obviously, if your letter and résumé don't arrive until the screening process is at step 3, you're out of luck. The same holds true if your dossier arrives when the screening process is at the end of step 4. Timing, then, is crucial. Too often, dossier requests from employers sit and gather dust in some "incoming" box on a desk in the placement office. Sometimes, one or two weeks will pass before your dossier is mailed out. The only loser is you.

EXERCISE 6-3

Directions:
Without referring back to Figure 6-3; answer the following questions.

1. What is an unsolicited letter?
2. What are its advantages?
3. What is one disadvantage?
4. What is a prototype?
5. What is a dossier?

Most likely, you were able to answer all or most of the questions correctly. Previewing, then, does provide you with a great deal of information. Now, suppose you were to return to Figure 6-3 and read the entire section. You would find it to be an easier task than without previewing.

Why Previewing Is Effective

Previewing helps you to make decisions. Just as a film preview helps you make decisions about whether you want to see a film, so does previewing help you make decisions about how you will approach the material. Based on what you discover about the assignment's organization and content, you determine which reasoning and thinking strategies will be necessary for learning the material.

❏ ❏ ❏
Thinking Critically . . . About Previewing

While previewing a reading assignment, you can make predictions about its content and organization. Specifically, you can anticipate what an assignment will contain and how it will be presented. Use the following suggestions to sharpen your critical thinking-previewing skills:

- Assess the difficulty of the material.
- Discover how it is organized.
- Identify the overall subject and how it is approached.
- Establish what type of material it is (practical, theoretical, historical background, or a case study).
- Look for logical breaking points where you might divide the assignment into portions, perhaps reserving a portion for a later study session.
- Identify points at which you might stop and review.
- Look for connections between the assignment and class lectures.

Previewing activates your thought processes. It puts your mind in gear, and initiates your thoughts on the subject. *Previewing activates your prior knowledge of the subject.* It helps you connect new material with what you already know. *Previewing provides you a mental outline of the chapter's content.* It enables you to see how ideas are connected, and since you know where the author is headed, reading will be easier than if you had not previewed.

EXERCISE 6-4

Directions:

Select a chapter that you have not read in one of your textbooks and preview it using the procedure described in this section. When you have finished, answer the following questions.

1. What is its overall subject?
2. What topics (aspects of the subject) does the chapter discuss? List as many as you can recall.
3. How difficult do you expect the chapter to be?
4. How is the subject approached? That is, is the material practical, theoretical, historical, research oriented, procedural?

ANALYZING A LEARNING TASK

By previewing an assignment, you acquire a substantial amount of information about it. The next step is to analyze that information and *think* about the about the assignment. Try to establish a focus and an approach or game plan. Four steps will guide you in analyzing assignments and developing a strategy for approaching them:

1. Discover what you already know.
2. Acquire needed background information.
3. Decide what to learn.
4. Select the best way to learn.

Discover What You Already Know

Once you have previewed an assignment, an important next step is to call to mind what you already know about the subject. There are several reasons for doing so. First, learning occurs more easily if you can relate new information to already stored information. Second, tasks become more interesting and meaningful if you can connect them to your own experience or to a subject you have already learned. Finally, material that is familiar and meaningful is easier to learn than that which is not. For example, it is easier to learn a list of real words (*sat, tar, can*) than a list of nonsense syllables (*sar, taf, cag*). Similarly, it would be easier to learn basic laws of economics if you had an example of each from your experience with which to associate them. Search your previous knowledge and experience for ideas or information to which you can connect the new material in an assignment.

To draw on, or activate, your prior knowledge and experience (not only facts, ideas, and concepts, but also experiences, observations, and impressions), think about the subject using one of the following techniques:

❑ Ask as many questions as you can about the topic and attempt to answer them.
❑ Divide the subject into as many features or subtopics as possible.
❑ Free-associate, writing down anything that comes to mind related to the topic. *Take notes*

A student studying a chapter on advertising in her business management text previewed the chapter and then asked herself the following questions:

❏ Who decides what an ad should say?
❏ What is the purpose of advertising?
❏ What persuasive devices are employed?
❏ Do laws govern advertising?
❏ Does the consumer absorb advertising costs?
❏ Is all advertising persuasive?

From these questions, she realized that she had a great deal of practical knowledge and experience that she could apply to chapter content. The questions focused her attention and made the chapter content more relevant.

EXERCISE 6-5

Directions:

Assume you have previewed a chapter in a sociology text on domestic violence. Activate your knowledge of the subject by using one of the three techniques suggested above.

EXERCISE 6-6

Directions:

Assume you have previewed a chapter in a business management text on employee motivation. To activate your previous knowledge and experience, experiment with all three of the techniques suggested above. Then answer the following questions.

1. Which technique seemed most effective? Why?
2. Might you choice of technique be influenced by the subject matter with which you are working?
3. Did you discover you knew more about employee motivation than you initially thought?

Acquire Background Information You Need

The next step after establishing what you already know is to determine if you need any information to accomplish the task. For example, while previewing a textbook chapter on building subroutines, you may discover that it requires knowledge of algorithms discussed in a previous chapter. Or you may notice that a chapter in a chemistry text uses numerous formulas previously discussed; a quick review of the earlier chapter that introduced the formulas is in order.

On occasion you may find you are lost, lacking completely the knowledge the author assumes you have. In an economics text, for example, a working knowledge of the concept of supply and demand may be assumed. In engineering or technical courses, familiarity with the metric system is necessary. If you lack knowledge or skill, take steps to remedy the situation. In most cases, you will need to refer to other written sources. You can acquire the additional information you need in numerous ways.

Check the appendix in your text. Textbook appendixes often contain supplementary information such as tables, metric conversions, documents, and so forth.

Obtain an easier, more basic text in the same field. Your college library or nearest public library will have introductory textbooks that explain in great detail the more basic concepts used in the field.

Look up terms in special dictionaries or encyclopedias. If you are having difficulty with terminology, check a subject area dictionary (see Chapter 12) for definitions and explanations of unfamiliar terms.

Consult reference materials. Ask a librarian whether there are handbooks or reference sources that might provide the information you need. If, for example, you are having difficulty in a writing class, and your instructor has not already assigned one, a handbook that reviews grammar, punctuation, and basic writing would be a valuable aid.

Obtain review books for the topic. Check your college bookstore to learn what review books are available. Especially for literature works, review books often explain historical context and literary allusions (reference to other literary works). They are not a substitute for close reading and careful analysis and interpretation, but they can help fill in necessary background.

EXERCISE 6-7

Directions:
Decide what course of action to take in each of the following situations.

1. You are taking a literature course and the assigned readings contain numerous unfamiliar references to Greek mythology as well as various biblical references.
2. While reviewing several graded papers in your freshman composition class, you notice an error pattern. You are misusing commas, and the instructor's symbols for "split infinitive" and "comma splice" appear frequently on your papers. Your only text for the course is a collection of essays.

Decide What to Learn

Research on how people learn has clearly established that we remember only what we *intend* to remember. For example, take a moment to sketch the face of a dollar bill. Or draw the dial or pushbuttons of a telephone, indicating which letters correspond with each number.

Why did you have difficulty with each of these tasks? You certainly have seen each of these items many times. Most likely, you could not recall the needed information because you never *intentionally* learned it. This principle of intention strongly influences and controls your learning. Unless you select a given piece of information as important, and then consciously work on storing it in your memory, you will quickly forget it. Learning, then, is a sifting and sorting process in which you identify what is necessary and important to learn and remember. Here are a few suggestions on deciding what to learn:

Follow your instructor's emphases. Notice the topics the instructor emphasizes in lectures, spends a great deal of time discussing, or seems interested in or excited about; these are likely to be important.

Use the structure and organization of your text to identify key ideas and concepts. Use the table of contents, chapter introductions, headings, summaries, and review questions as guides.

Review previous exams and quizzes. They indicate the type of information to learn.

Talk with other students who have taken the course.

Select the Best Way to Learn

Once you have analyzed a learning task, you are ready to select the best techniques to accomplish it. Many students just jump into an assignment, only to find out midway through it that a different approach would have produced better results and saved valuable time. Here is an example:

> Sarah was preparing for a midterm examination in human anatomy and physiology. As soon as the exam was announced, she began to prepare detailed outlines of each chapter. The day of the exam, in comparing notes with a classmate, she discovered that a system of testing herself by drawing and labeling diagrams and making tables and function charts would have been a more active and effective means of learning.

Suppose you are faced with the task of reviewing several chapters in your mass media and communications text in preparation for an essay exam. What strategy would you use to learn and remember as much as possible? Some students would use the same strategy they use for every other reading assignment: reread and underline. A better approach is to choose a strategy that fits your learning style, the nature of the material to be read, and the type of exam you anticipate. You might, instead, predict possible essay questions and organize information to answer each.

Here are a few suggestions to use in deciding how to approach an assignment:

Define the characteristics or nature of the task. State as explicitly as possible what you are expected to accomplish.

Identify your options. What strategies can you use? You will be able to answer this question more explicitly later, after you have worked through all the chapters of this book.

Try to match the strategy to the material. As you will see in later chapters, not all learning strategies are equally effective in all situations. To strike the best match, ask yourself questions such as these: (1) What types of thinking and learning are required? For example, is the task primarily one of problem solving, or does it require creative thought? (2) What level of recall is required (facts and details or just major concepts)? (3) Am I expected to make applications? (4) Am I expected to evaluate and criticize?

MONITORING AND REVISING YOUR LEARNING STRATEGIES

You maintain an awareness or check on how well you are performing many daily activities. In sports such as golf, tennis, or bowling, you know if you are playing a poor game; you actually keep score and deliberately try to correct errors and improve your performance. When preparing a favorite food, you often taste it to be assured it will turn out as expected. You know whether your car is clean after taking it through the car wash.

A similar type of checking should occur as you learn and study. You should be aware of, or *monitor,* your performance. You need to keep score of how effectively and efficiently you are learning. However, with the cognitive activities of reading, learning, and studying, you have very little observable evidence to suggest whether you are on the right track. Instead, you must develop a checking procedure that enables you to focus on clues and signals that provide information about your performance. Several monitoring techniques are described below.

Pacing

A first step in monitoring your learning is to evaluate the pace at which you are working. Ask the following questions:

- Do l slow down when ideas become complex, different, or confusing?
- Do I speed up when working with familiar concepts and ideas?
- Do I vary my pace to suit my purpose, slowing down when high retention and recall are needed and speeding up when material does not fit my purpose?

Establishing Checkpoints

Race car drivers make pit stops during races for quick mechanical checks and repairs; athletes are subject to frequent physical tests and examinations; theater troupes rehearse, even during the run of a play. These activities provide an opportunity to evaluate or assess performance and to correct any problems or malfunctions. Similarly, when studying and learning, you should stop and evaluate.

As you preview a textbook assignment, identify reasonable or logical checkpoints: point at which to stop, check, and, if necessary, correct your performance before continuing. Pencil a checkmark in the margin to designate these points. These checkpoints should be logical breaking points where one topic ends and another begins or where a topic is broken down into several subtopics. As you reach each of these checkpoints, stop and assess your work by asking two types of questions.

Recall Questions

Recall questions force active learning and check whether you have understood and can recall the information you have just read or reviewed. You can easily form a question for each chapter heading, as in the following examples from a data processing text:

❑ ❑ ❑

Heading	Question
Evaluating Storage and Retrieval Costs	How are storage and retrieval costs calculated?
Multiple Uses of Stored Data	What are the uses of stored data?
The Data Base Concept	What is the data base concept, and how is it used?

❑ ❑ ❑

Since a heading announces the subject of the section that follows it, questions based on the heading will test your recall of the key ideas presented about that subject.

The best time to pose and answer recall questions is *while you are reading*. As you finish each section, stop and take a moment to glance at the heading and recall the main points the section presented. Your success in answering your questions is a strong indicator of your level of comprehension and concentration.

Connection Questions

Connection questions require you to think: to draw together ideas and to discover relationships between the material at hand and other material in the same chapter, in other chapters, or in class lectures. Here are a few examples:

❏ What does this topic have to do with topics discussed earlier in the chapter?
❏ How does this reading assignment fit with the topics of this week's class lectures?
❏ What does this chapter have to do with the chapter assigned last week?
❏ What principle do these problems illustrate?

Connection questions enable you to determine whether your learning is meaningful and whether you are simply taking in information or whether you are using the information and fitting it into the scheme of the course. The best time to ask connection questions is before you begin and after you finish the chapter or each major section.

EXERCISE 6-8

Directions:
What recall and connection questions would you ask when reading an economics textbook chapter titled "The Distribution of Income"?[1] The major headings of two sections are

Income Distribution in the United States
Historical Changes in Adjusted Income
Age Distribution and Income
Rags to Riches: Mobility

Some Characteristics of Income Distribution
Family Income Characteristics
Poverty
Poverty During Recession
Race and Sex Discrimination: Wages
Programs to Alleviate Poverty

Using Internal Dialogue

Internal dialogue, mentally talking to yourself, is another excellent means of monitoring your learning. For reading and study, it involves rephrasing to yourself the message the author is communicating or ideas you are studying. If you are unable to express the ideas in your own words, then perhaps your understanding is incomplete. Internal dialogue might occur in a variety of other situations as well:

❏ While working on a math problem, you verbalize the steps you are following.
❏ You are reading a magazine article that argues convincingly that the threat of nuclear winter is real. As you finish reading each stage of the argument, you rephrase it in your own words.
❏ You are writing an essay exam, and after each answer you mentally review the points you think you have already made and then check to see if you have expressed each point clearly.

EXERCISE 6-9

Directions:
Describe a situation from your daily or academic experiences that illustrates each of the following situations.

1. You had no idea that your learning strategies were not working until it was too late.
2. You used internal dialogue to solve a problem or complete a task.
3. You deliberately altered your pace when completing a task.

Revising and Modifying Learning Strategies

As you monitor your learning, you may, at times, find that a particular strategy is not working. You may find that an assignment is taking too long, that you do not seem to be making the right connections, or that you are not mastering the material as you feel you should. Perhaps the best way to describe this situation is to say that nothing has "clicked." It is best to stop, assess the situation, and modify your approach.

Often a tried-and-true strategy that has always worked in the past fails when applied to a new type of learning. At first, the strategy may seem to be working as well as usual because you are so comfortable with it. Only later, when assessing your progress, do you realize that the strategy is not effective. For example, a student taking her first philosophy course approached the course by focusing on facts, as she had always done in other courses. She learned names and dates but found very few facts to learn. Eventually she realized her focus was too specific—she needed to focus on larger issues, theories, world views, and so forth.

The key to modifying your approach is to determine how the current situation differs from others in which you have used the strategy successfully. That difference pinpoints the problem. Next, you must alter your approach to accommodate that difference. Identify alternative approaches, evaluate each, and select the one most likely to succeed. It is also helpful to check with students who are doing well in the class to find out what learning strategies they are using.

SUMMARY

1. A systematic approach to learning emphasizes learning as an active, thinking process.
2. The individual variations in how learning occurs are known as learning styles.
3. Before beginning to learn, it is important to

   ❏ preview new material
   ❏ become generally familiar with its content and organization

4. Once you are familiar with a task

   ❏ analyze what is required and how best to approach it
   ❏ activate your previous knowledge
   ❏ acquire needed background information
   ❏ establish an intent to remember

5. In selecting an appropriate strategy, you should consider the nature of the material and the characteristics of your learning style.
6. As you read and study, monitor your progress by

   ❏ evaluating your pace

❏ asking questions
❏ using internal dialogue

7. You may need to revise your approach.

CLASS ACTIVITY

Activity I
Directions:
Each student should bring a text to class, and students, working in pairs, should follow these steps:

1. Each student chooses a chapter in his or her text that he or she has read recently.
2. Students exchange texts and preview the chapter chosen by their partners.
3. After previewing is complete, the textbook owner questions the previewer to discuss and evaluate the level and quality of information he or she acquired through previewing.

Activity II
Directions:
Each class member should bring two textbooks to class. These texts should be from elective courses or from fields that may be unfamiliar to other students in the class. Students exchange tests so that each student has a text from an unfamiliar field. Each student previews and then evaluates the text and field of study, using the following questions as guidelines:

1. What might make this subject difficult or complicated?
2. What kind(s) of learning seem(s) to be expected?
3. Is this similar to any familiar fields of study?
4. How is it different from a history or psychology text?
5. Discuss learning strategies that might be effective in the field.

FURTHER ANALYSIS

Directions:
Analyze the following situation and answer the questions below.

Assume you have been assigned a chapter on criminal behavior in your social problems textbook. A list of the headings of the first section is printed on p. 128. Your professor's lecture topic this week is "The Criminal Justice System." You have also been assigned a chapter in a supplementary reading, *Assault with a Deadly Weapon: The Autobiography of a Street Criminal.* Your professor has assigned a five-page research paper on any topic related to criminal behavior. You also know that this chapter will be included on the next hourly multiple choice exam. The text chapter headings are as follows:

What is Crime?
> Elements of the Legal Definition
> Defining Behavior as Criminal

Explanations for Criminal Behavior
> Physiological Explanations
> Psychological Explanations
> Sociological Explanations

1. Activate your previous knowledge on criminal behavior by listing questions, dividing your previous knowledge into subtopics, or free associating.
2. What background information might be necessary or helpful in handling these assignments and lectures?
3. Establish an intent to remember by listing types of information you think important.
4. What strategies would you use to read the chapter? to read the supplementary assignment?

DISCUSSION

1. In what everyday, routine situations do you use a form of previewing?
2. For what types of printed material do you feel previewing would be of limited use? For what types of material, other than textbooks, do you think previewing would be useful?
3. Discuss ways in which your professors clarify or help you identify what to learn in their courses.
4. What other factors, in addition to those discussed in this chapter, influence or control how easily and efficiently you learn?

FURTHER READING

Carrell, Patricia L., and Laura B. Monroe. "Learning Styles and Composition." *Modern Language Journal* 77(1993): 148.

Sonbuchner, Gail Murphy. *Help Yourself: How to Take Advantage of Your Learning Styles.* Syracuse, NY: New Readers, 1993.

C. E. Weinstein, E. T. Goetz, and P. A. Alexander, eds. *Learning and Study Strategies: Issues in Assessment, Instruction, and Evaluation.* San Diego, CA: Academic, 1988.

PART
□ □ □

3

MASTERING COURSE CONTENT

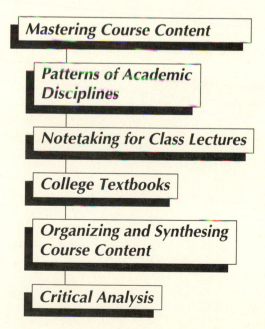

Mastering Course Content

Patterns of Academic Disciplines

Notetaking for Class Lectures

College Textbooks

Organizing and Synthesing Course Content

Critical Analysis

7

Patterns of Academic Disciplines

Learning Objectives

Discover how recognition of thought patterns contributes to course mastery

Recognize seven common academic thought patterns

This semester or term you are probably taking courses in several disciplines simultaneously. You may study English composition, biology, psychology, and philosophy all in one semester. Many students find it difficult to manage such a diverse course load. During one day you may write a descriptive essay, learn how cells divide, and study early schools of psychology. These tasks become mind boggling because you treat each course completely differently from every other. Consequently, you are forced to shift gears for each course, developing new approaches and strategies.

What few students realize is that a biologist and a psychologist, for example, think about and approach their subject matter in similar ways. Both may carefully define terms, examine causes and effects, study similarities and differences, describe a sequence of events, classify information, solve problems, and enumerate characteristics. While the subject matter and the language they use differ, the thought patterns are basically the same for each. Regardless of their field of expertise, then, researchers, textbook authors, and your professors all use standards patterns of thought to organize and express their ideas.

You might think of these patterns as learning blueprints. We have hundreds of blueprints, or preestablished operating instructions, that enable us to perform numerous everyday activities. These are sometimes referred to as *schema*. You may have a blueprint for riding a bicycle, swimming the crawl stroke, tying a shoelace, making pizza, or ironing a shirt. You have numerous academic blueprints as well: solving algebra problems, using the card catalog, or writing an English composition. These blueprints enable you to complete a task without analyzing it or rediscovering the best way to do it each time.

PATTERNS: GUIDES TO LEARNING

Familiarity with these basic thought patterns will enable you to approach all your courses more easily and effectively. You will find textbook chapters easier to read if you can identify the thought pattern(s) by which they are organized. Lectures will be easier to follow, and your notes will be better organized if you identify your professor's thought pattern.

Recognizing patterns will enable you to anticipate the author's or speaker's thought development. For example, from a heading or topic sentence alone, you often can predict the pattern of thought the section or paragraph will follow. If you read a heading "Types of Engineering Models," you might anticipate a classification pattern. Or suppose you read the following topic sentence:

When you are viewing an on-line computer system in action, it is as if you are watching a science fiction movie.

Here, you would anticipate a comparison-contrast pattern of development in the paragraph. If a speaker announced, "Today we'll consider the impact of stress upon health," you could anticipate the speaker to use a cause-effect pattern of development.

Patterns provide a strategy or framework for comprehending a message. Thought patterns indicate how ideas are organized. Familiarity with patterns enables us to grasp meaning more easily. If, for example, you establish that a lecturer intends to contrast two forms of media advertising, then the lecture will be easier to follow.

Patterns facilitate storage and retrieval of information in memory. Information that is grouped, chunked, or organized is easier to store than single, unrelated bits of information. Also, the manner in which information is stored in memory influences the ease with which it is retrieved. Patterns provide a vehicle for organizing information and function as retrieval clues for subsequent recall.

Patterns provide a means of understanding and analyzing assignments. Often an assignment seems difficult or confusing until you understand its function. Patterns provide a vehicle for organizing and expressing your ideas in a coherent, comprehensible form. As you write essay exam answers, class assignments, or terms papers, patterns provide a base or structure around which you can effectively express your thoughts.

ACADEMIC THOUGHT PATTERNS

Here are the commonly used thought patterns:

- ❑ Order or sequence
- ❑ Comparison and contrast
- ❑ Cause and effect
- ❑ Classification
- ❑ Problem-solution
- ❑ Definition
- ❑ Listing

The following section describes each pattern. In later chapters, you will see how these patterns are useful in taking lecture notes, reading textbooks, writing papers, and preparing for and taking exams.

Order or Sequence

If you were asked to summarize the plot of a film, you would mention key events in the order in which they occurred. In describing how to solve a math problem, you would detail the process step by step. If asked to list what you feel are your accomplishments so far this week, you might present them in order of importance, listing your most important accomplishment first, and so forth. In describing a building, you might detail the front, then the sides, then the roof. In each case, you present information in a particular sequence or order. Each of the above, then, illustrates a thought pattern known as order or sequence. Each form is described briefly below.

Chronology

Chronological order refers to the sequence in which events occur in time. This pattern is essential in the academic disciplines concerned with the interpretation of events in the past. History, government, and anthropology are prime examples, as well as other disciplines for which historical background is provided. In various forms of literature, chronological order is evident: the narrative form, used in novels, short stories, and narrative essays, centers on chronological order.

Speakers and writers often provide substantial clues that signal that this thought pattern is being used. These signals may occur within single sentences or as transitions or connections between sentences. Several examples of these signals follow. (Clue words that occur in phrases are italicized here to help you spot them.)

❏ ❏ ❏

In-sentence clues	*in* ancient times
	at the start of the battle
	on September 12
	the *first* Homo sapiens
	later efforts
Between sentence transitions	then, later, first, before, during, by the time, while, afterwards, as, after, thereafter, meanwhile, at that point

❏ ❏ ❏

Process

In disciplines that focus on procedures, steps, or stages by which actions are accomplished, the process pattern is often employed. These include mathematics, natural and life sciences, computer science, and engineering. The pattern is similar to chronology in that steps or stages follow each other in time.

Clues and signals often used in conjunction with this pattern are similar to those used for chronological order.

Order of Importance

The pattern of ideas sometimes expresses order of priority or preference. Ideas are arranged in one of two ways: from most important to least important, or from least to most important. Here are some commonly used clues that suggest this pattern.

❏ ❏ ❏

In-sentence clues	is *less* essential than . . . *more* revealing is . . . of *primary* interest
Between sentence transitions	first, next, last, most important, primarily, secondarily

❏ ❏ ❏

Spatial Order

Information organized according to its physical location or position or order in space uses a pattern that is known as spatial order. Spatial order is used in academic disciplines in which physical descriptions are important. These include numerous technical fields, engineering, and the biological sciences.

Diagramming is of the utmost importance in working with this pattern; in fact, often a diagram accompanies text material. For example, in studying the functioning of the various parts of the human eye, a diagram makes the process easier to understand. Lecturers often refer to a visual aid or chalkboard drawing when providing spatial description. Clue words and phrases that indicate spatial order include the following:

❏ ❏ ❏

In-sentence clues	the *center*, the *lower* portion, the *out side* area, *beneath* the surface
Between sentence transitions	next to, beside, to the left, in the center, externally

❏ ❏ ❏

EXERCISE 7-1

Directions:

Read each of the following opening sentences from a textbook reading assignment and anticipate whether the material will be developed using chronology, process, order of importance, or spatial order.

1. The rise of organizations of women both preceded and postdated the civil rights movements.[1]

2. As is common with all other cells, the neuron has a nucleus, a cell body, and a cell membrane, which encloses the whole cell.

3. As people move away from denial (they can no longer reject the fact that they are ill because their symptoms are growing so acute), anger (being angry is not helping symptoms), and bargaining (also ineffective; they are becoming worse, not better), they eventually arrive at a stage of really admitting to themselves that they are ill.[2]

4. Short fibers, dendrites, branch out around the cell body and a single long fiber, the axon, extends from the bell body.

5. The basic technique for input loop control involves using a flag to signal when the EOF record has been read.[3]

6. The battle for women's suffrage was fought mostly in the last years of the nineteenth and first years of the twentieth century.[4]

7. A newborn needs careful assessment to be certain that his musculoskeletal and neurological systems are intact.

8. The key consideration in determining whether a college education is a good investment is the opportunity cost, the cost of choosing college over other alternatives.

Comparison and Contrast

The *comparison* pattern is used to emphasize or discuss *similarities* between or among ideas, theories, concepts, or events, while the *contrast* pattern emphasizes *differences*. When a speaker or writer is concerned with both similarities and differences, a combination pattern is used. Comparison and contrast are widely used in the social sciences, where different groups, societies, cultures, or behaviors are studied. Literature courses may require comparisons among poets, among several literary works, or among stylistic features. A business course may examine various management styles, compare organizational structures, or contrast retailing plans.

A speaker or writer may be concerned with similarities, differences, or both similarities and differences. In turn, this concern will affect the organizational pattern. For example, suppose a professor of American literature is comparing two American poets, Whitman and Frost. Each of the following organizations is possible:

❑ Compare and contrast the two; that is, discuss their similarities, then their differences.

❑ Discuss characteristics of Whitman, then discuss characteristics of Frost, then summarize their similarities and differences.

❏ Discuss by characteristic. For example, first discuss the two poets' use of metaphor, then their use of rhyme, and then their common themes.

Clues, words, and phrases that reflect these patterns are listed below:

❏ ❏ ❏

Contrast

Within sentence clues	*unlike* Bush, Clinton . . .
	less rigid than . . .
	contrasted with
	differs from
Between sentence transitions	in contrast
	however
	on the other hand
	as opposed to

Comparison

Within sentence clues	. . . *similarities between*
	is *as* powerful *as* . . .
	like Bush, Clinton . . .
	both Bush and Clinton . . .
	Clinton *resembles* Bush *in that* . . .
Between sentence transitions	in a like manner
	similarly
	likewise
	correspondingly
	in the same way

❏ ❏ ❏

EXERCISE 7-2

Directions:

Read each of the following opening sentences from textbook reading assignments and anticipate whether a comparison, contrast, or combination pattern will be used.

1. Black Muslim religious practices closely follow those of Islam, a major religion of the Middle East and North Africa.
2. The majority of Americans will be better off in the year 2000 than we are today.

3. Two recent research reports have come to opposing conclusions about the dangers of hazardous waste pollution of the area's water table.
4. Both Werner (1994) and Waible (1995) focus on variability of genetic traces in pinpointing causes of cancer.
5. In the few areas on which they agree, the two authors dispute the credibility of each other's sources.

Cause and Effect

The cause and effect pattern expresses a relationship between two or more actions, events, or occurrences that are connected in time. The relationship differs, however, from chronological order in that one event leads to another by causing it. Information that is organized using the cause-effect pattern may

❑ explain causes, sources, reasons, motives, and action
❑ explain the effects, results, or consequences of a particular action
❑ explain both causes and effects

The cause and effect pattern is used extensively in many academic fields. All disciplines that ask the question "why," all that involve research, and all that search for explanations of the operation of the world around us use the cause and effect thought pattern. It predominates in science, technology, and social science.

In its simplest form, cause and effect is straightforward and direct. In other situations, causes and effects, or reasons and consequences, although not directly stated, can be inferred. For example, consider the following sentence:

Because wages are decreasing, the pace of inflation is slowing.

Decreasing wages is the cause or reason, and the slowing of inflation is the result or consequence. Notice, however, that the relationship is not directly stated, only implied.

Many statements expressing cause and effect relationships appear in direct order, with the cause states first and the effect following.

I couldn't find my keys, so I was late for class.

However, reverse order is sometimes used, as in the following statement:

I was late for class because I couldn't find my keys.

EXERCISE 7-3

Directions:

Identify the cause and the effect in each of the following statements.

1. Your buying decisions influence the prices farmers receive for their products.
2. A computer program is easy or difficult to run, depending in part on the data entry system you choose.
3. Recently, the Justice Department investigated charges that some airlines were using their computerized reservations systems to gain a competitive edge over smaller airlines.
4. Computer users suffer when poor, incompletely designed error-checking systems are marketed.
5. The threat of nuclear war has been with us for so long—nearly two generations—that we are in serious danger of forgetting the real dangers it poses.

The cause and effect pattern, however, is not limited to an expression of a single one cause-one effect relationship. There may be multiple causes, or multiple effects, or both multiple causes and multiple effects. For example, both slippery road conditions and your failure to buy snow tires (causes) may contribute to your car's sliding into the ditch (effect). In other instances, a chain of causes or effects may occur. For instance, missing the bus may force you to miss your 8:00 A.M. class, which in turn may cause you to not turn in your term paper on time, which may result in a penalty grade.

Clue words or phrases that suggest the cause and effect pattern include the following:

❑ ❑ ❑

Within sentence clues	causes, creates, leads to, stems from, produces, results in
Between sentence transitions	therefore, consequently, hence, for this reason, since

❑ ❑ ❑

EXERCISE 7-4

Directions:

For each of the following statements, determine whether it expresses single or multiple causes and single or multiple effects.

1. Acute stress may lead to an inability to think clearly, to organize, and to make decisions.
2. A mild stimulant, such as caffeine, appears to change a person's ability to maintain attention and concentration on relevant stimuli at hand.
3. Many peoples consider large families a blessing, or have religious objections to birth control, or are culturally ill suited to the regular use of birth control methods.[5]
4. Regional conflict, then, is at the base of the huge military bill of the Third World, together with ideological competition, and sometimes revolution, between Western oriented governments and Socialist movements.[6]
5. Geography and territorial position are among the most enduring determinants of national power and national defense.

Classification

Suppose you were asked to explain how a microcomputer operates by a friend who had never used one. You might start by describing the function of each major component: the monitor, the disk drives, the central processing unit, and so forth. By dividing a topic and discussing each of its components, you are using a pattern known as classification.

This pattern is widely used in many academic subjects. For example, a psychology text might explain human needs by classifying them into two categories: primary and secondary. Or in a chemistry textbook, various compounds may be grouped and discussed according to common characteristics, such as the presence of hydrogen or oxygen. The classification pattern divides a topic into parts, based on common or shared characteristics. Classification implies use of both the comparison and the contrast thought patterns, since it is on the basis of some similarity that items may be put into a class or category and on the basis of some differences that individual members of a class remain distinct from one another.

Here are a few examples of topics and the classifications or categories into which each might be divided:

Cars: sports, luxury, economy
Energy: kinetic, potential
Diseases: communicable, noncommunicable

Clue words and phrases that indicate the classification pattern are as follows:

❏ ❏ ❏

Within sentence clues	There are several *kinds* of . . .
	There are numerous *types* of . . .
	can be *classified as* . . .
	is *composed of* . . .
	comprises . . .
Between sentence transitions	finally, another, one type of . . .

❏ ❏ ❏

EXERCISE 7-5

Directions:
Divide each of the topics listed below into several groups or categories.

1. Emotions
2. Music
3. Discrimination
4. Laws
5. Literature

Problem-Solution

Many scientific and technical fields are concerned with defining problems and conducting research to test possible solutions. In the social and behavioral sciences this approach is also used. This problem-solution pattern forms the basis of the scientific method, a process used throughout the sciences to ask questions, test hypotheses, solve problems, and acquire new knowledge.

Problem-solution is a complicated thought process, involving several other patterns as well. Cause and effect are also involved, since the solution must have an effect on the problem. The "if . . . , then . . . " type of thinking involved in predicting possible solutions is basically a cause and effect relationship. Process, too, is involved, since problem solving involves step-by-step analysis of the problem.

In many texts, numerous forms of this pattern are found. Several solutions to a particular problem may be offered or various solutions may be discussed before the problem is fully defined, or various related problems may be discussed and numerous solutions offered. The clue words and phrases used within this pattern are as follows:

❏ ❏ ❏

Within sentence clues	since . . . , why . . . , would . . . , if . . . then, why does . . .
Between sentence transitions	since, whereas, consequently, as a result

❏ ❏ ❏

EXERCISE 7-6

Directions:

Predict which of the following textbook chapter headings is most likely to follow the problem-solution pattern.

1. Types of Consumer Research
2. Preventing the Spread of Infection
3. Factors That Influence Food Choice
4. Detecting Errors in Computer Programs
5. Procedures for the Administration of Oral Liquid Medicine

Definition

Each academic discipline has its own specialized vocabulary (see Chapter 12). One of the primary purposes of basic textbooks is to introduce students to this new language. Consequently, definition is a commonly used pattern throughout most introductory-level texts.

Suppose you were asked to define the word "comedian" for someone unfamiliar with the term. First, you would probably say that a comedian is a person who entertains. Then you might distinguish a comedian from other types of entertainers by saying that a comedian is an entertainer who tells jokes and makes others laugh. Finally, you might mention, by way of example, the names of several well-known comedians who have appeared on television. Although you may have presented it informally, your definition would have followed the standard, classic pattern. The first part of your definition tells what general class or group the term belongs to (entertainers). The second part tells what distinguishes the term from other items in the same class or category. The third part includes further explanation, characteristics, examples, or application.

Here are a few additional examples:

❑ ❑ ❑

	General Class	Distinguishing Characteristics
Opossum	animal	ratlike tail nocturnal habits
Prejudice	emotional attitude	involving a tendency to respond negatively to certain identifiable groups or group members

❑ ❑ ❑

EXERCISE 7-7

Directions:

Using the patterns described above, give a definition for each of the following.

1. Athlete
2. Cheating
3. Music
4. Credit rating
5. Discrimination

Listing

If asked to describe an exam you just took, you might mention its length, its difficulty, the topics it covered, and the types of questions it contained. These details about the exam could be arranged in any order; each detail provides further information about the exam, but each has no specific relationship to any other. This arrangement of ideas is known as *listing*, the presentation of pieces of information on a given topic by stating them one after the other.

This pattern is widely used in college textbooks in most academic disciplines. The listing pattern is the least structured pattern, but it is used frequently in several ways. In its loosest form, the pattern may be simply a list of items: factors that influence light emission, characteristics of a particular poet, a description of an atom, a list of characteristics that define poverty. Step-by-step procedures may also be presented using this pattern. Somewhat more structured is the use of listing to explain, support, or provide evidence. Support may be in the form of facts, statistics, or examples. For instance, the statement "The newest sexually transmitted disease to come to public awareness, AIDS, was first documented in 1981 and has spread rapidly since that time" would be followed by details about its discovery and statistics documenting its spread.

The clue words or phrases used for this pattern include the following:

❏ ❏ ❏

Within sentence clues	the second . . .
	. . . and . . .
	also
	there are several . . .
	(1) . . . , (2) . . . , and (3) . . .
	(a) . . . , (b) . . . , (c) . . .
Between sentence transitions	In addition,
	first, second, third
	finally
	another

❏ ❏ ❏

EXERCISE 7-8

Directions:
Identify the topics listed below that might be developed using the listing pattern.

1. Sources of Drug Information
2. Types of Computers
3. Problem Solving Techniques
4. Two Famous Twentieth-Century Composers
5. Obstacles to Creative Thought

Mixed Patterns

Patterns are often combined. In describing a process, a writer may also give reasons why each step must be followed in the prescribed order. A lecturer may define a concept by comparing it to something similar or familiar. Let's suppose your political science professor opens a lecture by stating that the distinction between "power" and "power potential" is an important one in considering balance of power. You might expect a definition pattern, in which the two terms are defined, but you might also anticipate the difference or "distinction" between the two terms to be discussed using a contrast pattern.

❏ ❏ ❏
Thinking Critically . . . About Patterns

When you learn to identify patterns, you see the ideas in a piece of writing or a lecture as a coherent set rather than as unconnected facts. Patterns focus your attention on concepts, larger ideas, and issues rather than on small, individual details.

Patterns, then, help you decide what is important and what is not. Here's a list of patterns and what they emphasize:

Pattern	*What is Important*
Order or Sequence	
• chronology	• dates and events
• process	• steps or procedures
• importance	• priorities
• spatial	• physical location
Comparison and Contrast	
• comparison	• similarities
• contrast	• differences
Cause and Effect	Sequence, actions, relationships, consequences, motives
Classification	Characteristics and distinguishing features
Problem-Solution	Causes, effects, solutions, outcomes
Definition	Terminology, examples

EXERCISE 7-9

Directions:

For each of the following topic sentences, anticipate two patterns that are likely to be evident in the paragraph.

1. On balance, then, there appear to be four discernible reasons for nuclear weapons development: security, prestige, regional dominance or equilibrium and reification of modern scientific development.[7]

2. Before examining the components of the balance of power, it will be useful to clarify five features about the international system that apply regardless of historical era or structural form.[8]

3. Industry, the second and more modern form of production, displaced feudalism.[9]

4. Like reinforcement, punishment comes in two varieties, positive and negative.[10]

5. The reasons for this huge increase in military expenditure in the Third World are many, and they go considerably beyond reasons of national grandeur. Perhaps most important is the degree to which the developing nations remain of interest to the super-powers.[11]

EXERCISE 7-10

Directions:

For each of the following lecture topics, anticipate and discuss what pattern(s) the lecture is likely to exhibit.

1. Conducting an Interview
2. Why Computers Use Binary-Coded Information
3. Functions of Money
4. Classical vs. Instrumental Conditioning
5. Narrowing a Research Paper Topic
6. Assigning Data to a Two-Level Table
7. Adolescence: The Failure to Cope
8. Cures for Inflation
9. Phillips Curves: Hypothetical and Actual
10. Apartheid: Tradition or Discrimination

EXERCISE 7-11

Directions:

For each of the following topic sentences, anticipate what pattern(s) that paragraph is likely to exhibit.

1. Should terrorism and hostage-taking be controlled by an international response team? If so, what policies and procedures should govern its actions?

2. Unlike Japan and the Western European countries, Canada has been relatively removed from the balance of terror.

3. More recently, however, the Japanese outlook has shifted. American withdrawal from the mainland of Asia after the Vietnam War, together with the uncertainties introduced to national security by the Nixon Doctrine, necessitates a larger measure of self-dependence.[12]

4. We may agree in theory with the ringing words of the Declaration of Independence that "all men are created equal"; but in the

concrete world of reality, the words are often obscured by conflicts.[13]

5. Writing in *Foreign Affairs* in 1947, foreign policy strategist George F. Kennan proposed a policy of containment. His containment doctrine called for the United States to isolate the Soviet Union, "contain" its advances, and resist its encroachments.[14]

6. Throughout the nuclear era much attention has been given to the various types of unintended nuclear war—war initiated by accident, error, or terrorist activity.

7. With the Doppler technique, high-frequency sound waves are "bounced off" body tissue; the rate and pitch at which they return demonstrate the movement and density of the underlying tissue.

8. The sections of a comprehensive history are introduction, chief concern, history of present illness, past medical history, family medical history, and review of systems.

9. In addition to nuclear devices, missiles and weapons for land, sea, and air warfare, arms designers have created a variety of weapons less well known but equally horrifying.[15]

10. Behaviorists see the individual as essentially passive, while cognitive psychologists maintain that the individual actively interacts with the environment.

APPLYING YOUR KNOWLEDGE OF PATTERNS

Now that you are familiar with the seven basic thought patterns, you are ready to use them to organize your learning and study and to shape your thinking. Subsequent chapters in this text will demonstrate the use of patterns in specific learning situations. In the next chapter, you will identify patterns in college lectures and use them to organize your note-taking. In Chapter 9 you will see that they are helpful in interpreting graphs, tables, and diagrams. Patterns are used in Chapter 10 to describe various techniques of mapping (using drawings to organize ideas). Chapter 13, "Study Strategies for Academic Disciplines," discusses predominant patterns in each discipline. When preparing for examinations (Chapter 14), you will need to organize thematic study as well as predict examination questions. In Chapter 15 the thought patterns involved in various types of examination questions are discussed. Finally, in Chapters 16 and 17 you will discover that patterns are useful in organizing and expressing your own ideas, as well as in synthesizing information for use in term papers.

SUMMARY

Recognition of an author's or speaker's thought pattern is an aid to comprehension and recall and also allows you to anticipate idea development. Seven patterns are common:

1. *Order or sequence.* The order or sequence pattern takes four forms. Chronology refers to the arrangement of events in time; process focuses on the order in which procedures or steps are accomplished; order of importance expresses priority or preference; spatial order refers to physical location, position, or order.
2. *Comparison and contrast.* This pattern emphasizes similarities or differences among ideas, concepts, people, or events.
3. *Cause and effect.* Casual relationships between two or more events or actions are shown with this pattern. Causes may be implied or directly stated, and often multiple causes or multiple effects are evident.
4. *Classification.* Classification is a process of dividing a topic into parts or categories, based on common or shared characteristics.
5. *Problem-solution.* This pattern focuses on the identification of a problem or problems and discussion of possible solutions.
6. *Definition.* An object or idea is explained by describing the general class or groups to which it belongs and how it differs from others in the same group (distinguishing characteristics).
7. *Listing.* The listing pattern is a means of presenting pertinent information about or in support of a topic either step by step or with no inherent order.

CLASS ACTIVITY

Directions:
While the thought patterns presented in this chapter are widely used in academic thinking, writing, and speaking, they also are important and frequent in our everyday lives. In groups of five or six, brainstorm to list as many daily activities or decisions as you can that involve one (or more) of the seven thought patterns discussed in this chapter.

FURTHER ANALYSIS

Directions:
Analyze the following situation and answer the questions that follow:

A student is given an assignment in art history class to write an essay discussing two paintings, one by Renoir, the other by Daumier. She has spent considerable time studying each painting, but she has no idea of how to begin the assignment. Although the paintings are obviously very different, she cannot seem to find an organizing principle on which to base her essay.

Feeling as if she is making no progress, she calls several friends and asks advice. One friend advises her to read some general background information on each artist. Another advises her to focus on her first impression of each painting and write about those impressions.

1. Evaluate the advice given by each friend.
2. What advice would you offer that would help the student complete this assignment?
3. What possible ways could the student organize her paper?

DISCUSSION

1. Consider each course you are taking this semester. What thought patterns are predominant in each?
2. From your experience, do essay exam questions seem to use these thought patterns? Think of essay questions you have read and consider the types of responses they required.
3. What connections do you see between the patterns discussed here and the type of essays you have written or are writing in English composition classes?
4. Assume you must read and take notes on seven articles, one representative of each of the seven patterns discussed in this chapter.
   a. How would you modify your reading strategy for each?
   b. How would you organize your notes for each?

FURTHER READING

Horowitz, Rosalind. "Text Patterns, Part I and Part II." *Journal of Reading,* 29 (1985)), 448-454, 634-541.

Levin, Gerald. *Prose Models,* 9th ed. New York: Harcourt, 1993.

8

Notetaking for Class Lectures

Learning Objectives

Learn a systematic approach to listening and lecture notetaking

Develop techniques for recording content and organization of lectures

Recognize various lecture styles

Identify and use instructors' thought patterns

Edit and review your notes

Class lectures are a primary source of information. They are a personalized explanation or interpretation of course content, and notetaking is your primary means of organizing and processing this material. Notetaking is a means of thinking and reasoning about course content and of identifying and recording important information using thought patterns as organizing principles. This chapter discusses listening and notetaking techniques, describes various lecture styles, demonstrates how to anticipate and identify lecturers' thought patterns, and presents systems for editing and reviewing your notes.

SHARPENING YOUR LISTENING SKILLS

During college lectures, listening is your primary means of acquiring information. Listening is also an essential skill in most careers. It is estimated that between 35 percent and 40 percent of a white-collar worker's day is spent listening. Yet research indicates that most adult students or employees do not listen efficiently. Rate the effectiveness of your listening skills by completing the questionnaire shown in Figure 8-1.

The Distinction Between Hearing and Listening

Have you ever found yourself not listening to a friend who is talking to you? Instead, perhaps you are thinking about something else entirely or about what you'll say next. Have you ever found yourself not listening to an instructor during class? In each case, the speaker's voice was loud and clear; you could *hear* but you were not *listening*. These two situations illustrate the distinction between hearing and listening. Hearing is a passive physiological process in which sound waves are received by the ear. In contrast, listening is an intellectual activity that involves comprehension and interpretation of incoming information. Listening is intentional—something you do deliberately and purposefully. It requires your attention and your concentration. Hearing, on the other hand, occurs without any thought or effort.

Tips for Effective Listening

Use the following suggestions to sharpen your listening skills:

Tune in. Focus your attention on the lecture or presentation before it begins. Recall what you know about the topic. Review related reading assignments while you are waiting for the lecture to begin.

Maintain eye contact with the lecturer. Except when writing notes, make eye contact with the lecturer. Eye contact improves communication; you will feel more involved and find it easier to stay interested in the lecture.

Stay active by asking mental questions. Keep your attention focused on the lecture by asking yourself questions. Here are a few examples: What key point is the lecturer making? How does it fit with previously discussed key points? How is the lecture organized? How will the lecturer prove the point?

Anticipate what is to follow. A good lecturer provides clues about his or her organization. Careful listeners, then, are able to predict or anticipate where the lecturer is leading up to or what topics will follow.

Figure 8-1
Rate Your Learning and Notetaking Skills

Directions:

Respond to each of the following statements by checking "Always," "Sometimes," or "Never."

	Always	*Sometimes*	*Never*
1. Do you tune in to a lecture before it begins by rereading previous notes or assigned material?	❑	❑	❑
2. Do the speaker's mannerisms or physical appearance distract you?	❑	❑	❑
3. Do you arrive at class on time or a few minutes early?	❑	❑	❑
4. Do you find yourself day-dreaming or thinking about something else while listening?	❑	❑	❑
5. Do you get tired or sleepy during a lecture?	❑	❑	❑
6. Do you try to record every-thing the lecturer says?	❑	❑	❑
7. Do you read the textbook assignment that is related to the lecture *before* attending the lecture?	❑	❑	❑
8. Do you tune out the lecturer if the topic is boring, technical, or overly complicated?	❑	❑	❑
9. Do your notes reflect the lecturer's organization?	❑	❑	❑
10. Do you edit (review and revise) your notes after each class?	❑	❑	❑

Stick with the lecture. When a lecture becomes confusing, complicated or technical, it is tempting to tune out, telling yourself you'll figure it out later by reading your textbook. Resist this temptation by taking detailed notes. These notes, when reviewed after the lecture, will be valuable as you try to straighten out your confusion.

Avoid emotional involvement. If the lecture is on a controversial issue or the lecturer mentions a topic or word that has emotional meaning for you, it is easy to become emotionally involved. When this occurs, your listening sometimes becomes selective—you hear what you want to hear. Instead, try to remain objective and open-minded. Your attention may be diverted by these topics unless you force yourself to concentrate on the speaker's position, not your own.

Use gaps and pauses in the lecture. Use this time to organize or summarize your notes.

Focus on content, not delivery. It is easy to become so annoyed, upset, charmed by, or engaged with the lecturer as a person that you fail to comprehend the message he or she is conveying. Force yourself to focus on the message, and disregard personal characteristics such as an annoying laugh or overused expressions.

Focus on ideas, not facts. If you concentrate on recording and remembering separate, unconnected facts, you are doomed to failure. Remember, your short-term memory is extremely limited in span and capacity, so while you are focusing on certain facts, it is inevitable that you will ignore some and forget others. Instead, listen for ideas, trends, and patterns.

Listen carefully to the speaker's opening comments. As your mind refocuses from prior tasks and problems, it is easy to miss the speaker's opening remarks, which may be among the most important. Here the speaker may establish connections with prior lecturers, identify his or her purpose, or describe the lecture's content or organization.

Attempt to understand the lecturer's purpose. If it is not stated explicitly, try to reason it out. Is the purpose to present facts, discuss and raise questions, demonstrate a trend or pattern, or present a technique or procedure?

Fill the gap between rate of speech and rate of thinking. It is natural for your mind to wander while a friend is talking. Although you may be interested in what he or she is saying, do you seem to have time to think about other things while listening? This is natural, since the rate of speech is much slower than the speed of thought. To listen most effectively in class, use this gap to think about the lecture. Anticipate what is to follow, think of situations where the information may be applied, pose questions, or make the information fit with your prior knowledge and experience.

Treat listening as a challenging mental task. We all know concentration and attention are necessary for reading, yet many of us treat listening as something that should occur without effort. Perhaps as a result of the constant barrage of the spoken word through radio, television, and social contact, we assume listening occurs automatically. Lectures, however, represent a concentrated form of oral communication that requires you to concentrate.

HOW TO START WITH AN ADVANTAGE

Some students regard lecture notetaking as a frustrating chore of handling an overwhelming rush of incoming information. Other students seem to approach it systematically, managing to process large amounts of information easily. Which it becomes for you depends largely on your approach. A few suggestions will enable you to approach lecturers confidently and efficiently—with distinct advantages over students who just appear in class with a pen.

Get Organized

Organization is the key to handling many situations, and this is especially true of lecture notetaking. Use the following tips to approach notetaking in an organized, systematic manner:

Organize a notebook for each course. Use standard size, $8\frac{1}{2}$ x 11 inches. Not enough information fits on a page in smaller notebooks, making review more difficult. Either spiral or looseleaf notebooks are acceptable; looseleaf types allow you to add class handouts, review sheets, and quizzes beside the notes to which they pertain.

Use ink. Pencil tends to smear and fade.

Date your notes for later reference.

Get used to sitting in the same place, preferably near the front of the room. You will feel more comfortable and less distracted if you have your own seat. Sitting near the front is especially important in large lecture halls. You will feel as if you are in more direct contact with the instructor and will be able to see as well as hear emphasis as you observe his or her facial expressions and gestures.

Make a point to attend all lecturers, even if attendance is not mandatory. Borrowing and copying a classmate's notes is not a substitute for attending the lecture, since it does not involve the key learning processes of identifying, organizing, and synthesizing information. If it is absolutely necessary to miss a class, be certain to borrow and photocopy several students' notes. Then, after you have reviewed each set, abstract from them your own set of notes. This procedure approximates the actual notetaking process by forcing you to think about, compare, and decide what is important.

Be Thoroughly Prepared for Each Lecture

Lecture notetaking will be easier if you are familiar with the topic of a lecture, key points, key terminology, and basic thought patterns. If you approach a lecture "cold," without advance preparation, you must devote considerable time and effort focusing on the topic, determining its organization, and assessing its relationship to other course content.

To prepare in advance, read related text assignments. It is tempting to delay reading an assignment until after the lecture because a text assignment seems easier once you have heard the lecture on the same topic. However, reading the text in advance will improve your comprehension of the lecture. At first it may seem to be a toss-up as to which it is best to do first. Remember, however, that your text is always available for rereading, study, and review, while each lecture is a one-time opportunity.

If you are unable to read an assignment completely before a particular lecture, preview it using the procedure described in Chapter 6 to obtain a basic familiarity, and plan to read it after the lecture.

Overcoming Common Problems

Instructors present lectures differently, use various lecture styles, and organize their subjects in different ways. Therefore, it is common to experience difficulty taking notes in one or more courses. Table 8-1 identifies common problems associated with lecture notetaking and offers possible solutions.

RECORDING APPROPRIATE CONTENT AND ORGANIZATION

The worst mistake you can make when taking notes is to try to record everything the instructor says. While this may seem to be the safest, most thorough approach, it interferes with, and often prevents, learning. If you are constantly writing, you have little time to think—to understand, assimilate, or react to what is being said. The effectiveness of notetaking as a learning strategy depends on active listening. As you eval-

Table 8-1
COMMON NOTETAKING PROBLEMS

Problem	Solution
"My mind wanders and I get bored."	Sit in the front of the room. Be certain to preview assignments. Pose questions you expect to be answered in the lecture.
"The instructor talks too fast."	Develop a shorthand system; use abbreviations. Leave blanks and fill them in later.
"The lecturer rambles."	Preview correlating text assignments to determine organizing principles.
"Some ideas don't seem to fit anywhere."	Record them in the margin or in parentheses within your notes for reassessment later during editing (see pp. 173–174).
"Everything seems important." or "Nothing seems important."	You have not identified key concepts and may lack necessary background knowledge (see Chapter 6)—you do not understand the topic.
"I can't spell all the new technical terms."	Record them phonetically, the way they sound; fill in correct spellings during editing (see pp. 173–174).

uate the relevance and importance of incoming information and make connections with other information presented, learning occurs. The following sections offer some general suggestions on recording and organizing information.

Identifying Main Ideas

The main ideas of a lecture are the points your instructor emphasizes and on which he or she elaborates. They are the major ideas that the details, explanations, examples, and general discussion support. Frequently, instructors give clues to what is important in a lecture. The following are a few ways speakers show what is important:

Points repeated. When an instructor repeats a statement, he or she is indicating to you that the idea or concept is important. Look for signals such as "This, you will recall . . . " or "As we saw last week in a different framework . . . "

Change in voice. Some lecturers change the tone or pitch of their voices when they are trying to emphasize major points. A speaker's voice may get louder or softer or higher or lower as he or she presents important ideas.

Change in rate of speech. Speakers may slow down as they discuss important concepts. Sometimes a speaker goes so slowly that he or she seems to be dictating information. If, for example, a speaker giving a definition pauses slightly between each word or phrase, it is a way of telling you that the definition is important and you should write it down.

Listing and numbering points. Lecturers often directly state that there are "three important causes" or "four significant effects" or "five possible situations" as they begin discussing a topic. These expressions are clues to the material's importance.

Writing on the chalkboard. Some lecturers write key words or outlines of major ideas on the chalkboard as they speak. Although not all important ideas are recorded on the chalkboard, you can be sure that if an instructor does take the time to write a word or phrase on the chalkboard, it is important.

Use of audiovisuals. Some instructors emphasize important ideas, clarify relationships, or diagram processes or procedures by using audiovisual aids. Movies, filmstrips, videotapes, or photographs emphasize or describe important ideas and concepts.

Direct announcement. Occasionally, an instructor will announce straightforwardly that a particular concept or idea is especially important. He or she may begin by saying, "Particularly important to remember is . . . " or "One important fact that you must keep in mind is . . . " The instructor may even hint that such information would make a good exam question. Be sure to mark hints like these in your notes. Emphasize these items with an asterisk or write "exam?" in the margin.

Nonverbal clues. Many speakers provide clues to what they feel is important through their movements and actions as well as their words. Some lecturers walk toward their audience as they make a major point. Others may use hand gestures, pound the table, or pace back and forth as they present key ideas. While each speaker is different, most speakers use some type of nonverbal clue.

At the beginning of each course, be sure to analyze each professor's means of emphasis. Think of this analysis as a means of tuning in or getting on the same wavelength as your professor.

EXERCISE 8-1

Directions:
Analyze the lecture style of one of your instructors. Attend one lecture, and as you take notes, try to be particularly aware of how he or she lets

you know what is important. After the lecture, analyze your instructor's lecture style, using the following questions.

1. How does he or she emphasize what is important?
2. What nonverbal clues are evident?

Then analyze your notetaking skills.

1. What notetaking problems did you encounter?
2. What can be done to overcome these problems?

Recording Details and Examples

A difficult part of taking notes is deciding how much detail to include. You cannot record everything because the normal speed of speech greatly exceeds the normal speed of writing. Some lecturers speak as fast as 90-125 words per minute. Therefore, you will have to be selective and record only particularly important details. As a rule of thumb, record a brief phrase to summarize each major supporting detail.

If an instructor gives you several examples of a particular law, situation, or problem, be sure to write down in summary form at least one example. Record more than one if you have time. While at the time of the lecture it may seem that you completely understand what is being discussed, you will find that a few weeks later you really do need examples to help you recall the lecture.

Reflecting the Lecture's Organization

As you record the main ideas and details, try to organize or arrange them so that you can easily see how the lecture was organized and recall the relative importance of ideas. A simple way to show a lecture's organization is to use a system of indentation. Retain a regular margin on your paper. Start your notes on the most important of the topics at the left margin. For less important main ideas, indent your notes slightly. For major details, indent slightly farther. Indent even farther for examples and other details. The rule of thumb to follow is this: The less important the idea, the further it should be indented. Your notes might be organized like this:

Major topic
        Main idea
            Detail
            Detail
                Example

> Main idea
>> Detail
>> Detail
>> Detail
> Major topic
>> Main idea
>>> Detail
>>>> Example

❏   ❏   ❏

Notice that the sample looks like an outline but is missing the Roman numerals (I, II, III), capital letters (A, B, C), and Arabic numerals (1, 2, 3) that usually enumerate an outline. This system of notetaking accomplishes the same goal as an outline—it stratifies information to show, at a glance, the relative importance of the various facts or ideas listed. If the organization of a lecture is obvious, you may wish to use a number or letter system in addition to indenting.

Since not all instructor's lectures follow a tightly organized pattern, it is not always possible to develop an outline. Try not to spend too much time during the lecture thinking about the outline format. Be primarily concerned with recording ideas; you can always reorganize your notes after the lecture.

The notes in Figures 8-2 and 8-3 were taken by two students on the same lecture. The notes in Figure 8-2 clearly indicate main ideas, important details, and examples and reflect the lecture's organization. The notes in Figure 8-3 are lengthy and do not emphasize key ideas. Read and evaluate each set of notes.

Taking Notes More Efficiently

If you record main ideas, details, and examples, using the indentation system to show the lecture's organization, you will take adequate notes. However, the following tips can help you make notetaking easier, make your notes more complete, and make study and review easier.

Leave blank spaces. To make your notes more readable and to make it easier to see the organization of ideas, leave plenty of blank space. If you know you missed a detail or definition, leave additional blank space. Fill it in later by checking with a friend or referring to your text.

Mark assignments. Occasionally, an instructor will announce an assignment or test in the middle of a lecture. As you jot it down, mark "Assignment" or "Test Date" in the margin so that you can find it easily and transfer it to your assignment notebook.

Figure 8-2
An Effective Notetaking Style

Marketing 101

Consumer Behavior

How Buyers Buy
2 factors involved:
    1. product adoption = consumer's decision to buy
defs   *2. product diffusion = rate of adoption by*
        consumers throughout market
prod w/ quick diffusion = good chance of success
   " " slow   " must sustain loss
until diff. increases
A. Types of Adopters – 5 classes, based on
    speed of adoption
    1) innovators – 1st to buy   young, bit eccentric
       rely on printed info rather than salespeople
    2) early adopters – socially, financially well-to-do.
       if this group doesn't buy – product will fail
    3) early majority adopters – careful, cautious
       – most influenced by sales people, ads
    4) late majority adopters – opinion followers
       rely heavily on friends, family
    5) Laggards – fearful of new, older people, less
       educated peers are primary source of info
B. Factors affecting Diffusion

Mark ideas that are unclear. If an instructor presents a fact or idea that is unclear, put a question mark in the margin. Later, ask your instructor or a classmate for a clarification.

Don't plan to recopy your notes. Some students take each day's notes in a hasty, careless way and then recopy them in the evening. These students feel that recopying helps them review the information and think it is a good way to study. Actually, recopying often becomes a mechanical process that takes a lot of time but very little thought. Time spent recopying can be better spent reviewing the notes in a manner that will be suggested later in this chapter.

Recognize that tape recording lectures requires review time. In an attempt to get complete and accurate notes, some students tape record their lectures. After the lecture, they play back the tape and take notes on

Figure 8-3
An Ineffective Notetaking Style

Marketing 101

    What Makes Buyers Buy What They Do
    There are two factors involved: product adoption and product
diffusion. Adoption — decision to buy. Diffusion means adoption
throughout the market.

    There are 5 classes of buyers
Innovators are the first to buy. They are young and eccentric and rely
on printed information rather than salespeople. People who are
socially and financially well off are early adopters. If this group
doesn't buy the product will fail. Early majority adopters are most
influenced by salespeople & ads.

    Late majority adopters are opinion followers who rely heavily on
information from friends and family. Laggards are older people who
are less educated and are the last to buy. Their peers are their
primary source.

    There are several factors that affect diffusion.

it, starting and stopping the tape as needed. In using the tape system, you spend at least an additional hour in playback for every hour spent in class to complete your notes. This procedure is time-consuming and inefficient in terms of the time spent relative to the amount of learning that occurs.

Generally, tape recording is not recommended. However, there are obvious exceptions. Foreign students often find the process valuable. Also, students who must spend large amounts of time commuting to campus find listening to tapes this time. Before you tape a lecture, be certain to obtain the permission of your instructor.

Try not to write complete sentences. Use as few words as possible. You will be able to record more information, and review will be easier.

Use abbreviations. To save time, try to use abbreviations instead of writing out long or frequently used words. If you are taking a course in psychology, you would not want to write out p-s-y-c-h-o-l-o-g-y each time the word is used. It is much faster to use the abbreviation "psych." Try to develop abbreviations for each subject area you are studying. The following abbreviations, devised by a student in business management, will give you an idea of the possibilities and choices you have. Notice that both common words and specialized words are abbreviated.

❏ ❏ ❏

Common Words	Abbre-viation	Specialized Words	Abbre-viation
and	+	organization	org.
with	w/	management	man.
compare	comp.	data bank	D.B.
comparison		structure	str.
importance	imp't.	evaluation	eval.
advantage	adv.	management by	MBO
introduction	intro.	objectives	
continued	cont'd.	management infor-mation system	MIS
		organizational de-velopment	OD
		communication	comm./
		simulation	sim.

❏ ❏ ❏

As you start to use abbreviations, be sure to begin gradually. It is easy to overuse abbreviations and end up with a set of notes that are almost meaningless.

WORKING WITH VARIOUS LECTURE STYLES

Not all instructors lecture in the same way or for the same purpose. In fact, two instructors teaching the same course who use the same text may exhibit very different lecture styles. Or a certain instructor may alternate between styles to achieve various purposes. Lectures may differ in focus, purpose, format, and organization, as well as content. While each instructor is unique, you will encounter four general lecture styles: factual, conceptual, analytical, and discussion.

The Factual Lecture Style

The factual lecture style centers around a straightforward presentation of information: facts, definitions, historical events, rules, principles, processes, and procedures. Many introductory-level course lectures fall into this category. The primary purpose of this type of lecture is to present and explain. As one psychology instructor tells his students: "You have to learn about psychology before you can think about and work within it." In other words, you must acquire a base of knowledge as you begin to study a new discipline. Here are a few examples of lecture topics using the factual style:

❏ ❏ ❏
Thinking Critically . . . About Lectures

Although listening to a lecture is demanding, try to *think about* the lecture as well as take notes on it. Here are a few suggestions:

Before the Lecture
1. Anticipate the content and focus of the lecture by referring to assigned readings and/or your course syllabus.
2. Think about how the lecture topic fits with the previous lecture.

During the Lecture
1. Keep your focus on ideas and concepts, not individual facts.
2. Jot in the margin any questions as they come to mind.

After the Lecture
1. Review your questions; if they are still unanswered, check your text, talk with another student, or consult your instructor.
2. Ask yourself questions about the lecture at each level of thinking (see p. 18). Focus especially on application, analysis, synthesis, and evaluation.

❏ ❏ ❏

Course	Lecture topic
Public speaking	Analyzing Your Audience
American government	The Structure of American Elections
Nursing	Fluid and Electrolyte Balance
Business communication	Strategies for Interviewing

❏ ❏ ❏

Here are a few suggestions for taking notes from factual lectures:

Be as accurate and complete as possible.

If you have difficulty recording all the needed information, leave blank spaces and fill in the information later. Check with a classmate, if necessary.

Don't waste time rewriting information that duplicates what is contained in your text; jot down the topic and a page reference.

The notes shown in Figure 8-1 were taken from a factual lecture.

The Conceptual Lecture Style

The conceptual lecture style focuses on the analysis and interpretation of information. It is concerned with ideas, trends, and concepts. Although factual information may provide the basis of this type of lecture, the focus is often on issues, policies, problems, and perspectives. This style is common in philosophy, special issue classes such as "Environmental Problems," sociology, and economics. Here are a few examples of lecture topics that employ a conceptual format:

❏ ❏ ❏

Course	*Lecture topic*
Social problems	Welfare: Myths and Realities
Ecology	Solving the World Food Shortage
Marketing and advertising	Controlling Consumer Behavior

❏ ❏ ❏

Use the following tips for taking notes on conceptual lectures:

Focus on concepts, or broad, organizing ideas. For example, it is much more important to record the concept that "impressionism, as an art form, dominated the last 20 years of the nineteenth century" than it is to record every fact your instructor gives you about impressionism.

Record only as much detail as you need to understand and recall the concept. Choose the most vivid or those that provide the strongest evidence.

Record key details on which your instructor spends the most time.

A sample set of notes from a conceptual lecture is shown in Figure 8-4.

The Analytical Lecture Style

The analytical style is used in courses that examine literary or artistic works, social issues, mathematical or scientific problems, or philosophical, moral, or religious issues. This style is evident in literature, art, math-

Figure 8-4
Conceptual Style Notes

<u>*Nuclear Arms Race & Third World Countries*</u>

basic attitude is one of resentment

1. *3ʳᵈ world countries are the poor getting poorer while watching rich countries get richer*
   ∴ *they deplore the expenditure of valuable economic & natural resources on "war games"*
2. *3ʳᵈ world knows that the US and S. Union have spent trillions on the arms race*
   ∴ *resent claims by these 2 countries that they lack eco. capability to assist them fight poverty*
3. *Super Powers attempt to establish influence in 3ʳᵈ world countries*
   ∴ *3ʳᵈ world countries feel "used" and suspicious of offers of "friendship".*

ematics, science, and philosophy courses, as well as in seminars that focus on a particular social issue, historical or literary period, or art form. In analytical lectures, close study followed by interpretation is the mode of presentation. Personal reaction is often important, as is assessment of value, worth, and aesthetic qualities. Search for reasons and interpretation of actions or published works are often involved.

Here are a few topics of lectures that use the analytical style:

❏ ❏ ❏

Course	Lecture topic
Literature	Steinbeck's Use of Symbolism
Philosophy	Mill's Theory of Utilitarianism
Business law	Antitrust Litigation: Three Illustrative Cases

❏ ❏ ❏

To take notes on analytical lectures, use the following suggestions.

Record themes, essential characteristics, theories, significance of related events, and important facts.

When analyzing a case, poem, story, or painting, make notes in the margin of the work as it is discussed.

Focus on the significance or importance of the work being analyzed.

Figure 8-5 shows a sample portion of notes taken on the analysis of Keat's poem "Ode on a Grecian Urn."

The Discussion Style

This form cannot be called a lecture style since the emphasis is not on the presentation of ideas but on their exchange. The purpose of class discussion is to involve students in thinking, reacting, and evaluating the topic at hand. Discussion-style classes are prevalent in disciplines that involve controversial issues or subjective evaluation.

For discussion classes, advance preparation is the key. In fact, you

Figure 8-5
Analytical Style Notes

John Keats (1795–1821)

theme of permanence
figures on urn never change

Ode on a Grecian Urn   1820
    refers to urn   *2 interpretations*
Thou still unravished bride of quietness,   *1. as yet*
    Thou foster-child of silence and slow time,   *2. motionless*
Sylvan historian, who canst thus express
rustic
woodland   A flowery tale more sweetly than our rhyme:
scene What leaf-fringed legend haunts about thy shape   *Tempe- beautiful rural*   5
        Of deities or mortals, or of both,   *valley in Greece*
            In Tempe or the dales of Arcady   *Valleys of Arcadia—*
        What men or gods are these? What maidens loth? *often symbolize pastoral*
    What mad pursuit? What struggle to escape?   *ideal*
feeling
of lack   What pipes and timbrels? What wild ecstasy?   10

    Heard melodies are sweet, but those unheard   *words don't quite express*
        Are sweeter; therefore, ye soft pipes, play on; *thought, what is imagined is*
    Not to the sensual° ear, but, more endeared,   *better than what is expressed*
        Pipe to the spirit ditties of no tone: — *imagined sounds*   *physical*
    Fair youth, beneath the trees, thou canst not leave
        Thy song, nor ever can those trees be bare; *— nothing will change*   15
            Bold Lover, never, never canst thou kiss,
    Though winning near the goal–yet, do not grieve;   *yet never will*
permanence   She cannot fade, though thou hast not thy bliss, *achieve the goal*
        For ever wilt thou love, and she be fair! . . .   20

need to spend more time preparing for a discussion than you do studying your notes afterward. Plan to spend considerable time reading, making notes, and organizing your thinking about the topic. Make lists of questions, points with which you agree or disagree, good or poor examples, and strong or weak arguments. These lists will provide a basis for your input into the discussion.

When participating in class discussion, students often neglect to take notes. While careful, detailed notetaking may not be as critical for class discussions as for lectures, try to keep a record of key points in the discussion. Not only will the notes be valuable for later review, they are also useful for immediate reaction and response during the discussion. If you have recorded someone's argument or objection, you are better prepared to defend or criticize it than to do so purely from memory.

You might also use your notes to outline or sketch a response before you present it. As you will see in Chapter 16, writing is a vehicle that clarifies your thinking. By informally outlining or jotting down the points you intend to make, you will organize and focus your thoughts, thus improving your contribution.

Discussion notes will be much less detailed and will reflect less organization than lecture notes. Think of them as a chronological record of the discussion, a list of ideas and topics discussed. After class, it is especially important to reread and edit discussion notes (see pp. 173–174).

EXERCISE 8-2

Directions:
Each student should bring notebooks from two courses he or she is currently taking. Students should exchange notebooks and identify the predominant style used in several lectures.

EXERCISE 8-3

Directions:
For each course in which you are currently enrolled, identify the predominant lecture style.

NOTETAKING AND LEARNING STYLE

While instructors vary in their lecture style, students also vary in their learning style. Do you recall the learning style questionnaire you completed in Chapter 6? Refresh your memory by reviewing the results on p. 109. Your learning style influences your listening skills and your notetaking ability. Certain lecture styles, too, may be easier for you to work with due to your learning style. Auditory learners, of course, are well-suited to listening and notetaking, while visual learners are less inclined to learn by listening. Nonspatial learners find the lecture mode more appropriate than spatial learners, who prefer a more concrete mode of presentation. Table 8-2 offers suggestions for adapting your listening and notetaking abilities for various aspects of your learning style.

USING THE LECTURER'S THOUGHT PATTERNS

If you approach lectures simply as a means of acquiring information, you are missing an important learning opportunity. Lectures provide you the opportunity to understand how the instructor approaches the subject

Table 8-2
ADAPTING NOTETAKING TO YOUR LEARNING STYLE

Learning Characteristic	Notetaking Strategy
Auditory	Take advantage of your advantage! Take thorough and complete notes
Visual	Work on notetaking skills; practice by tape recording a lecture; analyze and revise your notes
Creative	Annotate your notes, recording impressions, reactions, spin-off ideas, related ideas
Pragmatic	Reorganize notes during editing Pay attention to lecturer's organization
Social	Review and edit notes with a classmate Compare notes with others
Independent	Choose seating in close contact with instructor; avoid distracting groups of students
Applied	Think of applications (record as annotations) Write questions in the margin about applications
Conceptual	Discover idea relationships Watch for patterns
Spatial	Add diagrams, maps during editing
Nonspatial	Record lecturer's diagrams, drawings—but translate into language during editing

matter. They reveal how the instructor thinks: how he or she processes, organizes, and approaches the material. Understanding the lecturer's thought patterns will show you what to record and help you follow the lecturer's organization.

Understanding the instructor's thought processes is also an important advantage in completing assignments, taking exams, and writing papers. You will be better able to understand the purpose of an assignment, interpret exam questions accurately, or choose the appropriate focus for a paper. These skills will be discussed in greater detail in subsequent chapters.

Anticipating and Identifying Patterns in Lectures

The most common thought patterns used in lectures are those discussed in Chapter 7: sequence or order, comparison and contrast, cause and effect, classification, problem-solution, definition, and listening. Lecturers often use various devices to make their pattern of organization apparent.

Organizing Statements

At the beginning of a lecture, instructors frequently announce the topic and provide clues to their approach. For instance, a psychology instructor may open a lecture by saying:

> This morning we will define behaviorism by studying two of its leading advocates—B. F. Skinner and Watson. Both believed that . . .

From this statement you can predict a comparison and perhaps contrast pattern between Skinner and Watson, as well as discussion of the characteristics of behaviorism (listing pattern).

Transitions

Good speakers and lecturers use transitions to assist their audiences in anticipating and following their train of thought. As they move from point to point, they often use a transitional word or phrase to signal the change. These transitions are similar to those used in writing, except that they tend to be more direct and frequent than in written language. If, for example, a lecturer says "Consequently, we have . . . ," you can anticipate a cause and effect pattern.

Summary Statements

Similar to opening statements, summary statements provide strong clues about a lecture's organization. But since they come at the end of the lecture, the clues usually confirm patterns listeners have already identified.

Lecture Style

A lecturer's thought patterns are, to some extent, reflected in the style of lecture used. An instructor who uses a discussion style is more likely to employ cause and effect, comparison or contrast, or problem-solution patterns than to follow listing or sequence/order patterns, which seem more appropriate to a factual lecture style. For example, a political science class discussion on Third World countries might involve such topics as reasons for their growing importance or their effects on other countries.

PATTERNS AS AN AID TO ORGANIZING YOUR NOTES

Once you have identified a lecturer's predominant pattern, you can use that knowledge to organize you lecture notes. Notetaking tips for each pattern are presented in Table 8-3.

Table 8-3
USING PATTERNS IN LECTURE NOTETAKING

Pattern	Notetaking Tips
Comparison and contrast	Record similarities, differences, and basis of comparison; use two columns or make a chart.
Cause and effect	Distinguish causes from effects; use diagrams.
Sequence or order	Record dates; focus on order and sequence; use timeline for historical events; draw diagrams; record in order of importance; outline events or steps in a process.
Problem-solution	Record parameters of the problem; focus on nature of problem; record process of arriving at solution.
Classification	Use outline form; list characteristics and distinguishing features.
Definition	Record general group or class; list distinguishing characteristics; include several examples.
Listing	Record in list or outline form; record order of presentation.

EXERCISE 8-4

Directions:

For each lecture topic, predict what pattern(s) might be used.

Course	*Lecture title/topics*
American government	The Bill of Rights—Then and Now
Speech communications	Ways to Research Your Topic
Nursing	Transfusion Reactions
Human sexuality	Components of Interpersonal Intimacy
Engineering/ technology	The Rationale for the Use of Standard Parts

EXERCISE 8-5

Directions:

Review your notes from each class lecture you attended last week, and identify the predominant patterns used in each lecture. Substantiate your answer.

EDITING AND REVIEWING YOUR NOTES

You should not assume that your lecture notes are accurate and complete or that simply by notetaking you have learned the information the notes record. Two more steps are necessary: (1) you must edit your notes, making them thorough and accurate, and (2) you need to develop and use a system for study and review.

Editing Lecture Notes

Even experienced notetakers find that they often miss some information and are unable to record as many details or examples as they would like during a lecture. Fortunately, the solution is simple. Do not plan on taking a final and complete set of notes during the lecture. Instead, record just enough during the lecture to help you remember a main idea, detail, or example. Leave plenty of blank space; then, as soon as possible after class, review the notes. Fill in the missing information and expand the notes, adding any details or examples. The process of revising notes to make them more complete and accurate is called *editing*. Editing notes for a one-hour lecture should take no more than five or ten min-

Figure 8-6
Sample Edited Notes

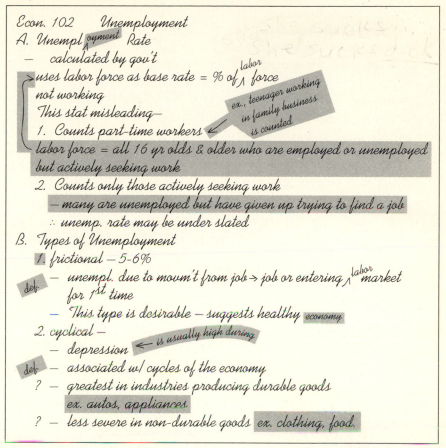

Econ. 102   Unemployment
A. Unempl_{oyment} Rate
  — calculated by gov't
  → uses labor force as base rate = % of ⟨labor⟩ force
  not working
  This stat misleading—   ex., teenager working
  1. Counts part-time workers ←   in family business
  labor force = all 16 yr olds & older who are employed or unemployed   is counted
  but actively seeking work
  2. Counts only those actively seeking work
    — many are unemployed but have given up trying to find a job
    ∴ unemp. rate may be under stated
B. Types of Unemployment
  1. frictional — 5-6%
  def. — unempl. due to movm't from job → job or entering ⟨labor⟩ market
        for 1st time
      — This type is desirable — suggests healthy economy
  2. cyclical —
    — depression ← is usually high during
  def. — associated w/ cycles of the economy
  ? — greatest in industries producing durable goods
       ex. autos, appliances.
  ? — less severe in non-durable goods ex. clothing, food.

utes. Some students find editing is easier when working with groups of two or three classmates. Group interaction and discussion provide a focus on the lectures, and one person may have recorded information that others did not.

The longer the time lapse between the notetaking and the editing, the more facts and examples you will be unable to recall and fill in.

The sample lecture notes in Figure 8-6 have been edited. The notes taken during the lecture are in dark print; the additions and changes made during the editing are in the shaded areas. Read the notes, noticing the types of information added during editing.

Use the Recall Clue System

The recall clue system helps make the review and study of lecture notes easier and more effective. It involves the following steps:

❏ Leave a 2-inch margin at the left side of each page of notes.
❏ Keep the margin blank while you are taking notes.
❏ After you have edited your notes, fill in the left margin with words and phrases that briefly summarize the notes. These *recall clues* should be words that will trigger your memory and help you recall the complete information in your notes.

These clues function as memory tags. They help you retrieve information that is labeled with these tags. Figure 8-7 shows a sample of notes in which the recall clue system has been used.

To study your notes using the recall clues, cover up the notes with a sheet of paper, exposing only the recall clues in the left margin. Next read the first recall clue and try to remember the information in the portion of the notes beside it. Then slide the paper down and check that portion to see if you remembered all the important facts. If you remembered only part of the information, cover up that portion of your notes and again check your recall. Continue checking until you are satisfied that you can

Figure 8-7
Recall Clue system

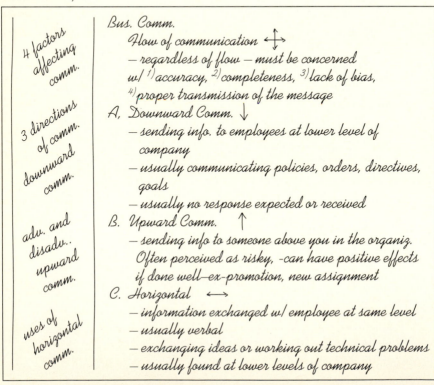

remember all the important facts. Then move on to the next recall clue on the page, testing and checking again.

A variation on the recall clue system that students have found effective is to write questions rather than summary words and phrases in the margin. The questions trigger your memory and enable you to recall the information that answers your question. With the questions you can test yourself, thereby simulating an exam. They also force you to think and actively respond to course content.

SUMMARY

1. Class lectures are a primary source of learning. Effective listening and notetaking skills are essential.
2. Notetaking can be improved by

   ❏ getting organized
   ❏ preparing for each lecture
   ❏ overcoming common notetaking problems

3. Recording information and organizing it effectively are the keys to retention of lecture content.
4. Notes should

   ❏ contain main ideas
   ❏ include key details and examples
   ❏ be organized to reflect the lecture's organization

5. Lectures differ in content, organization, and purpose. These are four general lecture styles:

   ❏ factual
   ❏ conceptual
   ❏ analytical
   ❏ discussion

6. Lectures often reflect one or more basic thought patterns.
7. Anticipating the lecturer's thought patterns helps in recording and organizing notes.
8. Editing class notes reinforces learning.
9. Recall clues are an aid to study and review.

CLASS ACTIVITY

Activity I:

Reading and listening are both receptive communication skills. Working in small groups of three or four students, discuss how reading and listening are similar and how they differ. Consider factors such as purpose, process, types of thinking, interference, recall, and retention. One student should record each group's findings and report those to the class. After each group has reported, the class may consider the question: Are some people better listeners than readers, and vice versa? Discuss why this may be true.

Activity II:

Each student should bring to class a notebook or a set of notes from a recent lecture. Working in small groups, students should exchange and evaluate one another's notes, using the checklist shown in Table 8-4.

FURTHER ANALYSIS

Directions:

Figure 8-8 shows the notes a student took for a psychology lecture on stress. Review the notes and then critique them using the checklist shown in Table 8-4. Make specific suggestions for improvement.

Figure 8-8
Notes from a Psychology Class

> *Coping with stress is a problem solving activity done by direct action —*
> *behavior that masters it. Palliation — way of addressing symptoms of stress*
> *stress and your ability to cope is affected by cognitive appraisal —*
> *also by sympathetic support —*
>
> *Predictability —*
> *— more stress if unpredictable advance notice helps*
>
> *Control affects the intensity of stress*
> *experiment by Brady showed monkeys more stressed by control than non-control*
> *— used "executive monkey"*
>
> *Relaxation involves muscle tension control*
> *— headaches, hypertension insomnia*
> *— at least 30 minutes/day progressive relaxation*

Table 8-4
NOTETAKING CHECKLIST

	Yes	No
1. Notes are titled and dated.	☐	☐
2. A separate line is used for each key idea.	☐	☐
3. Less important ideas are indented.	☐	☐
4. Abbreviations and symbols are used.	☐	☐
5. The organization of the lecture is apparent.	☐	☐
6. Words and phrases (not entire sentences) are recorded.	☐	☐
7. Examples and illustrations are included.	☐	☐
8. Sufficient explanation and detail are included.	☐	☐
9. Adequate space is left for editing.	☐	☐
10. Marginal space is available for recall clues.	☐	☐

DISCUSSION

1. A student complained that her computer science professor spends each class reading his notes aloud. She is having difficulty taking notes and maintaining interest. What suggestions would you offer?
2. A classmate who missed all her classes last week due to a skiing injury has asked to borrow your notebook for your medical terminology course over the weekend. How would you respond?
3. Identify and list factors that interfere with effective listening. Then discuss how each can be controlled.
4. Discuss how listening to music differs from and is similar to listening to a lecture.
5. Table 8-1 lists common notetaking problems. Discuss additional problems and offer possible solutions.

FURTHER READING

Anderson, Thomas H., and Bonnie B. Armbruster. "The Value of Taking Notes During Lectures." *Teaching Reading and Study Strategies,* eds. Rona F. Flippo and David C. Caverly. Newark, DE: International Reading Association, 1991. 86–165.

9

College Textbooks: Thinking and Learning Strategies

Learning Objectives

Discover keys to textbook organization

Use textbook features as aids to learning

Learn techniques for reading graphic material

Develop strategies for approaching supplemental reading assignments

Each semester you will spend hours reading, reviewing, and studying textbooks. The course textbook is often the focal point of a college course. Class lectures are often coordinated with reading assignments in the course text, written assignments require you to apply or evaluate ideas and concepts presented in the textbook, and term papers explore topics introduced in the text.

This chapter presents strategies for using textbooks as efficiently as possible. It discusses organization of the textbook; describes its unique features; presents strategies for studying graphs, tables, and diagrams; and discusses how to handle supplementary reading assignments.

KEYS TO OVERALL TEXTBOOK ORGANIZATION

When you first purchase a textbook, it may seem like an overwhelming, unmanageable collection of facts and ideas. However, textbooks are highly organized, well-structured sources of information. They follow specific patterns of organization and are uniform and predictable in format and style. Once you become familiar with these structures, you will come to regard them as easy-to-use resources and valuable guides to learning. Various features of textbooks make their organization and purpose understandable and explicit.

Preface

Traditionally, a textbook begins with an opening statement, called a *preface,* in which the author describes some or all of the following:

- ❏ Author's reasons for writing the text
- ❏ Intended audience
- ❏ Major points of emphasis
- ❏ Special learning features
- ❏ Structure or organization of the book
- ❏ Distinctive features
- ❏ Suggestions on how to use the text
- ❏ Author's qualifications
- ❏ References or authorities consulted

Reading the preface gives you a firsthand impression of the author and his or her attitudes toward the text. Think of it as a chance to get a glimpse of the author as a person.

Some authors include, instead of or in addition to a preface, an introduction titled "To the Student." Written specifically for you, it contains information similar to that of a preface. The author may include an introduction "To the Instructor" as well. Although it often may be quite technical, discussing teaching methodologies and theoretical issues, it may contain information of interest to students as well. Figure 9-1 presents a portion of the preface of a freshman composition text.

EXERCISE 9-1

Directions:
Read or reread the preface or introduction to the student in this book and in one of your other textbooks. Using the list above as a guide, identify the types of information each provides.

Figure 9-1
Sample Preface

PREFACE

Where there is too much,
something is missing.

We have tried to keep this proverb in mind; we hope we have
written a compact book rather than an undiscriminating one.

The book is designed for college courses in which students
write essays, instructors read them, and students and instructors
together discuss them. We hope we offer a practical guide to all
three activities. The student, looking for information about choosing a topic, writing an analysis, constructing a paragraph, using a
semicolon, can use the text as a guide to writing the week's essay.
The instructor, after reading the essay, can suggest chapters or
passages the student should consult in revising the essay or in
writing the next one. Students and instructors together can discuss
the exercises, the techniques used in the reprinted essays, the assumptions we make and the suggestions we offer.

Although we include discussions and examples of description and narration, we emphasize analysis, exposition, and argument because those are the chief activities, usually rolled into
one, that we all engage in, both in school and later. When students write reports for a course, or professors write reports for a
committee, or psychiatric social workers write case studies, most
of what they write is exposition, a statement of what's what; usually they have come to see what's what by analyzing or dividing
the subject into parts, and because they want to be believed, they
construct as persuasive an argument as possible.

Table of Contents

The table of contents is an outline of the textbook's main topics and
subtopics. It shows the organization of the text and indicates the interrela-
tions among the topics. Often, it reveals thought patterns used throughout the text.

Besides using the table of contents to preview a text's overall content
and organization, be sure to refer to it before reading particular chapters.
Although chapters are organized as separate units, they are interrelated.

To understand a given chapter, note what topics immediately precede and follow it.

Recent textbooks include a brief table of contents, listing only unit and chapter titles, followed by a complete table of contents that lists sub-headings and various learning aids contained within each chapter. The brief table of contents is most useful for assessing the overall content and structure of the entire text, while the complete one is more helpful when studying individual chapters.

In the brief table of contents from an adolescent psychology textbook shown in Figure 9-2, you can see that the text divides the subject of adolescence into three primary topics. The first section defines and describes adolescence from various points of view. The second focuses on six aspects of normal adolescent development, and the third considers three problem areas. The thought pattern used to organize the textbook's contents is classification.

Figure 9-3 is an excerpt from a detailed table of contents from the same textbook. The chapter outlined examines the influence of physical and physiological change on adolescents. Two thought patterns are evident: classification, and comparison and contrast.

EXERCISE 9-2

Directions:
Turn to the table of contents of one of your textbooks. Choose a unit or part that you have not read. Use the table of contents to predict the thought pattern(s) for each chapter.

Appendix

The appendix of a textbook contains supplementary information that does not fit within the framework of the chapters. Often, the appendix offers valuable aids. For example, an American government text contains three appendixes.

Appendix 1   The Declaration of Independence
Appendix 2   The Constitution of the United States of America
Appendix 3   Beyond the Call of Duty: Data and Documents

The textbook includes appendixes 1 and 2 for the readers' convenience, since the text refers to each frequently. Appendix 3 lists and explains additional sources of information for each chapter.

Figure 9-2
A Brief Table of Contents

The textbook includes appendixes 1 and 2 for the readers' convenience, since the text refers to each frequently. Appendix 3 lists and explains additional sources of information for each chapter.

Glossary

The glossary is a multidictionary of specialized vocabulary used throughout the text. Uses of the glossary are discussed in Chapter 12.

Index

At the very end of many texts, you will find an alphabetical subject index, listing topics covered in the text along with page references. Al-

Figure 9-3
Excerpt from a Complete Table of Contents

though its primary function is to allow you to locate information on a specific topic, it also can be used as a study aid for final exams. If you have covered most or all of the chapters in the text, then you should be familiar with each topic indexed. For example, suppose the index of an accounting textbook listed the following:

Purchases
  determining the cost of, 169-170
  of equipment for cash, 17-18, 36-37, 200
  of merchandise for cash, 201-202
  of merchandise on credit, 163-168

To review for an exam, look at each entry and test your recall. In the accounting textbook example, you would ask yourself: How is the cost of purchases determined? How are equipment purchases using cash recorded? What are the procedures for purchases of merchandise on credit?

Some texts also include a name index that allows you to locate references to individuals mentioned in the text. The checklist in Figure 9-4 is provided to help you quickly assess a textbook's content and organization.

EXERCISE 9-3

Directions:

Use the checklist in Figure 9-4 to analyze the content and organization of one of your textbooks.

TEXTBOOKS: GUIDES TO LEARNING

Most college textbooks are written by college professors who are experienced teachers. They understand how students learn, and they know which topics and concepts usually cause students difficulty. Their purpose in writing is not only to present information but to help students learn it. Consequently, a textbook contains numerous learning aids: chapter previews, marginal notes, special-interest boxes or inserts, review questions, lists of key terms, summaries, and references. A textbook is a guide to learning, a source that directs your attention, shows you what is important, and leads you to apply your knowledge. Learning will be easier if you use the textbook's learning aids to your best advantage.

Chapter Preview

Research in educational psychology indicates that if readers have some knowledge of content and organization of material *before* they begin to read it, their comprehension and recall increase. Consequently, numerous textbooks begin each chapter with some kind of preview. Previews take several common forms.

Chapter Objectives

In some texts, the objectives of each chapter are listed beneath its title, as is done in this book. The objectives are intended to focus your attention on important ideas and concepts. They are usually listed in the order in which the topics appear in the chapter, presenting an abbreviated outline of the main topics.

Figure 9-4
Assessing Your Textbook's Learning Features

Directions:
Mark "yes" or "no" after each of the following statements.

	Yes	No
Preface		
The purpose of the text is stated.	☐	☐
The intended audience is indicated.	☐	☐
The preface explains how the book is organized.	☐	☐
The author's credentials are included.	☐	☐
Distinctive features are described.	☐	☐
Major points of emphasis are discussed.	☐	☐
Aids to learning are described.	☐	☐
Table of Contents		
Brief table of contents is included.	☐	☐
The chapters are grouped into parts or sections.	☐	☐
Thought pattern(s) throughout the text are evident.	☐	☐
Appendix		
Useful tables and charts are included.	☐	☐
Supplementary documents are included.	☐	☐
Background or reference material is included.	☐	☐
Glossary		
The text contains a glossary.	☐	☐
Word pronunciation and meaning are provided.	☐	☐
Index		
A subject index is included.	☐	☐
A name index is included.	☐	☐

Chapter Outline

Other texts provide a brief outline of each chapter's contents. Formed from the headings and subheadings used throughout the chapter, the outline reflects both content and organization of the chapter. A sample outline, from a text on human development, is shown in Figure 9-5. As you study a chapter outline, pay attention to the sequence and progression of topics and look for thought patterns.

Chapter Overview

Some textbook authors provide a preview paragraph in which they state what the chapter is about, discuss why certain topics are important, focus the reader's attention on important issues, or indicate how the chapter relates to other chapters in the book. Overviews may be labeled

Figure 9-5
A Chapter Outline

_34_

Fractionalization of the Family Unit

Introduction

Study of the Family
    Theoretical approaches
    Levels of family functioning
        Level I: Infancy, or the chaotic family
        Level II: Childhood, or the intermediate family
        Level III: Adolescence, or the family
            with problems
        Level IV: Adulthood, or the family
            with solutions
        Level V: Maturity, or the ideal Family

Stressors to the Family Bond
    Acute stressors–crisis situations
    Chronic stressors–long-term situations
    Cultural stressors in contemporary life

Results of Family Stress
    Physical abuse
    Separation or divorce

Maximizing Family Potentials
    Assessment of and approach to families
    Facilitating intrafamily communication

Conclusions

"Chapter Preview," "Overview," or as in the sample shown in Figure 9-6 from an American government text, with a less obvious title such as "Memo."

Each type of preview can be used to activate and monitor your learning before, during, and after reading the chapter.

Before reading

❏ Use the chapter preview to activate your prior knowledge of the subject. Recall what you already know about the subject by trying to anticipate the chapter's main points.
❏ Use chapter previews to predict the predominant thought patterns.
❏ Use previews to anticipate which portions or sections of the chapter will be most difficult or challenging.

While reading

❏ Use the preview as a guide to what is important to learn.
❏ Mark or underline key information mentioned in the preview.

After reading

❏ Use the preview to monitor the effectiveness of your reading.
❏ Test your ability to recall the key information.
❏ Review immediately any material you were unable to recall.

EXERCISE 9-4

Directions:

Refer to the chapter outline in Figure 9-5 to answer the following questions.

1. What do you remember about stressors to the family bond? Activate your prior knowledge by listing crises that might strain family togetherness.
2. What predominant though pattern(s) do you predict the chapter will use?
3. Which section do you feel will be the most difficult to read and learn? Justify your choice.

Figure 9-6
A Chapter Preview

10   **Interest Groups**

MEMO

Like parties and elections, interest groups are a linkage institution. And like these other linkage institutions, they have been dramatically reshaped by our high-technology politics. In this chapter, we will see how.

Interest groups–sometimes called special interests, pressure groups, or lobbies–seek favorable public policies from government and want to side-track unfavorable ones. No part of the government is immune from interest groups.

Frankly, interest groups these days have had bad press. People usually think of them as representing some narrow, special, and selfish interest. Press and public alike suspect that they exert a corrupting influence on our political system. I, for one, believe these charges are partially true but greatly oversimplified. There is a significant bias in the interest group system; not all groups are created equal. But interest groups are a vital part of our political system.

Keep the following in mind as we discuss groups and government:

■ The American political system teems with an amazing array of groups. Some of them will seem trivial to you, but they have interests and members work to achieve their policy goals.

■ Groups, unlike parties, view the whole political system as fair game. Lobbying, electioneering, litigation, and appeals to the public are major group strategies.

■ Small groups, curiously, have a distinct advantage over large ones.

■ We can try to understand interest groups by looking at them from the perspectives of democratic theory, elite and class theory, pluralism, and hyperpluralism.

297

EXERCISE 9-5

Directions:

Refer to the chapter preview in Figure 9-6 to answer the following questions.

1. What do you know about interest groups? Activate your prior knowledge by listing several special-interest groups with which you are familiar.

2. What predominant thought pattern(s) do you predict the chapter will use?

Figure 9-7
Marginal Notations

Free goods: Things that are available in sufficient quantity to fill all desires.

You may feel that some things are not scarce and that the best things in life–such as love, sunshine, and water–are free. In economic terms, **free goods** are goods that are available in sufficient supply to satisfy all possible demands. But are many things truly free? Surface water is usually unfit for drinking except in areas far from human habitation. Water suitable for drinking must be raised to the surface from deep wells or piped from reservoirs and treatment plants, operations involving resources that are scarce even when water itself is not. Scarcity of winter sun in the North results in costly winter vacations in warm states. And if you think love is free. . . .

Economic goods: Scarce goods.

Costs: The value of opportunities forgone in making choices among scarce goods.

All scarce goods–from television to chlorinated water–are called **economic goods**. Their scarcity leads to **costs**. While it is customary to associate cost with the money price of goods, economists define cost as the value of what individuals have to forgo to acquire a scarce good. Since all unlimited wants cannot be met with scarce resources, individuals have to make choices–between, for instance, more steaks and more computer games; societies may have to choose between safer highways and more accurate missiles.

Marginal Notations

Textbooks used to have wide empty margins, useful to students for jotting notes. Recently, some textbook authors have taken advantage of this available space to offer commentary on the text; pose questions based on the text; provide illustrations, examples, and drawings; or identify key vocabulary. Figure 9-7, excerpted from an economics text, illustrates one type of marginal notation. In the excerpt, brief definitions of key terms are given in the margin next to the sentence in which the term is first introduced.

The best way to approach marginal notes is usually to refer to them once you have read the text to which they correspond. Often marginal notes can be used to review and check your recall. If the marginal notes are in the form of questions, go through the chapter, section by section, answering each question. Test your ability to define each key term in your own words.

Special-Interest Inserts

Modern textbooks may contain, at various points within or at the end of the chapters, brief articles, essays, or commentaries that provide a practical perspective or an application of the topic under discussion. Usually these inserts are set apart from the text using boxes or shaded or colored print. Usually, too, the inserts are consistently titled throughout the text, often suggesting their function, such as "Focus," "Counterpoint," "Today's Problems." In a sociology textbook, in a chapter on drug abuse, a vivid narrative of the life of a drug addict may be included. Or, in an economics text, specific situations that apply key concepts may be included.

Make use of article inserts in the following ways:

❏ Read the insert *after* you have read the text material on the page.
❏ Determine the purpose of the insert and mark in the margin the concept or principle to which the insert refers.
❏ When reviewing for exams, especially essay exams, quickly review the chapter inserts, especially if your instructor has emphasized them.

EXERCISE 9-6

Directions:
Read the box insert in Figure 9-8, which is taken from a banking and finance text chapter on investment opportunities. Then answer the following questions.

1. What investment principle does this special-interest box illustrate?
2. How useful do you feel this insert would be in preparing for an exam?
3. Do you feel the example of the Hunt brothers will make the concept of diversification come alive and seem real? Give reasons for your answer.

Questions for Review

Some textbook chapters conclude with a set of review questions. Read through these questions *before* you read the chapter. They serve as a list of what is important in the chapter. Usually the questions are listed in the order in which the topics appear in the chapter, forming an outline.

As you read and locate answers in the text, be sure to underline or mark them. Review questions are a useful but by no means a sufficient re-

Figure 9-8
A Special Interest Insert

Box 5.1

**The Dangers of Not Diversifying:
The Hunt Brothers and the Silver Crash**

In early 1979, two Texas billionaires, W. Herbert Hunt and his brother. Nelson Bunker, decided that silver was a bargain. As Herbert has stated, "I became convinced that the economy of the United States was in a weakening condition. This reinforced my belief that investment in precious metals was wise . . . because of the rampant inflaction."* Not accustomed to doing things in a small way, the Hunts invested over $1 billion in silver.

Spurred on by their purchases, the price of silver began to climb from $6 per ounce to over $50 per ounce by January 1980. Unfortunately for the Hunts, the good times

were not to last: After some decline from January to February, the silver market crashed in March 1980 and the price of silver fell to near $10 an ounce. Because of their failure to diversify, the Hunt brothers' losses from the silver crash were so large (estimated to be over $500 million) that they found themselves in some financial difficulty. As a result they went into debt to the tune of $1.1 billion, mortgaging not only the family's holdings of Placid Oil Company, but also 75,000 head of cattle, a stable of thoroughbred horses, paintings, jewelry, and even such mundane items as irrigation pumps and lawn mowers.

Clearly, Nelson and Herbert Hunt paid a heavy price for not diversifying, but at least Nelson retained his sense of humor. When asked in 1980 how he felt about his losses, he said, "A billion dollars isn't what it used to be."

---

*Quoted in G. Christian Hill, "Dynasty's Decline: The Current Question About Hunts of Dallas: How Poor Are They?" *Wall Street Journal* (November 14, 1984). The quote from Nelson following is also found in this article.

---

view. These questions often test only factual recall of specific information. They seldom require you to pull together ideas, compare, assess causes, or react to the information presented.

Lists of Key Terms

Lists of key terms are often found at the end of each chapter. Usually, only specialized terms that are introduced for the first time in that chapter are included. Glancing through the list before reading the chapter will familiarize you with them and make reading go more smoothly.

Chapter Summaries

Reading the end-of-chapter summary is useful both *before* and *after* you read a chapter. Before reading, the summary will familiarize you with the chapter's basic organization and content. After the chapter, it provides an excellent review and helps you tie together, or consolidate, the major points covered in the chapter.

Suggested Readings or References

Many textbook authors provide a list of suggested readings at the end of each chapter or section. This list refers you to additional sources,

---

Table 9-1
EVALUATION LIST

Chapter preview
What preview format is used?
What is its primary purpose?
What thought pattern(s) is evident?
How could it get used for review?

Marginal notes
What format is used?
How can they be used for study and review?

Special-interest inserts
How do they relate to chapter content?
How much importance should you place on them?

Review questions
Do the questions provide an outline of chapter content? (Compare them with chapter headings.)
What types of thinking do they require? Are they primarily factual, or do they require critical thinking?

Key terminology
How many, if any, words are already familiar?
How difficult do you predict the chapter will be?

Chapter summary
Does it list the main topics the chapter will cover?
Is a thought pattern evident?

Suggested readings
What types of sources are listed?
To which topics do they refer?

both books and periodicals, that provide more information on topics discussed in the chapter. References given in this list provide a useful starting point when researching a topic discussed in the chapter.

The evaluation list shown in Table 9-1 will enable you to quickly assess the learning aids a chapter provides.

EXERCISE 9-7

Directions:
Use the evaluation list shown in Table 9-1 to analyze how the author of one of your current textbooks guides your learning.

STUDYING GRAPHS, TABLES, AND DIAGRAMS

Significant portions of textbooks in the sciences, economics, and business are devoted to graphs, tables, and diagrams. These graphics present a visual picture of a given situation and summarize a great deal of information in a relatively small space.

It is tempting to skip over graphs, tables, and diagrams; stopping to study a graph takes time and seems to break your flow. Because they do not present information in verbal form (there are no statements to underline or remember), some students think they are unimportant. Actually, graphics are often *more* important than the paragraphs that surround them. They are included to call your attention to, emphasize, and concisely describe a situation. Graphics require time and effort to prepare and are expensive to include in a text. Consequently, graphics often indicate what the author thinks is important.

How to Read Graphics

Here are some general suggestions for reading graphics:

Read the title or caption. The title often tells you what situation or relationship is being described.

Determine how the graphic is organized. If you are working with a table, note the column headings. For a graph, notice what is marked on the vertical and horizontal axes.

Note any symbols and abbreviations used.

Determine the scale or unit of measurement. Note how the variables are measured. For example, does a graph show expenditures in dollars, thousands of dollars, or millions of dollars?

Identify the trend(s) or pattern(s) the graph is intended to show. The following sections will discuss this step in greater detail.

Read any footnotes. Footnotes printed at the bottom of a graph or chart indicate how the data was collected, explain what certain numbers or headings mean, or describe statistical procedures.

Check the source. The source of data is usually cited at the bottom of the graph or chart. Unless the information was collected by the author, you are likely to find a research journal or publication listed from which the data were taken. Identifying the source is helpful in assessing the reliability of the data.

Identifying Thought Patterns in Graphics

All graphics describe some type of relationship. Not coincidentally, these relationships correspond to the thought patterns studied earlier, in Chapter 7.

Tables: Comparison and Classification of Information

Sociologists, psychologists, economists, and business analysts frequently use tables to organize and present statistical evidence. A table is an organized display of factual information, usually numbers or statistics. Its purpose is to classify information so that comparisons can be made between or among data.

Take a few minutes now to study the table in Figure 9-9, using the suggestions listed above. Then analyze the table, using the following steps.

Determine how the data are classified or divided. This table classifies the use of five types of energy source from 1875 to 2000. Notice that this table contains both column (top to bottom) and row (left to right) headings. Note also that the footnote indicates the source of the data.

Figure 9-9
Example of a Table

Changing emphasis on world energy sources[a]

| Energy source | Percentage contribution to total energy used | | | | | |
	1875	1900	1925	1950	1975	2000 (est.)
Wood, vegetation	60	39	26	21	13	5
Coal	38	58	61	44	27	21
Oil	2	2	10	25	40	39
Natural gas	<1	1	2	8	15	15
Other sources (mainly hydroelectric and nuclear)	<1	<1	1	2	5	20

[a]Data compiled from U.N. and other sources.

Make comparisons and look for trends. This step involves surveying the rows and columns, noting how each compares with the others. For example, by looking at the horizontal column for wood, we can see a steady decline in wood usage since 1875. Be certain to compare columns and rows, noting both similarities and differences and focusing on trends.

Draw conclusions. This final step is to decide what the data presented are intended to show. You can conclude from Figure 9-9 that wood and coal usage are steadily declining, that oil usage increased until 1950 and then declined, and that natural gas and hydroelectric and nuclear energy sources are steadily increasing. Often, you will find clues, or sometimes direct statements, in the paragraphs that correspond to the table. The portion of the text that refers you to the table often makes a general statement about what the table is intended to show.

Once you have drawn your conclusions, be sure to stop, think, and react. For example, you might consider what the data in Figure 9-9 suggest about the future of nuclear power plants, the risk of nuclear accidents, or the relationships of world powers with oil-producing countries.

EXERCISE 9-8

Directions:

Study the table shown in Figure 9-10 and answer the questions that follow.

1. What change of direction or focus has community health nursing taken?
2. How has the service emphasis changed?
3. What thought patterns are evident in this table?

Figure 9-10
Example of a Table

Development of Community Health Nursing

Stages	Focus	Nursing Orientation	Service Emphasis	Institutional Base (Agencies)
District nursing (1860–1900)	Sick poor	Individual	Curative: beginning of preventive	Voluntary: some government
Public health nursing (1900–1970)	Needy public	Family	Curative: preventive	Government: some voluntary
Emergence of community health nursing (1970–present)	Total community	Population	Health promotion: illness prevention	Many kinds: some independent practice

Figure 9-11
A Linear Graph

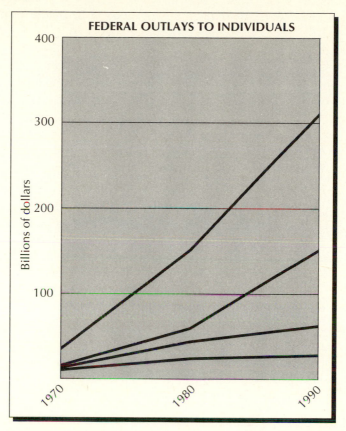

Graphs: Relationships Among Variables

Graphs depict the relation between two or more variables, such as price and demand or expenditures over time. Put simply, they are pictures of relationships between two or more sets of information. As you read and study in various academic disciplines, you will encounter many seemingly different types of graphs. They are all variations of a few basic types.

Linear graphs. For linear graphs, information is plotted along a vertical and a horizontal axis, with one or more variables plotted on each. The resulting graphs allows easy comparison between the variables. A sample linear graph is shown in Figure 9-11. The line graph displays federal expenditures to individuals from 1970 to 1990. It enables you to compare the amount spent on four categories of individuals over a period of twenty years.

Figure 9-12
Relationships Shown by Graphs

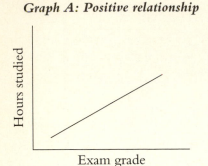

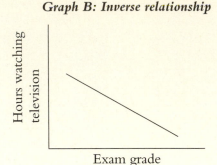

Graph C: Independent relationship

    In addition to yearly comparison, the graph also allows you to deter-
mine the general trend or pattern among the variables. Generally, this
graph shows an overall increase in each of the four categories. You can see
that retirement and medical care expenditures have increased dramatically, while public assistance and other have changed very little over the
twenty-year period.
    A linear graph can show one of three general relationships: positive,
inverse, or independent. Each of these is shown in Figure 9-12.
Positive relationships. When both variables increase or decrease simultaneously, the relationship is positive and is shown on a graph by an up-
wardly sloping line. Graph A shows the relation between how long a student studied and exam grades. As the time spent studying increases, so do
the exam grades.
Inverse relationships. Inverse relationships occur when, as one variable

increases, the other decreases, as shown in Graph B. Here, as exam grades increased, the amount of time spent watching television decreased. The inverse relationship is shown by the line or curve that slopes downward and to the right of point or origin.

Independent relationship. When the variables have no effect upon or relationship to one another, the graph appears as in Graph C. In this graph you can see that the amount of coffee drunk while studying had no effect upon exam grades.

From these three relationships, you probably realize that linear graphs may suggest a cause and effect relationship between the variables. A word of caution is in order here: Do not assume that since two variables change, one is the cause of the other. Once you have determined the trend and the nature of the relationship a linear graph describes, be sure to jot these down in the margin next to the graph. These notes will be a valuable timesaver as you review the chapter.

EXERCISE 9-9

Directions:

What type of relationship (positive, inverse, or linear) would each of the following linear graphs show?

1. In a graph plotting effective use of study time versus college course grades, what type of relationship would you expect?
2. In a graph plotting time spent reading versus time spent playing tennis, what relationship would you predict?
3. What type of relationship would be shown by a graph plotting time spent checking a dictionary for unknown words versus reading speed?

Circle graphs. A circle graph, also called a pie chart, is used to show whole-part relationships, or to show how given parts of a unit have been divided or classified. Figure 9-13 presents a circle graph that might be included in a corporate financial report. In this graph, revenue income is divided or classified into four categories. Circle graphs often are used to emphasize proportions or to show relative size or importance of various parts.

Figure 9-13
A Circle Graph

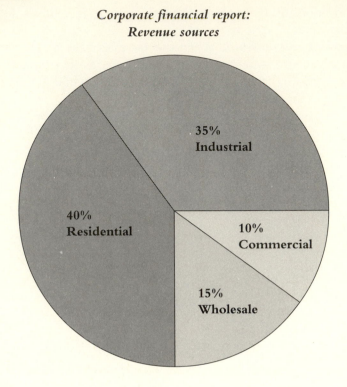

Corporate financial report:
Revenue sources

35%
Industrial

40%
Residential

10%
Commercial

15%
Wholesale

Bar graphs. A bar graph is often used to make comparisons between quantities or amounts. Figure 9-14 presents bar graphs that compare the level of effectiveness for easy and difficult tasks. It also compares the effectiveness in the presence of others versus working alone.

Diagrams: Explanations of Process

Diagrams are often included in technical and scientific as well as business and economic texts to explain processes. Diagrams are intended to help you to visualize, to see relationships between parts, and to understand sequence. Figure 9-15, taken from an engineering text, describes the Bourdon gauge, an instrument for measuring mechanical pressure.

The gauge functions using an expansion tube, the outside of which is exposed to the atmosphere. The inside is connected so as to be at the

Figure 9-14
A Bar Graph

*The Effects
of the Presence of Others
on Task Performance*

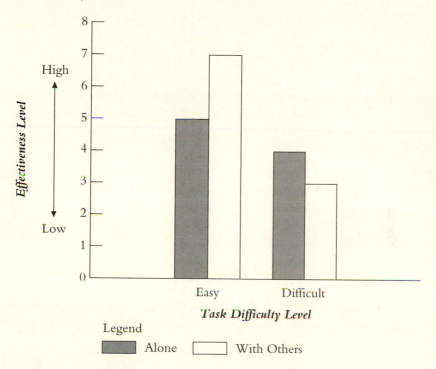

Legend

▓ Alone   ☐ With Others

same pressure as that which is to be measured. As the expansion tube straightens or contracts, it moves the pivot, which in turn moves the gauge needle.

Reading diagrams differs from reading other types of graphics in that diagrams often correspond to fairly large segments of text, requiring you to switch back and forth frequently between the text and the diagram, determining to which part of the process each paragraph refers.

Because diagrams of process and the corresponding text are often difficult, complicated, or highly technical, plan on reading these sections more than once. Use the first reading to grasp the overall process. In subsequent readings, focus on the details of the process, examining each step and understanding its progression.

Figure 9-15
A Mechanical Diagram

FUNDAMENTALS OF FLUID MECHANICS

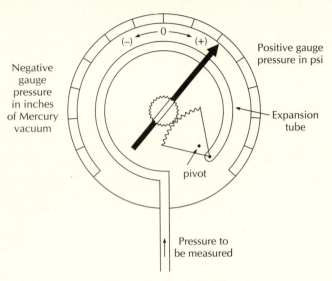

Bourdon gauge (reading in English units)

One of the best ways to study a diagram is to redraw the diagram without referring to the original, including as much detail as possible. Or test your understanding and recall of the process explained in a diagram by explaining it, step by step in writing, using your own words.

EXERCISE 9-10

Directions:

Study Figure 9-16. Then answer the questions that follow.

1. What is the purpose of the diagram?
2. What control does the executive branch exert over the judicial branch?
3. How does the judicial branch influence the legislative branch?
4. If a president were convicted of a criminal act, what branch would handle his removal from office?
5. Now test your knowledge of the procedure by drawing your own diagram without referring to the original.

Figure 9-16
A Conceptual Diagram

7 Separation of Powers and Checks and Balances in the Madisonian System

The president can veto congressional legislation

LEGISLATIVE BRANCH
The Congress
• House
• Senate

House and Senate can veto each other's bills.

Congress approves presidential appointments and controls the budget. It can pass laws over the president's veto and impeach and remove the president from office.

EXECUTIVE BRANCH
The President

Executive office of the president; executive and cabinet departments; independent government agencies.

The Senate confirms the president's appointments; Congress can impeach and remove judges from office.

The Court can declare presidential acts unconstitutional.

The Court can declare laws unconstitutional.

The president appoints judges.

JUDICIAL BRANCH
The Supreme Court of the United States

Circuit Courts of Appeals
District Courts

SUPPLEMENTAL READING ASSIGNMENTS

In addition to the textbook, many professors assign supplemental readings. These assignments are drawn from a variety of sources: other textbooks, paperbacks, newspapers, periodicals, scholarly journals, reference books. If the reading is not available as a paperback that you can purchase, a visit to the library is usually necessary. Often, your professor will place the required book or periodical *on reserve* in the library. This designation means the book is held at the reserve desk, where its use is restricted to a specified period of time.

❏ ❏ ❏
Thinking Critically . . . About Graphs and Statistics

Analyzing Statistics

The purpose of many graphs, charts, and tables is to display statistics in an easy-to-read format. A critical reader should look as closely at statistics as at any other type of information. While statistics may seem like hard facts, they can be misleading and deceiving.

Here is an example. Many graphics report averages—average salaries, average costs, average weights, or average educational levels. Did you know that an average can be computed three different ways with, at times, three very different results? The terms *median, mode,* and *mean* are all used to report averages. Let's say you want to report the average temperature for one week in your town or city. The daily temperatures are 69, 70, 70, 94, 95, 95, 96.

The mean temperature is 84.1.
The median temperarture is 94.
The mode is 70.

These are very different numbers. Here's how they were calculated:

Mean: total the daily temperatures and divide by 7.
Median: arrange the temperatures from low to high and take the middle-most temperature (the one with three higher and three lower temperatures).
Mode: choose the temperature that occurs most frequently.

This is just one example of why caution is needed when interpreting statistics. There are many others. (In the example above, for instance, how was the daily temperature calculated? Was it the daily high, daily low, 24-hour "average"?)

Since statistics are subject to manipulations and interpretation, study graphics with a questioning, critical eye.

Supplemental assignments present the following:

❏ new topics not covered in your text
❏ information not covered in the text
❏ updated information
❏ alternative points of view
❏ applications or related issues
❏ realistic examples, case studies, or personal experiences

Reading supplemental assignments requires different skills and strategies from those for reading textbooks. Unless the assignment is made in another textbook, you may find the material is not as well or as tightly organized as in a textbook. It may also be less concise and factual.

Analyzing the Assignment

First determine the purpose of the assignment: How does it relate to existing course content? Listen carefully as your professor announces the assignment; important clues are often provided at this time. Next, determine the type and level of recall that is necessary. If, for example, the purpose of an assignment is to present new important topics not covered in your text, then a high level of recall is required. If, on the other hand, an assignment's purpose is to expose you to alternate points of view on a controversial issue, then key ideas are needed, but highly factual recall is not. Or, if an assignment is given to help you understand real life experience, key ideas are all that may be necessary.

Choosing Reading and Study Strategies

Depending upon the purpose of the assignment and the necessary level and type of recall, you should read one assignment quite differently from another. Your choices range from a careful, thorough reading to skimming to obtain an overview of the key ideas presented. Before you begin, you need to select a study strategy to enable you to retain and recall the information. Table 9-2 lists examples of supplementary assignments and their purposes and suggests possible reading and study approaches for each. The table demonstrates that strategies should vary widely to suit the material and the purpose for which it was assigned.

Nonprint Supplemental Assignments

On occasion, a professor may make an assignment in nonprint materials, such as videotapes, films, lectures, or television documentaries. Approach these assignments as you approach printed assignments. It is particularly important to determine your purpose and to take adequate notes at the time, since it is usually extremely time consuming or, as in the case of a lecture, impossible to review the material later. Making notes on nonprint materials is, in some ways, similar to taking notes on class lectures. Refer to Chapter 8 for suggestions on lecture notetaking. In the case of films, dramatic recreations, or performances, your notes should reflect your impressions as well as a brief review of content.

Table 9-2
STRATEGIES FOR SUPPLEMENTAL READINGS

Assignment	Purpose	Reading Strategy	Study Strategies
Historical novel (American hitory course)	To acquaint you with living conditions of the historical period	Read rapidly, noting trends, patterns, characteristics; skip highly detailed descriptive portions	Write a brief synopsis of the basic plot; make notes (including some examples) of life-style, living conditions (social, religious, politi cal, as well as economic)
Essay on exchange in Moroccan bazaars (street markets) for economics course	To describe system of barter	Read for main points, noting process, procedures, and principles	Underline key points
Article titled "What Teens Know About Birth Control" assigned in a maternal care nursing course	To reveal attitudes toward and lack of information about birth control	Read to locate topics of information, misinformation, and lack of information; skip details and examples	Prepare a 3-column list: information, misinformation, and lack of information

SUMMARY

1. Textbooks contain numerous features to enable you to read, study, and learn their content as efficiently as possible.
2. The preface and table of contents provide keys to the overall organization, while the appendix, glossary, and index serve to organize and supplement the content, making it more easily accessible.
3. Textbook learning aids include

   ❏ chapter previews
   ❏ marginal notes
   ❏ special-interest inserts

- ❏ review questions
- ❏ lists of key terminology
- ❏ references

4. Textbook chapters often use graphics, including graphs, tables, and diagrams for a visual representation of information. All graphics express a relationship:

- ❏ Tables compare and classify information.
- ❏ Graphs express relations among variables.
- ❏ Diagrams explain processes.

5. In addition to textbook reading, professors often make collateral reading assignments as well. In reading these assignments you must

- ❏ analyze the assignment
- ❏ determine its purpose and relationship to other course content
- ❏ choose appropriate learning strategies

CLASS ACTIVITY

Directions:

Each student should bring two textbooks to class. Working in groups of three, students should complete each of the following activities.

1. Students should exchange texts and review each text using the lists on pp. 186 and 196. Then each student should identify the text that provides the strongest learning aids and justify his or her choice to the group. Collectively the group should agree on the "best" textbook.
2. Each group should appoint a group spokesperson who will present and describe the group's choice to the class. Depending on class size, the class might also identify the text with the strongest learning aids from among those chosen by each group.

FURTHER ANALYSIS

Directions:

Analyze the following situation and answer the questions below.

A business student is finding his ecology textbook overwhelmingly difficult and technical. He says he recognizes that the text contains numerous learning features, but despite these aids he is unable to master several assigned chapters per week. The student spends six hours per week; he reads each chapter, then rereads and outlines it in detail. Then he studies the outline, memorizing portions of it. The student described his problem to his professor, and she advised him to take a more active approach to his study.

1. Using your knowledge of textbook learning and study and thinking skills, evaluate this student's learning strategy.
2. Suggest how the student might learn more actively. How might the learning aids be used to promote more accurate learning?

DISCUSSION

1. Explain why reading a chapter overview increases your comprehension and recall of chapter content.
2. What do you consider to be the primary difference between a textbook and any other type of nonfiction book?
3. Discuss whether the following student complaints are justifiable:
   a. A student criticized her business management professor because she assigned textbook chapters but did not discuss them in class.
   b. A student felt he had wasted money because he was required to purchase a textbook for a course in which the professor assigned fewer than half of the chapters.
   c. A student complained that she would not have had to purchase the text at all since all material on the exam was discussed in class.
   d. Students in a sociology course were concerned that the instructor distributed a two-page supplemental reading list but did not make specific assignments. Instead, he advised students to "sample" as many readings as possible.
4. Six students in a physics class will be without textbooks for three weeks because the bookstore ran out of the text and has to reorder. How should these students handle this problem?

FURTHER READING

Caverly, David C., and Vincent P. Orlando. "Textbook Study Strategies." *Teaching Reading and Study Strategies*. Eds. Rona F. Flippo and David C. Caverly, Newark, DE: International Reading Association, 1991. 86-165.

McWhorter, Kathleen T. *Efficient and Flexible Reading*. 4th ed. New York: Harper-Collins, 1995.

Organizing and Synthesizing Course Content

Learning Objectives

Develop techniques for underlining textbook material

Use a marginal annotation system

Take effective notes from text

Learn mapping techniques

Use computers to integrate information

Have you ever wondered how you will learn all the facts and ideas your textbooks include and instructors present? The key to handling the volume of information presented in each course is a two-step process. First, you must reduce the amount to be learned by identifying what is important, less important, and unimportant to learn. Then you must organize and synthesize the information to make it more meaningful and easier to learn. This chapter describes two strategies for reducing the information—textbook underlining and marginal annotation—and three means of organizing information—notetaking, mapping, and computer integration.

TEXTBOOK UNDERLINING AND ANNOTATION

Textbook Underlining

Textbook underlining or highlighting is an extremely efficient way of making textbook review manageable. Especially when combined with annotation, it is a quick and easy way to review so that you do not have to reread everything when studying for an exam. If you highlight 20 percent of a chapter, you will be able to avoid rereading 80 percent of the material. If it normally takes two hours to read a chapter, you should be able to review an underlined chapter in less than a half hour. Underlining, by itself, however, is not a sufficient study method. The hour and a half you save, then, can be spent studying what you do not know, organizing and synthesizing the information, and preparing for your exam.

How to Underline

To underline textbook material most effectively, apply the guidelines below:

Begin by analyzing the task. Preview the assignment and define what type of learning is required. This will determine how much and what type of information you need to underline.

Assess your familiarity with the subject. Depending on your background knowledge, very little or thorough underlining might be necessary. Do not waste time underlining what you already know. In chemistry, for example, if you already have learned the definition of a mole, then do not underline it.

Read first; then underline. Finish a paragraph or headed section before you underline. Each idea may seem important as you first encounter it, but you must see how it fits with the others before you can judge its relative importance.

Use the boldface headings. Headings are labels that indicate the overall topic of a section. These headings serve as indicators of what is important to underline. For example, under a heading "Objectives of Economic Growth," you should be certain to underline each objective.

Underline main ideas and only key supporting details.

Avoid underlining complete sentences. Underline only enough so that your underlining makes sense when you reread it. Notice that in Figure 10-1, an excerpt from a criminology text, only key words and phrases are underlined.

Maintain a reasonable pace. If you have understood a paragraph or section, then your underlining should be fast and efficient.

Figure 10-1
Sample Underlining

LOSING DATA THROUGH NONREPORTING

Much information on crime is lost because individuals simply do not bring suspicious events to the attention of police. Estimates in recent years indicate that even with serious crimes such as robbery, rape, and burglary, a considerable proportion of offenses are not brought to police attention — perhaps as high as 75 percent.[19] Most often cited are the figures compiled from a survey of 10,000 households conducted in 1965 and 1966 on behalf of the President's Commission on Law Enforcement and the Administration of Justice. Many more people responding to this survey reported having been victimized than official statistics would indicate should be the case. Apparently, many victims of crime do not report their experiences to the police. *Victimization rates* (the number of incidents in which persons are victims of crime per 100,000 people) were around 3 1/2 times the crime rate officially published for rape, triple the rate published for burglary, and about double the official rates for robbery and aggravated assault.[20] Other recent studies of victimization support the general findings of this first study, namely, that official rates are significantly lower than rates of victimization for most crimes. One exception is auto theft. Here, official rates and victimization rates are similar. This is largely because victims must report the offense to collect insurance. . . .

Why, of all people, do the victims of crime not report their victimization to the police? Two of the more common explanations given by the victims themselves are that they felt "nothing could be done anyway," or they felt that the police would not want to be bothered with their problems. Another reason often given is that the incident was a private matter, and the victim would rather keep it that way.[21] Can you think of other reasons why victims might not report offenses to the police?

Develop a consistent system of underlining or highlighting. Decide, for example, how you will mark main ideas, how you will distinguish main ideas from details, and how you will underline new terminology. Some students use a system of single and double underlining, brackets, asterisks, and circles to distinguish various types of information; others use different colors of ink, or combinations of pens and pencils. The specific coding system you create is unimportant; what is important is that you devise some consistent approach to underlining. At first, you will need to experiment, testing out various systems. However, once you have settled on an effective system, use it regularly.

Adopt a 15–25 percent rule of thumb. Although the amount you underline will vary from course to course, depending on your purposes, try to underline no more than between 15 and 25 percent of any given page. If you exceed this figure, you may not be sorting ideas as efficiently as possible. Remember, the more you underline, the smaller your timesaving dividends will be as you review. Figure 10-1 provides an example of effective underlining.

Overcoming Common Pitfalls

Underlining, if done properly, is one of the biggest timesavers of all. However, if done incorrectly, underlining can waste valuable time and leave you inadequately prepared to review for an exam. Here are a few common mistakes to avoid:

Underlining without a defined purpose. Some students underline because they feel it will help them learn, rather than to identify specific information for subsequent review. Consequently, their review is unfocused and does not produce results. Be certain, then, to carefully assess the nature of the material and what you are expected to learn. For example, in a political science course, are you focusing on trends, facts, solutions to problems, or making comparisons and contrasts?

Underlining too much. This is the most common problem that students face. Operating under the tired, worn out "rather safe than sorry" or "too much is better than too little" rules, they tend to underline almost every idea on the page.

Underlining nearly everything is about as effective as underlining nothing, since no sorting occurs: Key ideas are not distinguished from other, less important ones. Underlining too much can become a way of escaping or postponing the issue at hand—determining what is necessary to learn and recall.

Underlining too little. Underlining less than 10 percent per page may be a signal that you are having difficulty comprehending the material. Test your comprehension by trying to express the content of a given section in your own words. If you understand what you read but are underlining very little, then you may need to refine or redefine your purpose for reading.

The Added Benefits of Underlining

Underlining is beneficial for several reasons. The process of underlining forces you to sift through what you have read to identify important

❏❏❏
Thinking Critically . . . About Underlining

Underlining, like any other learning strategy, deserves evaluation. To evaluate whether you are underlining effectively use the following suggestions:

1. Select a sample page, underline it, and reread only your underlining. Then ask yourself the following questions:
   a. Does my underlining convey the key idea of the passage?
   b. Can I follow the author's train of thought and progression of ideas by reading only my underlining?
   c. Is the underlining appropriate for my purposes?
2. Compare your underlining with that of another student; while you will see individual differences, both sets of underlining should reflect the same key ideas.

information. This sifting or sorting is an active thought process; you are forced to weigh and evaluate what you read. Underlining keeps you physically active while you are reading. The physical activity helps to focus your concentration on what you are reading. Underlining can help you discover the organization of facts and ideas as well as their connections and relationships. Underlining demonstrates to you whether you have understood a passage you have just read. If you have difficulty underlining, or your underlining is not helpful or meaningful after you have finished reading, you will know that you did not understand the passage.

A word of caution: Do not assume that what is underlined is learned. You must process the information by organizing it, expressing it in your own words, and testing yourself periodically.

EXERCISE 10-1

Directions:
Choose a two- or three-page section from one of your textbooks and underline it using the guidelines suggested in this chapter. Then evaluate the effectiveness of your underlining in preparation for an objective exam on the material.

Marginal Annotation

In many situations, underlining alone is not a sufficient means of identifying what to learn. It does not separate main ideas from examples or either of these from new terminology. Nor does it provide you any opportunity to comment on or react to the material. Therefore, you may need to make marginal annotations as well as to underline. Table 10-1 suggests various types of annotation used in marking a political science textbook chapter.

Figures 10-2 and 10-3 present two copies of the same paragraph. The first copy has been underlined, while the second, both underlining and annotation are used. Notice how the second version (Figure 10-3) more clearly conveys the meaning of the passage.

Figure 10-2
Underlining

> ***Influencing Public Opinion: Easy to Assume, Hard to Prove.*** Common sense suggests that long exposure to anything is likely to influence opinion. The average American spends twenty-eight hours and twenty-two minutes weekly glued to "the tube." (Contrary to popular opinion, teenagers are the least frequent TV viewers.) Thus Americans spend more time watching television than in any other single activity besides sleeping and working! On the average night, 100 million Americans–more than half the adult population–will be watching television.
>
> Because of its pervasiveness, it is easy to *overestimate* the effects of the technotronic media on opinion change. For one thing, the vast majority of what people watch on television and read about in the papers is essentially nonpolitical. "Sitcoms," the NFL, *Hill Street Blues*, and *Star Search* are not exactly high political drama. Even watching television news produces only about as much information as a single newspaper page.
>
> In the early days of research on media impact, it was assumed that there would be direct, visible impacts of the media on public opinion, but efforts to prove such direct effects usually failed. Most media effects are subtle; the most obvious is on "agenda setting." People pay attention to what the media pays attention to; what the media says is important, we assume is important. Because the media sets our priorities, we tend to adopt its world view of political issues.[31]

Figure 10-3
Underlining and Annotation

> *Influencing Public Opinion: Easy to Assume, Hard to Prove.* Common sense suggests that long exposure to anything is likely to influence opinion. The average American spends twenty-eight hours and twenty-two minutes weekly glued to "the tube." (Contrary to popular opinion, teenagers are the least frequent TV viewers.) Thus Americans spend more time watching television than in any other single activity besides sleeping and working! On the average night, 100 million Americans—more than half the adult population—will be watching television.
>
> Because of its pervasiveness, it is easy to *overestimate* the effects of the technotronic media on opinion change. For one thing, the vast majority of what people watch on television and read about in the papers is essentially nonpolitical. "Sitcoms," the NFL, *Hill Street Blues*, and *Star Search* are not exactly high political drama. Even watching television news produces only about as much information as a single newspaper page.
>
> In the early days of research on media impact, it was assumed that there would be direct, visible impacts of the media on public opinion, but efforts to prove such direct effects usually failed. Most media effects are subtle; the most obvious is on "agenda setting." People pay attention to what the media pays attention to; what the media says is important, we assume is important. Because the media sets our priorities, we tend to adopt its world view of political issues.[31]

Margin annotations:
- amount of TV watching
- TV watching nonpolitical little effect on public opinion
- major effect: agenda setting

Summary Words

Writing summary words or phrases in the margin is another valuable form of annotation. It involves pulling together ideas and summarizing them in your own words. This process forces you to think, monitor your comprehension, and evaluate as you read, and it makes remembering easier.

Figure 10-4 illustrates effective use of summary phrases to annotate a sample passage. First read the passage, and then study the marginal summary clues.

Summary clues are most effectively used in passages that contain long and complicated ideas. In these cases, it is simpler to write a summary phrase in the margin than to underline a long or complicated state-

Figure 10-4
Passage Annotated with Summary Phrases

The Deepening Shadow of Joblessness

joblessness rose during economic growth periods

The specter of massive unemployment, as we saw in Chapter 3, is no stranger to American life. Even if we ignore the Great Depression and consider only the years since World War II, unemployment has been a perennial problem that has receded only to return again in disturbingly recurrent cycles. Even during what we now regard with some nostalgia (and some truth) as an era of unparalleled economic growth and promise in the 1940s, 1950s, and 1960s, the jobless rate rose to the neighborhood of 6 percent (and even beyond) in 1949, 1958, and 1961. In the latter two years, joblessness was higher than it was in 1978 and 1979, years we regard as ones of economic decline.

1980's highest rate

Nevertheless, by the 1980s it was apparent that the job problem had been worsening over time. The jobless rate reached levels higher than any since the Great Depression; in early 1983 the number of unemployed in the United States was roughly equal to the entire Canadian labor force. Moreover, the peaks of unemployment had become progressively higher, while economic recovery hadn't brought the jobless rates down as significantly as in the past. Each successive recession of the 1970s and 1980s began with a higher level of unemployment than the one before; the level of joblessness just *before* the 1981-1982 recession began was much higher than any experienced in postwar America in any recession year before 1975.

eco. recovery hasn't reduced rates

problems of definition & measurement

The severity of the job problem is hidden, as we've seen, by the conventions of measurement and definition. An unemployment rate of around 10 percent means that roughly 11 million individuals are officially counted as out of work. But the true number of the jobless also includes the more than 1.5 million "discouraged" workers and the several million others who are "out of the labor force" but want to work. And even the lower figure of 11 million individuals out of work means that *25 to 30 million people in families* are touched by the unemployment of one or more members.

ment of the main idea and supporting details. To write a summary clue, try to think of a word or phrase that accurately states in brief form a particular idea presented in the passage. Much like recall clues in lecture notes (Chapter 8), summary words should trigger your memory of the content of the passage.

EXERCISE 10-2

Directions:
Review the textbook excerpt used in Figure 10-1 and add annotation.

EXERCISE 1-3

Directions:
Underline and annotate a five-page portion of one of your textbooks. Bring the text to class and exchange texts with a classmate. Reading only what you have underlined and annotated, the classmate should, if your work is effective, grasp the key ideas of each section.

NOTETAKING TO ORGANIZE AND CONDENSE INFORMATION

Although underlining is usually a fast and efficient method of identifying and locating key information to be learned; it does little to help you organize information and relate or pull together ideas. Underlining is of limited use in situations such as the following:

❏ Texts that deal with presentation and subsequent analysis of literary works or other documents
❏ Collections of readings (for example, "Readings in Psychology")
❏ Anthologies of literature
❏ Texts in technical fields such as electrical engineering
❏ Courses in which the text is used very selectively with only specific pages or sections assigned
❏ Very difficult, complicated material
❏ Reference materials that cannot be removed from the library

Notetaking, then, is a step that can either follow or replace underlining and annotating, depending on the type of material and your purpose for reading. Notetaking has a number of benefits. It provides a truer test of your understanding of the material than does underlining. While underlining requires you to *recognize* what is important, notetaking requires

Table 10-1
MARGINAL ANNOTATIONS

Types of Annotation	Example
Circling unknown words	. . . redressing the apparent (asymmetry) of their relationship
Marking definitions	*def* [To say that the balance of power favors one party over another is to introduce a disequilibrium.
Marking examples	*ex* [. . . concessions may include negative sanctions, trade agreements . . .
Numbering lists of ideas, causes, reasons, or events	components of power include ① self-image, ② population, ③ natural resources, and ④ geography
Placing asterisks next to important passages	* [Power comes from three primary sources . . .
Putting question marks next to confusing passages	? ⟶ war prevention occurs through institutionalization of mediation . . .
Making notes to yourself	*Check def in soc text* power is the ability of an actor on the international stage to . . .
Marking possible test items	⌐ There are several key features in the relationship . . .
Drawing arrows to show relationships	[. . . natural resources . . ., . . . control of industrial manufacture capacity
Writing comments, noting disagreements and similarities	*Can terrorism be prevented through similar balance?* war prevention through balance of power is . . .
Marking summary statements	*sum* [the greater the degree of conflict, the more intricate will be . . .

you to *express* it in words—a more difficult task that involves a higher level of thinking. Notetaking enables you to organize the material for easier learning.

Notetaking forces you to decide at once what is important. Since you cannot possibly record everything, you are forced to be selective. As you write, you have time to reflect on the ideas you are recording. This is a form of rehearsal, and it facilitates learning.

The outline form is often used for notetaking because it provides a visual representation of thought patterns and reflects the organization and development of ideas. When an outline is mentioned, many students react negatively, thinking of a rigid, formal, "Roman numeral I, II, capital letter A, B . . ." structure. Actually, this is only one form of outline notes; an outline is an adaptable, versatile structure that can take a variety of shapes and forms. Outline notes may be highly detailed or consist of a brief list of items; they may exhibit careful organization or be loosely structured. The type you write depends on how and why you are writing them.

The purpose of outline notes is to reflect the shape of a subject. Think of it as a sketch or drawing that shows general features but lacks the exact detail of a photograph.

Developing Outline Notes

Classification is the primary thought pattern involved in preparing an outline. Developing an outline involves two steps: (1) identifying how ideas relate and (2) grouping ideas together according to their connections. An effective outline, then, accomplishes two things:

- ❏ It shows the relative importance of ideas.
- ❏ It shows the relationships among these ideas.

An outline uses a listing order and a system of indentation as shown in Figure 10-5. A quick glance at the outline indicates what is most important, what is less important, and how ideas support or explain one another. Here are a few suggestions for developing an effective outline.

Concentrate on the relative importance of ideas. Do not worry about the numbering and lettering system. How you number or letter an idea, or whether you label it at all, is not as important as showing what other ideas it supports or explains.

Be brief. Use words and phrases, never complete sentences.

Use your own words. Don't lift most of the material from the text or lecture notes.

Make sure subentries are relevant. All the information you place in sublists beneath a heading should support or explain the heading.

Figure 10-5
Outline Notes

Time Management
   — Analyze your time commitments —
   hours per week
      — ex. class, part-time job,
      transportation
   — Analyze Your Efficiency
      — notice wasted time, duplication
      of effort.
      — notice time traps
      ex-making small decisions
   — Principles of Time Management
      1) Use peak periods of concentration
      2) do difficult tasks first

Align headings to reflect their relative importance. Headings with the same indentation on the page should be of equal importance.

How Much Information to Record

Before you begin writing an outline, determine how much information you need to include. An outline can be very brief and cover only major topics, or, at the other extreme, it can be very detailed, providing an extensive review of precise, factual information.

How much detail you include in an outline should vary with and be determined by your purpose for making it. For example, you need include very little detail in the outline for a supplemental reading that your instructor has assigned to show you the author's viewpoint and general approach to a problem. On the other hand, your outline of a section of an anatomy and physiology text for an upcoming objective exam must be much more detailed. To find the right amount of detail to include, ask yourself questions such as "What do I need to know?" or "What type of test situation am I preparing for?"

When to Use Outline Notes

Outline notes are particularly appropriate and effective in a number of situations.

Difficult material. Outlining difficult or confusing material forces you to sort ideas, see connections, and express them in your own words, and it thus aids comprehension.

Interpreting and reacting. When you are asked to write and evaluation of, reaction to, or critical interpretation of an article or essay, it is helpful to write a brief outline of the factual content. Your notes will reflect development and progression of thought and help you analyze the writer's ideas.

Order and process. In courses where order or process is important, outline notes are particularly useful. In data processing, for example, where sets of programming commands must be performed in a specified sequence, outline notes would organize the information.

Classification. In the natural sciences, where classifications are important, outlining is a helpful way to record and sort information. In botany, for example, you can use outline notes to list plant subgroups within each botanical category and keep track of similar characteristics.

EXERCISE 10-4

Directions:
Write a brief set of outline notes reflecting the organization and content of one or two pages of one of your textbooks.

MAPPING TO SHOW RELATIONSHIPS

Mapping is a process of drawing a diagram to picture how a topic and its related ideas are connected. It is a method of organizing and consolidating information, often to emphasize a particular thought pattern. The degree to which you will find mapping useful will depend on the courses you are taking, since some types of information are more easily learned by using visual or organizational maps than others. The effectiveness of mapping will also depend on your individual learning style.

This section describes a general mapping procedure, called idea maps, and discusses five types of specialized maps: time lines, process diagrams, part and function diagrams, organization charts, and comparison and contrast charts. Each utilizes one of the thought patterns discussed in Chapter 7.

Idea Maps

An idea map of Chapter 9, on textbooks, is shown in Figure 10-6. Take a moment now to refer to Chapter 9 before studying the map.

Basically an idea map is a form of outline that presents ideas spatially rather than in list form. Use the following steps in constructing an idea map:

Figure 10-6
Sample Idea Map

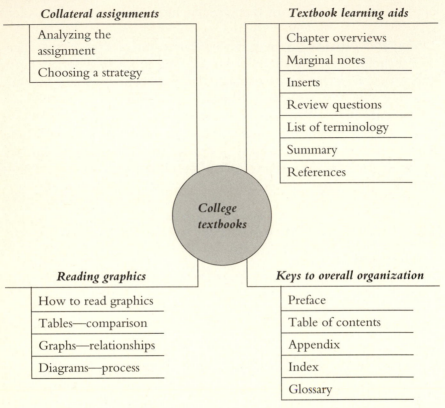

❏ Identify the topic and write it in the center of the page.
❏ Identify ideas, aspects, parts, and definitions that relate to the topic. Draw each on a line radiating from the central topic.
❏ As you discover details that further explain an idea already recorded, draw a new line branching from the idea it explains.

EXERCISE 10-5

Directions:
Choose a section of a chapter in this text that you have already read. Draw an idea map reflecting its overall content and organization.

Idea maps can be drawn to organize any set of information. For example, you could draw a map to reflect chapter content. However, you

Figure 10-7
A Sample Idea Map

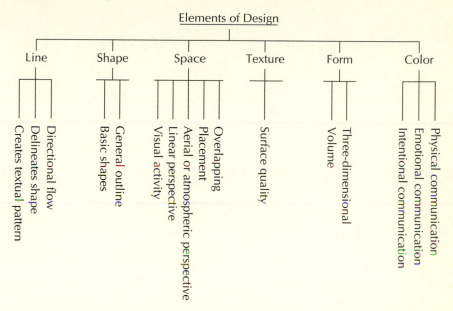

can also draw maps to organize a section of a chapter, integrate several sets of lecture notes, or relate text and lecture notes on the same topic.

Idea maps can be simple or complex, brief or detailed, depending on the material you are mapping and on your purpose for mapping. Figure 10-7 shows a map an art student drew to integrate information on elements of design. Figure 10-8 shows a more detailed map of the cardiovascular system drawn for an anatomy and physiology course.

Specialized Maps

Each of the following maps relates to a specific thought pattern.

Time Lines

When studying a topic in which the sequence or order of events is a central focus, a time line is a useful way to organize the information. To map a sequence of events, draw a single horizontal line and mark it off in year intervals, just as a ruler is marked off in inches. Then write events next to the correct year. For example, the time line in Figure 10-9 was developed for an American history course in which the Vietnam War was being studied. The time line shows clearly the sequence of events and helps you visualize their order.

Figure 10-8
A Sample Idea Map

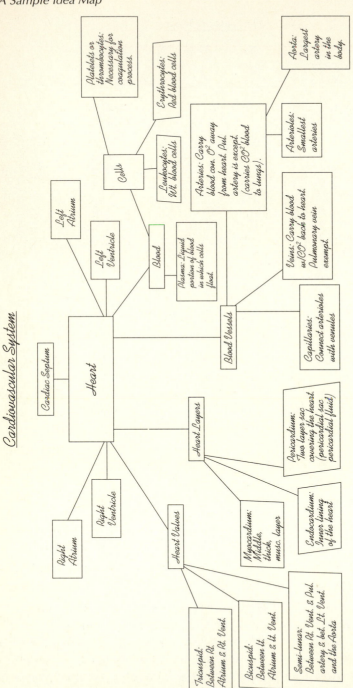

Figure 10-9
A Time Line

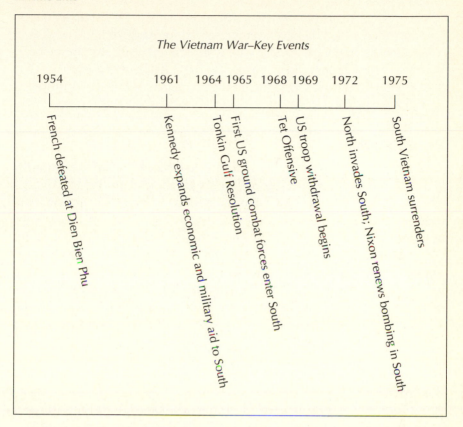

The Vietnam War–Key Events

1954   1961   1964 1965   1968 1969   1972   1975

French defeated at Dien Bien Phu

Kennedy expands economic and military aid to South

Tonkin Gulf Resolution

First US ground combat forces enter South

Tet Offensive

US troop withdrawal begins

North invades South; Nixon renews bombing in South

South Vietnam surrenders

EXERCISE 10-6

Directions:

The following passage reviews the ancient history of maps. Read the selection and then draw a time line that will help you to visualize these historical events. (Remember that B.C. refers to time before Christ and numbers increase as time moves back from history.)

In Babylonia, in approximately 2300 B.C., the oldest known map was drawn on a clay tablet. The map showed a man's property located in a valley surrounded by tall mountains. Later, around 1300 B.C., the Egyptians drew maps that detailed the location of Ethiopian gold mines and that showed a route from the Nile Valley. The ancient Greeks were early mapmakers as well, although none remains for us to examine. It is estimated that in 300 B.C. they drew maps showing the earth to be round. The Romans drew maps to tax land and to plan military tactics. The Romans drew the first road maps, a few of which have been preserved for study today. Claudius Ptolemy, an Egyptian scholar who lived around 150 A.D., drew one of the most famous ancient maps. He drew maps of the world as it was known at that time, including 26 regional maps of Europe, Africa, and Asia.

Process Diagrams

In the natural sciences as well as other courses such as economics and data processing, processes are an important part of the course content. A chart that depicts the steps, variables, or parts of a process will make learning easier. For example, the diagram in Figure 10-10 might be used by a biology student. It describes the food chain and shows how energy is transferred through food consumption from lowest to highest organisms. Notice that this student included an example as well as the steps in the process in order to make the diagram clearer. Figure 10-11 shows a more complicated process diagram. It describes the process for a person charged with a misdemeanor. Alternatives at each step are shown.

EXERCISE 10-7

Directions:
The following paragraph describes the process through which malaria is spread by mosquitoes. Read the paragraph and then draw a process diagram that shows how this process occurs.

Figure 10-10
A Process Diagram

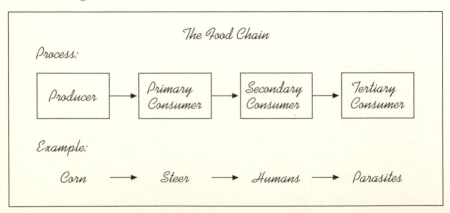

Figure 10-11
A Process Diagram

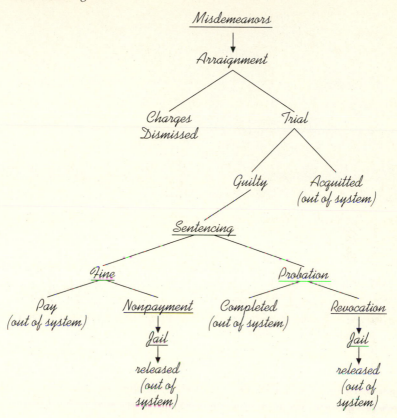

Malaria, a serious tropical disease, is caused by parasites, or one-celled animals, called protozoa. These parasites live in the red blood cells of humans as well as in the female anopheles mosquitoes. These mosquitoes serve as hosts to the parasites and carry and spread malaria. When an anopheles mosquito stings a person who already has malaria, it ingests the red blood cells that contain the malaria parasites. In the host mosquito's body, these parasites multiply rapidly and move to its salivary glands and mouth. When the host mosquito bites another person, the malaria parasites are injected into the victim and enter his or her blood stream. The parasites again multiply and burst the victim's blood cells, causing ane mia.

Part and Function Diagrams: Classification

In courses that deal with the use and description or classification of physical objects, labeled drawings are an important learning tool. In a hu-

Figure 10-12
A Sample Part and Function Diagram

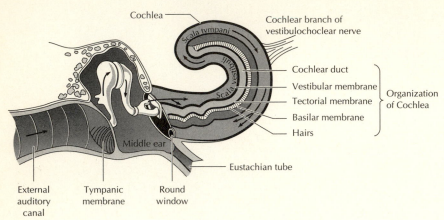

man anatomy and physiology course, for example, the easiest way to learn the parts and functions of the inner, middle, and outer ear is to draw the ear. To study, sketch the inner ear, and test your recall of each ear part and its function. A sample drawing is shown in Figure 10-12.

EXERCISE 10-8

Directions:

The following paragraph describes the earth's structure. Read the paragraph and then draw a diagram that will help you to visualize how the interior of the earth is structured.

At the center is a hot, highly compressed *inner core,* presumably solid and composed mainly of iron and nickel. Surrounding the inner core is an *outer core,* a molten shell primarily of liquid iron and nickel with lighter liquid material on the top. The outer envelope beyond the core is the *mantle,* of which the upper portion is mostly solid rock in the form of olivine, an iron-magnesium silicate, and the lower portion chiefly iron and magnesium oxides. A thin coat of metal silicates and oxides (granite) called the *crust,* forms the outermost skin.[1]

Organizational Charts

When reviewing material that is concerned with relationships and structures, organizational charts are useful study aids. In a business management course, suppose you are studying the organization of a small

Figure 10-13
An Organizational Chart

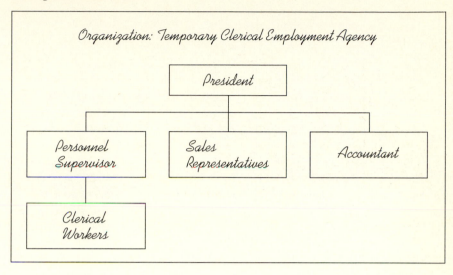

temporary clerical help firm. If you drew and studied the organizational chart shown in Figure 10-13, the structure would become apparent and easy to remember.

EXERCISE 10-9

Directions:
The following paragraph describes one business organizational structure that is studied in business management courses. Read the paragraph and then draw a diagram that will help you visualize this type of organization.

It is common for some large businesses to be organized by *place*, with a department for each major geographic area in which the firm is active. Businesses that market products for which customer preference differs from one part of the country to another often use this management structure. Departmentalization allows each region to focus on its own special needs and problems. Often the president of such a company appoints several regional vice-presidents, one for each part of the country. Then each regional office is divided into sales districts, each supervised by a district director.

Comparison and Contrast Charts
A final type of visual aid that is useful for organizing factual information is the comparison and contrast chart. This method of visual organization divides and groups information according to similarities or common

Figure 10-14
A Comparison and Contrast Chart

Market Survey Techniques			
Type	Cost	Response	Accuracy
Mail	usually the cheapest	higher than phone or personal interview	problems with misunderstanding directions
Phone	depends on availability of 800 number	same as personal interview	problems with unlisted phones and homes w/out phones
Personal interview	most expensive	same as phone	problems with honesty when asking personal or embarrassing questions

characteristics. Suppose in a business course on marketing and advertising you are studying three types of market survey techniques: mail, phone, and personal interview surveys. You are concerned with factors such as cost, level of response, time, and accuracy. To learn this information in an efficient manner, you could draw a chart such as the one shown in Figure 10-14.

EXERCISE 10-10

Directions:
The following passage describes the major physical differences between humans and apes. Read the selection and then arrange the information into a map that would make the information easy to learn.

Numerous physical characteristics distinguish man from apes. While apes' bodies are covered with hair, man's body has relatively little hair. While apes often use both their hands and feet to walk, man walks erect. Apes' arms are longer than their legs, while just the reverse is true for man. Apes have large teeth, necessary for devouring coarse, uncooked food, and long canine teeth for self-defense and fighting. By comparison, man's teeth are small and short. The ape's brain is not as well developed as that of man. Man is capable of speech, thinking, and higher-level reasoning skills. These skills enable man to establish culture, thereby placing the quality and level of man's life far above that of apes.

Man is also set apart from apes by features of the head and face. Man's facial profile is vertical, while the ape's profile is *prognathous,* with jaw jutting outward. Man has a chin; apes have a strong lower jaw, but no chin. Man's nostrils are smaller and less flaring than those of the ape. Apes also have thinner, more flexible lips than man.

Man's upright walk also distinguishes him from apes. Man's spine has a double curve to support his weight, while an ape's spine has a single curve. Man's foot is arched both vertically and horizontally, but, unlike the ape's, is unable to grasp objects. The torso of man is shorter than that of apes. It is important to note that many of these physical traits, while quite distinct, differ in degree rather than in kind.

LEARNING WITH COMPUTERS

Computers are part of our everyday lives—you probably do not go through an ordinary day without either being in direct contact with one or being influenced by one. As only a few examples, telephone numbers are dialed by computer; many cars have computers on board; your banking or checking account is computer controlled; and check-out scanners of larger stores are operated using a computer. Computers have become increasingly important in education as well. On many campuses, computers are readily available for student use.

Some students are reluctant to use computers, despite their importance in our society. Here are a few facts that may help you feel more comfortable using them:

- ❏ You do not have to be mechanical or good with machines to use computers.
- ❏ You do not have to program them. The software is preprogrammed and ready to use.
- ❏ Software is designed to be used by people who know very little about computers; clear, step-by-step directions are provided.
- ❏ To operate most personal computers, you just turn them on, insert the disk(s), and follow the directions printed on the screen. Some training is helpful in using some of the software, especially word processing (see below).

Colleges vary widely in the computer services available to students. Some colleges encourage students to purchase their own computers. Others have computer labs located in classroom buildings and dormitories. Others may have more limited computer facilities, with use restricted to students taking certain courses. Find out what services are available on your campus. Visit your college's computer facilities or computer lab. Ask what is available and when someone is available to assist you. Some colleges offer workshops; others offer assistance by student aides who are familiar with computers.

Computers can save you time and help you learn more efficiently. Because they store information that you type in, you can make changes in the information without retyping the entire work. This function is known as word processing. One of the most practical academic uses of computers, then, is in writing papers. See Chapters 16 and 17 for a more detailed description.

A computer's word processing capability also makes it a useful study and learning aid. The following sections offer suggestions for using the computer to organize your study. To make the most of these suggestions, you will need access to a computer on a daily basis.

Organizing Notes from Textbook Reading

As you take notes from reading, your notes tend to follow the organization of the text. That is, the order of ideas in your notes parallels the order of ideas presented in the text. At times, it is useful to reorganize and rearrange your notes. (See Thematic Study in Chapter 14). For example, you may want to pull together information on a certain topic that is spread throughout one or more chapters.

The computer's word processing and cut-and-paste functions enable you to rearrange and reorganize notes or outlines easily without retyping. You must type your notes initially, but you can edit and review them as you type.

Organizing Lecture Notes

Lecture notes are, of course, recorded by hand as you listen to the lecture. Typing your notes into the computer is a means of editing and review. Then, once your notes are entered, you can rearrange and reorganize as suggested above.

Integrating Text and Lecture Notes

A continual problem students wrestle with is how to integrate lecture and textbook notes. Some try leaving blank space in their lecture notes to add textbook notes; others try a 2-column approach, taking lecture notes on half the page and leaving the remaining column blank for textual notes. Neither system works extremely well, though, since one never knows how much space to leave, and some space is always wasted, since lecture and text do not always parallel one another.

The computer offers an ideal solution to the integration of textual and lecture notes. The cut-and-paste option allows you to move pieces (sections) of your notes to any desired place in the document. Thus, you can easily integrate text and lecture notes on each major topic. In Chapter 14, you will discover how to use these sets of notes to prepare for exams.

SUMMARY

Digesting the great volume of information in college courses is a two-step process

1. To identify what is important to learn, use

   ❑ textbook underlining
   ❑ marginal annotation

2. To organize, condense, and synthesize information, making it more meaningful and easier to learn, use

   ❑ outline notetaking to reflect organization and development of thought
   ❑ mapping, a visual representation or picture, to organize information and emphasize relationships among ideas

3. Five types of idea maps are

   ❑ time lines
   ❑ process diagrams
   ❑ part and function diagrams
   ❑ organizational charts
   ❑ comparison and contrast charts

4. Computers are useful tools for organizing information and integrating text and lecture notes.

CLASS ACTIVITY

Directions:
Working in groups of three, students should complete the following steps.

1. Each group should choose one academic discipline and read the corresponding section in Chapter 13 of this text. Assume this material will be included on an exam.
2. One group member should underline and annotate the section; another should make outline notes; the third member should draw a map of its content.
3. Group members should review and critique one another's work and discuss the following questions:
   a. Which of the three methods used seemed most effective for this material?
   b. Might your answer to the above question depend on the type of exam you would have (objective or essay)?
   c. What advantages did each method seem to offer? What were its limitations?
   d. Make a generalization about situations in which each can be used most effectively.

FURTHER ANALYSIS

Directions:
Analyze the following situation and answer the questions that follow.

A student who is taking a course in human anatomy and physiology failed the first multiple choice exam. She describes her main problem by saying, "I can't concentrate. Besides, the text is difficult and uninteresting." She also says that everything seems important, and if she used underlining, she would have most of each page underlined. The text already contains a detailed outline at the end of each chapter, so she feels she would be wasting her time by making outline notes.

1. Do you agree that underlining is not an effective strategy?
2. Should the student make outline notes? If so, what use, if any, should she make of the end-of-chapter outline?
3. What additional learning strategies do you recommend?
4. What strategies will help this student concentrate?

DISCUSSION

1. For which of your current courses do you think mapping would be most effective? In what types of courses would the technique be ineffective?
2. Outlining is a process of organizing information. In what non-academic situations might outlining be a useful technique?
3. How is the method you choose to organize information related to your learning style? (See pp. 104–113).
4. In what career or job-related circumstances might the skills presented in this chapter be important?

FURTHER READING

Buzan, Tony. *Use Both Sides of Your Brain.* New York: Dutton, 1991.

Caverly, David C., and Vincent P. Orlando. "Textbook Study Strategies." *Teaching Reading and Study Strategies.* Eds. Rona F. Flippo and David C. Caverly, Newark, DE: International Reading Association, 1991, 86–165.

Heimlich, Joan A. and Susan D. Pittleman. *Semantic Mapping: Classroom Applications.* Newark, DE: International Reading Association, 1986.

11

□ □ □ ▬▬▬▬▬▬▬▬▬▬▬

Critical Analysis of Course Content

Learning Objectives

Learn to synthesize information

Recognize and evaluate subjective content

Develop critical questioning strategies

Apply course content

Textbooks and class lectures typically contain large numbers of facts, definitions, statistics, examples, dates, places, and events. It is easy to become overwhelmed by the sea of factual information. You fall into a rote learning mode, trying to absorb as much information as possible and, as a result, neglect other more important aspects of study. In fact, many multiple choice and essay exam questions are designed *not* to measure your factual recall, but to test your ability to think about and use what you have learned—to analyze, synthesize, evaluate and apply course content.

In many introductory courses, you rely on your textbook as the primary source of written information. However, when you take more advanced courses, you will find yourself working with many new kinds of material: research articles, essays, critiques, reports, and analyses. To these, you will be expected to respond critically by discussing, criticizing, interpreting, and evaluating the authors' ideas. You may need to assess the accuracy and completeness of information, identify persuasive techniques, or evaluate an argument. The overall purposes of this chapter are to encourage you to pull together course content, to evaluate what you are reading and learning, to grasp implications, and to make applications.

SYNTHESIZING INFORMATION

Many writing assignments require you to synthesize, or pull together, information from a variety of sources. Synthesis is often required for in-class assignments, essay examinations, and term papers. Synthesizing is creating something new from a number of sources. Synthesizing information is a process of examining and inferring relationships among sources and then making those relationships explicit, usually in writing. Synthesis is also a process of combining information and ideas to create or develop a new idea, focus, or perspective.

Synthesis is required in a variety of academic situations:

- ❑ Integrating text and lecture notes on the same topic
- ❑ Summarizing information from several sources
- ❑ Reading several magazine articles on the same controversial issue and discussing pros and cons
- ❑ Answering an essay exam questions based on notes, lectures, and class discussion of the same topic

Here are a few more specific examples of assignments that require synthesis. Notice that each implies a thought pattern.

Mass Communications
> Discuss how the use of television may have affected public opinion toward the Vietnam War. Refer to at least three sources.

Literature
> Select two twentieth–century American writers whose work you feel was influenced by the liberal attitudes of the 1960s. Discuss how this influence is evident in their writings.

Each of these assignments requires you to combine information or ideas to produce a unified, coherent response. Each assignment, too, focuses on a type of relationship or thought pattern. The mass communications assignment asks you to infer a cause and effect relationship between television and public opinion. The literature assignment requires comparison and contrast between two writers.

The thought patterns you learned in Chapter 6 will be useful in synthesizing information. If, for example, you are synthesizing two or more articles that explain cultural differences in the status of women in the Middle East as compared to the United States, you can expect each article to use a comparison-contrast and possibly a cause-effect pattern. The articles will contrast women's status in the two regions and possibly explain why the differences exist. One effective way to integrate the information, then, is to use patterns. You might make a comparison-contrast chart of differences and then rearrange it by grouping the differences according to categories such as public/social behavior, role in the family, dress, legal rights, and so forth. If the articles detail reasons for the differences, you might add a third column titled "Why?" or "Reasons."

The thought patterns most helpful in synthesizing are cause-effect, comparison-contrast, problem-solution, and classification. Figure 11-1 lists suggestions for using each of these four patterns to synthesize information.

EXERCISE 11-1

Directions:
Analyze the following assignment by identifying the thought pattern(s) and notetaking strategies to use in synthesizing the information:

Using the periodical collection in the campus library, read three reports of a current national news event in *Time, U.S. News and World Report,* and one other periodical of your choice. Examine each, identifying factors such as completeness of coverage, political or social viewpoint, amount of detail. Write a one-page paper evaluating the completeness and accuracy of each source.

RECOGNIZING AND EVALUATING SUBJECTIVE CONTENT

Textbooks are generally reliable, trustworthy, and accurate sources of information. You cannot assume the same for all other print materials. Many articles and essays are not written to present information clearly and directly; instead, they may be written to persuade you to accept a particular viewpoint, offer an opinion, or argue for one side of a controversial issue. Consequently, you must often recognize and separate factual information from subjective content. Subjective content is any material that involves judgment, feeling, opinion, intuition, or emotion rather than factual information. For example, "It is raining outside" is a fact. "It will rain before sundown" is a subjective statement. The second statement involves judgment, based on some evidence, while the first is verifiable.

Figure 11-1
Synthesizing Information Using Patterns

Pattern	*Suggestions*
Cause-effect	1. Is the same cause-effect relationship described in all sources? 2. Can you construct a chain of events or happenings, each dependent on one another? 3. How do sources differ in attributing cause or describing effects?
Comparison-contrast	1. Identify ideas that are similar. Discover points of similarity. 2. Look for differences. Determine how and why the ideas or information differs. 3. Draw charts outlining similarities and differences.
Problem-solution	1. Is the problem defined the same way in each source? 2. What are the similarities and differences among solutions?
Classification	1. Use to organize information into broad types or categories. 2. Look for similarities and differences among ideas. How are members of a group similar? How are they distinguishable from one another? 3. Look for overlap among categories. 4. List features of each category.

Suppose a business management professor assigns a portion of *Ia-cocca: An Autobiography* in which Lee Iacocca, president of the Chrysler Corporation, describes how he attained his leadership position. In such a book you might expect to find a blend of personal experience, opinion, and reminiscence, as well as theories about and insights into corporate management strategy. Or suppose you are doing research for a term paper on the political career of former President Ronald Reagan. As you consult various sources, you will observe that some are factual, concise, and well documented, while others make general statements for which little or no support or documentation is provided. You will also encounter conflicting viewpoints on the Reagan era. Authors may also propose theories or hypotheses that explain Reagan's actions or decisions.

Recognizing and evaluating subjective content involves distinguishing between fact and opinion, identifying generalizations, evaluating viewpoints, understanding theories and hypotheses, weighing data and evidence, and being alert to bias.

Distinguishing Between Fact and Opinion

Facts are statements that can be verified—that is, proven to be true or false. *Opinions* are statements that express feelings, attitudes, or beliefs and are neither true or false. Here are a few examples of each:

❏ ❏ ❏

Facts:	1. Martin Luther King, Jr., was assassinated in 1968.
	2. Native Americans in the Great Plains were primarily meat eaters; herds of buffalo provided their main source of food.
Opinions:	1. If John F. Kennedy had lived, the United States would have made even greater advancements against the spread of communism.
	2. By the year 2000, food shortages will be a major problem in most Asian countries.

❏ ❏ ❏

EXERCISE 11-2

Directions:
Identify each of the following statements as either fact or opinion.

1. Between 1945 and 1990, 203,432 persons were arrested for homicide in Mexico.
2. Job orientation should begin before an employee starts to work.
3. All the states have developed laws that require hospitals and health care workers to report each incidence of communicable or infectious disease.
4. A major step in developing assertive behavior is evaluating your own strengths and weaknesses.
5. The immune deficiency in AIDS (Acquired Immune Deficiency Syndrome) results from a decreased number of certain white blood cells called T-helper lymphocytes.

6. People caught in the throes of romantic love are drawn to thoughts of marriage as moths are drawn to light.
7. The state should curtail the liberty of the individual.
8. An infection is an illness produced by the action of microorganisms in the human body.
9. Virtue is its own reward.
10. A prominent theory among biologists is that humans are by nature instinctively aggressive.

A special case within the realm of fact and opinion is that of *informed opinion* or testimony, the opinion of an expert or authority. Ralph Nader represents expert opinion on consumer rights, for example. Textbook authors, too, often offer informed opinion, as in the following statement from an American government text.

> Ample evidence indicates voters pay attention to economic conditions in making up their minds on election day: not only to their personal circumstances—whether they are employed or how secure their job is—but also to national economic circumstances.[1]

The author of this statement has reviewed the available evidence and is providing his expert opinion as to what the evidence indicates.

The ability to distinguish between fact and opinion is an essential part of critical thinking. Factual statements from reliable sources can be accepted and used in drawing conclusions, building arguments, and supporting ideas. As you write papers, participate in class discussions, and answer exam questions, you will use facts to support your ideas. Opinions, however, must be considered as one person's point of view that you are free to accept or reject. With the exception of informed ones, opinions have little use as supporting evidence. Still, they are useful in shaping and evaluating your own thinking. Exposure to both contradictory and supporting opinions provides background against which you can evaluate your own thinking.

A goal in many courses is to enable students to reexamine their existing beliefs, attitudes, and opinions. Expect your professors to ask challenging questions such as Why do you think so? What evidence do you have to support that opinion?

EXERCISE 11-3

Directions:

For each of the materials listed below, discuss and predict whether it will contain primarily fact or opinion.

1. A book titled *Move Your Shadow: South Africa, Black and White,* written by Pulitzer prize–winning reporter Joseph Lelyveld, who lived in South Africa in the 1960s and again in the 1980s
2. An article by Isaac Asimov, "Advertising in the Year 2000"
3. A book titled *The Nazi Doctors: Medical Killing and the Psychology of Genocide* by Robert Lifton
4. An article in the *New England Journal of Medicine* titled "Control of Health Care Costs in the 1990s"
5. A book titled *Secrets of Strong Families,* by Nick Stinnett, which describes how to keep a family happy and together.

Evaluating Differing Viewpoints

College widens your horizons. It provides you with an opportunity to encounter new ideas and viewpoints. Some of these ideas may force you to reexamine your own values and beliefs and to reevaluate how you think about a particular issue. Within the structure of a course, an instructor may examine a controversial or current topic or issue by asking you to examine or compare differing viewpoints. A sociology professor may, for example, assign several supplementary readings, each of which takes a different stance on capital punishment. Or, in an English literature class, you may consider various interpretations of Vonnegut's *Slaughterhouse Five.*

In examining differing viewpoints, try the following suggestions:

❏ Deliberately put aside or suspend temporarily what you already believe about a particular issue.
❏ Discover what similarities and differences exist among the various viewpoints.
❏ Identify the assumptions on which each view is based.
❏ Look for and evaluate evidence that suggests the viewpoint is well thought out.
❏ To overcome the natural tendency to pay more attention to points of view with which you agree and treat opposing viewpoints superficially, deliberately spend more time reading, thinking about, and examining ideas that differ from your own.
❏ To analyze particularly complex, difficult, or very similar viewpoints, write a summary of each. Through the process of writing, you will be forced to discover the essence of each view.

Evaluating differing viewpoints is an essential critical thinking skill because it enables you to pull together divergent ideas and integrate differing, even contradictory, sources. The skill is valuable as you research topics, examine social and political issues, and resolve controversy.

EXERCISE 11-4

Directions:

Determine how the three viewpoints on gun control expressed in statements 1 to 3 differ.

1. Guns don't kill people, people kill people. Gun laws do not deter criminals. (A 1976 University of Wisconsin study of gun laws concluded that "gun control laws have no individual or collective effect in reducing the rate of violent crime.") A mandatory sentence for carrying an unlicensed gun, says Kates, would punish the "ordinary decent citizens in high-crime areas who carry guns illegally because police protection is inadequate and they don't have the special influence necessary to get a 'carry' permit." There are fifty million handguns out there in the United States already; unless you were to use a giant magnet, there is no way to retrieve them. The majority of people do not want guns banned. A ban on handguns would be like Prohibition—widely disregarded, unenforceable, and corrosive to the nation's sense of moral order. Federal registration is the beginning of federal tyranny; we might someday need to use those guns against the government.[2]

2. People kill people, but handguns make it easier. When other weapons (knives, for instance) are used, the consequences are not so often deadly. Strangling or stabbing someone takes a different degree of energy and intent than pulling a trigger. Registration will not interfere with hunting and other rifle sports but will simply exercise control over who can carry handguns. Ordinary people do not carry handguns. If a burglar has a gun in his hand, it is quite insane for you to shoot it out with him, as if you were in a quick draw contest in the Wild West. Half of all the guns used in crimes are stolen; 70% of the stolen guns are handguns. In other words, the supply of handguns used by criminals already comes to a great extent from the households these guns were supposed to protect.[3]

3. [Statement by Edward Kennedy] We all know the toll that has been taken in this nation. We all know the leaders of our public life and of the human spirit who have been lost or wounded year after year. My brother, John Kennedy, and my brother, Robert Kennedy; Medgar Evers, who died so that others could live free; Martin Luther King, the apostle of nonviolence who became the victim of violence; George Wallace, who has been paralyzed for nearly nine years; and George Moscone, the mayor

of San Francisco who was killed in his office. Last year alone, we lost Allard Lowenstein, and we almost lost Vernon Jordan. Four months ago, we lost John Lennon, the gentle soul who challenged us in song to "give peace a chance." We had two attacks on President Ford and now the attack on President Reagan.[4]

Evaluating Generalizations

Each of the following statements is a generalization:

- ❏ College freshmen are confused and disoriented during their first week on campus.
- ❏ Typewriter keyboards and computer terminal keyboards are similar.
- ❏ The courts, especially those in large cities, are faced with far more criminal cases than they can handle.

A generalization is a statement made about a large group or class of items based on observation or experience with a portion of that group or class. By visiting campuses and observing and talking with freshman students, you could make the generalization that freshmen are confused and disoriented. However, unless you observed and talked with *every* college student, you could not be absolutely certain your generalization is correct. Similarly, unless you contacted each large city court, you could not be certain of the accuracy of the third statement. A generalization, then, is a reasoned statement about an entire group based on known information about part of the group. It involves a leap from observed evidence to a conclusion that is logical but unproven.

In many courses you will be expected to read and evaluate generalizations, as well as to make them yourself. Often generalizations are followed by evidence that supports them, as in the following excerpt from a sociology text:

An act considered deviant in one time period may be considered nondeviant in another. Cigarette smoking, for example, has a long history of changing normative definitions. Nuehring and Markle (1974) note that in the United States between 1895 and 1921, fourteen states completely banned cigarette smoking and all other states except Texas passed laws regulating the sale of cigarettes to minors. In the early years of this century, stop-smoking clinics were opened in several cities and antismoking campaigns were widespread. Following World War I, however, cigarette sales increased and public attitudes toward smoking changed. Through the mass media, the tobacco industry appealed to women, weight-watchers, and even to health seekers. States began to realize that tobacco could be a rich source of revenue, and by 1927 the fourteen states that banned cigarettes had repealed their laws. By the end of World War II, smoking had become acceptable, and in many contexts it was thought socially desirable.[5]

The excerpt begins with two generalizations. The second generalization (sentence 2), which is supported throughout the remainder of the paragraph, is made in support of the first generalization, stated in the opening sentence.

Because writers do not always have the space to describe all available evidence on a topic, they often draw the evidence together themselves and make a general statement of what it shows. Generalizations that stand alone without any evidence to attest to their accuracy appear to be unsupported. The following paragraph makes numerous generalizations about the elderly.

The lifestyles of the elderly vary greatly, depending on their social class and income. Women and blacks are the groups most likely to live in poverty. The most common source of income for the aged is Social Security. A minimal income is available to those not on Social Security through the Supplemental Security Income program. Income and class level greatly influence the health of the elderly.[6]

Without supporting evidence, you cannot evaluate the accuracy of the generalizations unless you research the topic yourself. You are left to rely on the credibility of the author to make accurate generalizations. In textbooks, where the author is an authority in his or her field, credibility is seldom a problem. However, when reading other information sources, do not assume automatically that all generalizations are supportable.

In many courses, you will be required to make generalizations by applying your knowledge to related, similar situations. Generalizing is an important skill—one that makes your learning usable and relevant in a variety of situations. Here are a few instances that require you to generalize:

❏ Solving math problems similar to sample problems solved in class
❏ Summarizing your experience with part-time jobs to make a generalization about the benefits of work experience
❏ Applying methods you learned in child psychology to control your niece's temper tantrums

Your generalization is usable and relevant when your experiences are sufficient in number to merit a generalization.

EXERCISE 11-5

Directions:

Indicate which of statements 1 through 10 are generalizations. Then indicate what support or documentation would be necessary for you to evaluate their worth and accuracy.

1. McDonald's is the largest owner of real estate in the world.
2. John Lennon's last book, *Skywriting by Word of Mouth,* will be hailed as a work of literature by those who appreciate brilliant, innovative writing.
3. Big money can be made in every corner of the world, including the world of legitimate drug consumption.
4. Floor space in department stores is valued at $500 per square foot.
5. Creative products including paintings, engineering design plans, or Monty Python skits are revised and revised again until they take final shape.
6. Intimacy is established through effective verbal communication.
7. Criminal law is divided into felonies and misdemeanors.
8. The kidney produces an enzymelike substance known as renin that raises blood pressure.
9. Quackery refers to the use of unproved or disapproved methods or devices to diagnose or treat illnesses.
10. Heroin costs the addict more than $100 a day.

Testing Hypotheses

Suppose you arrive three minutes late to your data processing class and find the classroom empty. You notice that the instructor's notes are on her desk and that most of all of the students have left their jackets or notebooks behind. So you form a hypothesis, a supposition to account for the observed circumstances and explain the absence of the class and instructor. You might hypothesize that the class went across the hall to the lab, for instance. A hypothesis, then, is a statement based on available evidence that explains an event or set of circumstances.

Here are a few examples of situations involving formulation of hypotheses:

❏ A nursing student is asked by her supervisor why she thinks patient X refuses to take his medication.
❏ A chemistry student must explain in her laboratory report why her experiment failed to produce expected results.

❏ A literature professor assigns a paper that requires you to develop and support a consistent theory explaining the symbolism used throughout a short story.

It is important to recognize that hypotheses are simply *plausible* explanations. They are always open to dispute or refutation, usually by the addition of further information. Or their plausibility may be enhanced by the addition of further information.

As you read textbook assignments, participate in class discussions, and conduct library research, you will frequently encounter hypotheses. In a political science course, for example, you might be asked to evaluate a theory or hypothesis that explains Stalin's popularity in Russia after Lenin's death. Or in a business and finance course, a class discussion may center on theories by Keynes and Friedman that explain why people choose to hold and not spend money. As a critical reader, you must assess the plausibility of each hypothesis. This is a two-part process. First, you must evaluate the evidence provided. Then you must search for information, reasons, or evidence that suggests the truth or falsity of the hypothesis. Ask questions such as these:

❏ Does my hypothesis account for all known information about the situation?
❏ Is it realistic—that is, within the realm of possibility and probability?
❏ Is it simple, or less complicated than its alternatives? (Usually, unless a complex hypothesis can account for information not accounted for by a simple hypothesis, the simple one has greater likelihood of being correct.)
❏ What assumptions were made? Are they valid?

EXERCISE 11-6

Directions:
Develop hypotheses to explain each of situations 1 through 3.

1. Bill Cosby's book *Fatherhood* appeared on the *New York Times* best seller list for several months.
2. McDonald's has expanded its operations to numerous foreign countries. It has become England's largest food service organization.
3. There has been a recent increase in the number of children per couple in the United States.

Weighing the Adequacy of Data and Evidence

Many writers who express their opinions, state viewpoints, make generalizations, or offer hypotheses also provide data or evidence in support of their ideas. Your task as a critical reader is to weigh and evaluate the quality of this evidence. You must look behind the available evidence and assess its type and adequacy.

In assessing the adequacy of evidence, you must be concerned with two factors: the type of evidence being presented and the relevance of that evidence. The following can be considered evidence:

- ❏ Personal experience of observation
- ❏ Statistical data
- ❏ Examples, particular events, or situations that illustrate
- ❏ Analogies (comparisons with similar situations)
- ❏ Informed opinion (the opinions of experts and authorities)
- ❏ Historical documentation
- ❏ Experimental evidence

Each type of evidence must be weighed in relation to the statement it supports. Evidence should directly, clearly, and indisputably support the case or issue in question.

Here are a few examples of situations that would require you to assess the adequacy of evidence:

- ❏ In an exam you are asked to write an essay to defend or criticize the 1989 decision of the United States to take military action against Panama.
- ❏ For a business retailing class you are asked to evaluate three interior store design proposals and rationales submitted by three contractors and recommend the best in terms of sales productivity.
- ❏ For a nursing course you are required to criticize three alternate nursing plans for the care of a patient whose postsurgical condition you just viewed on videotape.

EXERCISE 11-7

Directions:
Indicate the type(s) of evidence that would be appropriate to support each of the following assignments.

1. An editorial in a community college campus newspaper opposing the building of a rifle range for training local police cadets
2. A term paper for a business management course on theories of leadership
3. An essay exam answer to the following question: Discuss whether public financing of campaigns should be extended to include congressional candidates
4. A critique of a film shown in a criminal justice course
5. A psychology class assignment to visit the snack bar to monitor and observe body language in a student conversation for ten minutes

ASKING CRITICAL QUESTIONS

Suppose you received a phone call from someone saying you had just won a new car, and all you need do is pay a $200 claim fee to take ownership. Would you immediately write a check, or would you be suspicious and question the caller? Perhaps you would hang up, knowing it couldn't be true. As consumers we tend to be wise, alert, and critical— even suspicious. As readers, however, we tend to be much more tolerant and accepting. Many readers readily accept information and ideas presented in written form. This section of the chapter suggests questions that will help you become a more critical reader and thinker.

What Is the Source of the Material?

Determine from what book, magazine, reference book, or newspaper the material you are reading was taken. Some sources are much more reliable and trustworthy than others; knowledge of the source will help you judge the accuracy, correctness, and soundness of the material. For example, in which of the following sources would you expect to find the most accurate and up-to-date information about word processing software?

❏ an advertisement in *Business Week*
❏ an article in *Mademoiselle*
❏ an article in *Software Review*

The best source would be Software Review, a periodical devoted to the subject of computers and computer software. *Mademoiselle* magazine does not specialize in technical information, and the advertisement in *Business Week* is likely to present only advantages of a particular brand of software.

Suppose you were conducting research for a term paper on the effects of aging on learning and memory. Articles from professional or scholarly journals, such as the *Journal of Psychology,* would be more useful and reliable than articles in newsstand periodicals.

To evaluate a source consider the following:

❏ its reputation
❏ the audience for whom the source is intended
❏ whether references or documentation are provided

What Are the Author's Credentials?

Not everything that appears in print is accurate and competently reported. Also, there are varying levels of expertise within a field. Consequently, you must assess whether the material you are reading is written by an expert in the field who can knowledgeably and accurately discuss the topic. In some materials, the author's credentials are footnoted or summarized at the end of the work. In journal articles, the author's college or university affiliation is often included. Authors also may establish their expertise or experience in the field within the material itself.

Why Was the Material Written?

As you read, try to determine why the author wrote the material. In textbooks, the author's primary purpose is to inform (present information). However, other material may be written to entertain, amuse, or persuade. If the author's purpose is to persuade or convince you to accept a particular viewpoint or take a specific action (such as to vote against an issue), then you will need to evaluate the reasoning and evidence presented.

Is the Author Biased?

Read each of the following statements and determine what they have in common:

❏ Shelley is by far the best English poet.
❏ Laboratory experiments using live animals are forms of torture.
❏ The current vitamin fad is a distortion of sound medical advice.

Each statement reflects a *bias*—a partiality, preference, or prejudice for or against a person, object, or idea.

Much of what you read and hear expresses a bias. In many newspapers and magazine articles, nonfiction books, advertisements, and essays you will find the attitudes, opinions, and beliefs of the speaker or author revealed. As you listen to a history lecture, for example, you may discover the professor's attitude or bias toward particular historical figures, political decisions, or events. As you read biased material, keep two questions in mind: What facts has the author omitted, and what additional information is necessary.

Some writers reveal their attitudes directly by stating how they feel. Others do so less directly, expressing their attitudes through the manner in which they write. Through selection of facts, choice of words, and the quality and tone of description, they convey a particular feeling or attitude. This process is called *slanting*. Its purpose is to convey a certain attitude or point of view toward the subject without expressing it explicitly. Following are two examples of slanting. The first, from commercial advertising, clearly suggests an attitude toward the product. The second statement expresses strong feelings against sports-hunting.

❏ Clear, crisp, and incomparably delightful. Peterki's Vodka.
❏ How can a sportsman, solely for his own pleasure, delight in the mutilation of a living animal?

Notice that each statement is one-sided. Other facts, such as the disadvantages of Peterki's (price, aroma, or lack of smoothness), are not mentioned. Neither are arguments that favor sports-hunting included. Notice, too, the use of favorable, positive words to describe the vodka—"clear, crisp," and "delightful"—while the negative word "mutilation" is used to describe hunting.

As you read or listen to slanted materials, keep the following questions in mind:

❏ What facts were omitted? What additional facts are needed?
❏ What words create positive or negative impressions?
❏ What impression would I have if different words had been used?

EXERCISE 11-8

Directions:
In each of the following statements, underline the words and phrases that reveal the writer's bias. Indicate what additional information you would need to evaluate each.

1. Now you can have room and comfort as well as a world-class road car for under $10,000.

2. The country has wasted a lot of money on purposeless space exploration.
3. The drunken behavior of sports fans at playoff games is a disgrace and insult to players and fans alike.
4. Shakespeare exhibited creative genius far beyond his contemporary playwrights by revealing insights into human behavior and its motivation.
5. Highgate University offers competitive, athletic opportunities in football and basketball; its focus on academic excellence is unyielding; its emphasis on scholarship outstanding; its commitment to equal opportunity admirable.

Does the Author Make Assumptions?

An assumption is an idea or principle the writer accepts as true and makes no effort to prove or substantiate. Usually, it is a beginning or premise upon which he or she bases the remainder of the work. For example, an author may assume that television encourages violent behavior in children and proceed to argue for restrictions on watching TV. Or a writer may assume that abortion is morally wrong and suggest legal restrictions on how and when abortions are performed.

Does the Author Present an Argument?

An argument is a logical arrangement and presentation of ideas. It is reasoned analysis, a tightly developed line of reasoning that leads to the establishment of an end result or conclusion. Arguments are usually developed to persuade the reader to accept a position or point of view. An argument gives reasons that lead to a conclusion. You will encounter them in various forms in various types of courses. Here are a few examples:

❏ An astronomy professor argues that extraterrestrial life is a statistical probability.
❏ An editorial in the college newspaper proposes that all grades be eliminated for first-semester freshmen.
❏ A supplementary reading assignment for a political science course argues that terrorism is a necessary and unavoidable outgrowth of world politics.

Analyzing arguments is a complex and detailed process to which major portions of courses in logic are devoted. As a starting point, you might use the following guidelines as you encounter and analyze arguments:

- ❏ Analyze the argument by simplifying it and reducing it to a list of statements.
- ❏ Are the terms used clearly defined and consistently applied?
- ❏ Is the thesis (the point to be made) clearly and directly stated?
- ❏ Are facts provided as evidence? If so, are they verifiable?
- ❏ Is the reasoning sound? (Does one point follow from another?)
- ❏ Are counterarguments recognized and refuted or addressed?
- ❏ What persuasive devices or propaganda techniques does the author use (examples: appeal to emotions, name-calling, appeal to authority)?

EXERCISE 11-9

Directions:

Analyze and evaluate each of the following arguments by referring to the preceding list of questions.

1. Capital punishment deters crime. It also makes certain that the killer will never commit another crime. Therefore, capital punishment should be widely and consistently applied.

2. Voluntary euthanasia, permitting a person to elect to die, should never be legalized. First of all, our religious and cultural traditions and principles oppose it. Also, providing a terminally ill patient with the option to make a death decision adds to the person's pain and anguish. Finally, death decisions are irreversible, and we all have heard of cases in which unexpected miraculous recoveries occur.

3. Sex education classes in public schools should be banned. They create interest in sex where it did not previously exist. Further, they encourage sexual deviance by making everything about sex seem natural. Also, these filthy classes detract from the parental authority and autonomy.

4. Once the emotionalism surrounding abortion is lessened, and abortion is examined in a rational manner, it would seem apparent that abortion can be morally justifiable. Prior to the time of viability, the mother's right to autonomy and self-determination about her own body supersedes the rights of an unborn, potential human being.[7]

5. Of course dangers exist, but compared with the dangers of not proceeding with the development of nuclear power, they seem to me on about the level of the tanks of cooking gas of my youth. The gas tanks on 125th Street *could* have blown up.

Atomic containment may be breached, sometime, somewhere. But while Americans fret about these possibilities, they seem oblivious to the certain dangers of a failure to meet the threat posed by the end of the Petroleum Age. To maintain our own standard of living; to provide for a world that increasingly demands a chance to achieve that standard, we must accept the nuclear alternative.[8]

❏ ❏ ❏
Thinking Critically . . . About Arguments

While an argument is a reasoned presentation of facts, it does require close scrutiny and evaluation by the reader. Most importantly, you must evaluate the author's logic. You must also be alert for persuasive techniques he or she may use and for errors in reasoning he or she may make. Here are a few to be alert for:

1. *Circular reasoning.* Circular reasoning occurs when an author supports a conclusion by giving a reason that says the same thing. Here is an example of circular reasoning. Conclusion: Gun control legislation needs serious and drastic revision. Supporting Reason: Our country cannot afford to continue without legislative revisions. Notice that this writer did *not* answer the question, "Why is revision needed?"

2. *Emotional appeals.* Writers often attempt to appeal to the readers' emotions, in order to persuade them to accept a conclusion. For example, an author may argue against animal fur coats by describing an animal's face or behavior.

3. *Testimonial.* An author may argue in part that a conclusion is correct because a famous or well-known person endorses it. For example, a writer may cite a former U.S. president's opinion on the abortion issue. However, unless the famous person is an authority on the issue at hand, the person's endorsement is not relevant to the argument. Because a U.S. president is not an expert on abortion, his opinion is not relevant.

4. *False cause.* This reasoning error occurs when one incorrectly assumes that two events are casually related just because they follow each other in time. If a drop in unemployment occurs immediately following a mayor's election, for example, a writer may attribute the decrease to the mayor's election. Unless the mayor took specific action to create jobs, the two events, although close in time, may be unrelated.

SUMMARY

1. Critical analysis involves the careful and deliberate integration and evaluation of ideas or information.
2. Synthesizing information is a process of

   ❏ examining and inferring relationships among sources
   ❏ making those relationships explicit, usually in writing

3. Recognizing and evaluating subjective content involves

   ❏ distinguishing fact from opinion
   ❏ evaluating differing viewpoints
   ❏ evaluating generalizations
   ❏ testing hypotheses
   ❏ weighing the adequacy of data and evidence

4. Critical questions useful in evaluating reading materials include the following:

   ❏ What is the source of the material?
   ❏ What are the author's credentials?
   ❏ Why was the material written?
   ❏ Is the author biased?
   ❏ Does the author make assumptions?
   ❏ Does the author present an argument?

CLASS ACTIVITY

Directions:

Each student should write a one-page response to the following assignment. Working in pairs, students should complete each of the following steps:

> Assignment: Agree or disagree with the following statement:
> Any person on welfare for more than a year lacks motivation

and initiative.

1. Students should exchange and read each other's papers.
2. Students should identify or evaluate the paper using the following questions:
   a. Does the writer express opinions?
   b. Does the writer's viewpoint differ from your own? If so, how can you objectively evaluate the viewpoint?
   c. Does the writer make generalizations? If so, underline them.

   d. What types of evidence does the writer provide to support his
      or her ideas?
   e. Is the writer biased? Is his or her paper slanted?
   f. Evaluate the writer's argument. Is it logical and consistent?

FURTHER ANALYSIS

Directions:
Analyze the following situation and answer the questions that follow.

An English instructor gave his class the following assignment:
Locate three articles on a current controversial issue. One of
the three must express a different viewpoint from the other two.
Write a two-page paper that critically evaluates each article.

One student in the class located three articles on censorship
but did not know how to approach the assignment. He summarized
each article and then wrote a paragraph describing how one article
differed from the other two. The instructor refused to accept and
grade this student's paper, saying that he had not completed the assignment.

1. Why was the student's paper unacceptable?
2. How should he have approached the assignment?
3. On what bases or using what criteria might the student have
   evaluated the articles?

DISCUSSION

1. Critical analysis involves evaluation and judgment. What occu-
   pations and professions rely heavily upon these skills? Should
   courses in critical thinking be required for degrees in these
   fields?
2. Select an editorial from your local or campus newspaper. Analyze it carefully, answering the following questions:
   a. Is the article primarily fact or opinion?
   b. What types of evidence, if any, does the author use to support
      his or her position?
   c. Identify any generalizations.
   d. Identify instances of bias or slanting.
   e. Evaluate the writer's argument.
   f. What alternative viewpoints could be taken on this subject?

FURTHER READING

Barry, Vincent E., and Joel Rudinow, *Innovation to Critical Thinking.* 3rd ed. New York: Harcourt, 1991.

Browne, M. Neil, and Stuart M. Keeley. *Asking the Right Questions.* Englewood Cliffs, NJ: Prentice 1993.

Chaffee, John. *Thinking Critically,* 3rd ed. Boston: Houghton 1993.

Mayfield, Marlys. *Thinking for Yourself: Developing Critical Thinking Skills Through Writing.* Belmont, CA: Wadsworth, 1994.

PART

4

APPLYING YOUR SKILLS TO ACADEMIC DISCIPLINES

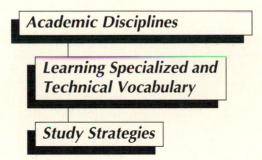

Academic Disciplines

Learning Specialized and Technical Vocabulary

Study Strategies

12

□ □ □ ▆▆▆▆▆▆▆▆▆▆▆▆▆▆▆▆▆

Learning Specialized and Technical Vocabulary

Learning Objectives

Focus on terminology as a key to course mastery

Use mapping to learn new terminology

Recognize core prefixes, roots, and suffixes

Learn how to develop a course master file

Have you noticed that each sport and hobby has its own language—a specialized set of words with specific meanings? Baseball players and fans talk about slides, home runs, errors, and runs batted in. Wine enthusiasts may discuss a wine's tannin, nose, bouquet, and finish. Each academic discipline also has its own language. For each course you take, you encounter an extensive set of words and terms that are used in a particular way in that subject area. This chapter discusses how specialized terminology is tied integrally to course mastery and suggests approaches for learning it.

TERMINOLOGY: THE KEY TO COURSE MASTERY

Each academic discipline has its own set of specialized words that enable accurate and concise description of events, principles, concepts, problems, and occurrences. One of the first tasks you face in a new course is to learn the specialized language of that course. This task is especially important in introductory courses in which the subject is new and unfamiliar. In an introductory computer science course, for instance, you often start by learning how a computer functions. From that point, many new terms are introduced: bit, byte, field, numeric characters, character positions, statements, coding, format, and so forth.

Specialized Terminology in Class Lectures

Often the first few class lectures in a course are devoted to acquainting students with the nature and scope of the field and to introducing them to its specialized language. Check your notes for the first few classes of the courses you are taking this semester. How many new or specialized terms were introduced?

You can see, then, that many disciplines devote considerable time to presenting the language of the course carefully and explicitly. Be sure to record accurately each new term for later review and study. Good lecturers give students clues to what terms and definitions are important to record. Some instructors make a habit of writing new words on the chalkboard, as a means of emphasis. Other instructors may emphasize new terms and definitions by slowing down, almost dictating so that you can record definitions. Still other instructors may repeat a word and its definition several times or offer several variations of meaning.

As a part of your notetaking system (see Chapter 9), develop a consistent way of easily identifying new terms and definitions recorded in your notes. You might circle or draw a box around each new term; or, as you edit your notes, underline each new term in red; or mark "def." in the margin each time a definition is included. The particular mark or symbol you use is a matter of preference; the important thing is to find some way to mark definitions for further study.

EXERCISE 12-1

Directions:
Estimate the number of new terms that each of your instructors introduced during the first several weeks for each of your courses. Now, check

the accuracy of your estimates by reviewing the first two weeks of your class notes for each course you are taking. How many new terms and definitions were included for each course?

Specialized Terminology in Textbooks

The first few chapters within a textbook are generally introductory, too. They are written to familiarize you with the subject of study and acquaint you with its specialized language. In one particular economics textbook, 34 new terms were introduced in the first two chapters (40 pages). In the first two chapters (28 pages) of a chemistry book, 56 specialized words were introduced. A sample of the words introduced in each text is given below. From these lists, you can see that some of the words are words of common, everyday usage that take on a specialized meaning; others are technical terms used only in the subject area.

❏ ❏ ❏

New terms: Economics text	*New terms: Chemistry text*
capital	matter
ownership	element
opportunity cost	halogen
distribution	isotope
productive contribution	allotropic form
durable goods	nonmental
economic system	group (family)
barter	burning
commodity money	toxicity

❏ ❏ ❏

Textbook authors use various means to emphasize new terminology. In some textbooks, new vocabulary is printed in italics, boldface type, or colored print. Other texts indicate new terms in the margin of each page. Still the most common means of emphasis, however, is the "New Terminology" list or "Vocabulary" list that appears at the beginning or end of each chapter.

Since textbook chapters (especially introductory ones) are heavily loaded with new specialized vocabulary, you should develop a system for marking new terminology as it is introduced.

Occasionally in textbooks you may find a new term that is not defined or that is not defined clearly. In this case, check to see if the text contains a glossary, a comprehensive list of terms introduced throughout the text, found at the back of the text. If so, it may provide a thorough explanation of the word. Make a note of the meaning in the text margin.

The glossary is particularly useful at the end of the course when you have covered all or most of the chapters. Use it to test your recall of terminology; read an entry, cover up the meaning, and try to remember it; then check to see if you were correct. As you are progressing through a course, however, the glossary is not an adequate study aid. A more organized, systematic approach to learning unfamiliar new terms is needed.

EXERCISE 12-2

Directions:
Review the first chapter from two of your texts and then answer the following questions.

1. How many new terms are introduced in each?
2. If your text contains a glossary, is each of these new terms listed?
3. Are most new words technical terms, or are they words from everyday usage to which a specialized meaning is attached?
4. How does each textbook author call your attention to these new terms?

Learning New Terminology

The following is a demonstration that makes an important point about learning new terminology. Follow the directions as listed.

Step 1

Read the following paragraphs from a computer science textbook; you will be able to refer back to the passage when completing the remaining steps.

7.4.1 Hash Functions
The hash function takes an element to be stored in a table and transforms it into a location in the table. If this transformation makes certain table locations more likely to occur than others, the chance of collision is increased and the efficiency of searches and insertions is decreased. The phenomenon of some table locations being more likely is called *primary clustering*. The ideal hash function spreads the elements uniformly throughout the table—that is, does not exhibit pri-

mary clustering. In fact, we would really like a hash function that, given any z, chooses a random location in the table in which to store z; this would minimize primary clustering. This is, of course, impossible, since the function h cannot be probabilistic but must be deterministic, yielding the same location every time it is applied to the same element (otherwise, how would we ever find an element after it was inserted?!). The achievable ideal is to design hash functions that exhibit pseudo-random behavior—behavior that appears random but that is reproducible.

Unfortunately, there are no hard and fast rules for constructing hash functions. We will examine four basic techniques that can be used individually or in combination. The properties of any particular hash function are hard to determine because they depend so heavily on the set of elements that will be encountered in practice. Thus the construction of a good hash function from these basic techniques is more an art than anything amenable to analysis, but we will present general principles that usually prove successful, pointing out their pitfalls as well.[1]

Step 2

Complete Quiz 1, referring to the passage as needed.

Quiz 1
1. Into what form does a hash function transform an element?
2. Define the term "primary clustering."
3. Describe an ideal hash function.
4. Why are the properties of a hash function difficult to determine?
5. What is "pseudorandom" behavior?

Step 3

Check your answers using the Answer Key at the end of the book. No doubt you did quite well. But did you really *understand* what you read? Let's find out.

Step 4

Complete Quiz 2, referring to the passage as needed.

Quiz 2
1. Give an example of an element to be stored in a table.
2. Define the term "transformation."
3. Define z and h.
4. In what situations might "primary clustering" be important?

Unless you have already taken courses in computer programming, you probably could not answer these questions. Why not? You did well with Quiz 1; how is Quiz 2 different? Quiz 2 tested your *understanding* of the terms used in the passage. Quiz 1 only asked you to locate information in the passage; it measured your ability to find answers—not to understand their meaning.

The differences between Quiz 1 and Quiz 2 illustrate the difference between merely manipulating new terminology and really understanding it. Many students fall into the trap of convincing themselves that they have learned new terminology when, actually, all they have learned is how to find answers. Often the answers lack real meaning to such students. You will know you have really mastered the terminology of a particular course when you begin to *think*, as well as speak and write, using those terms.

EXERCISE 12-3

Directions:

Select a beginning chapter that you have already read from one of your textbooks. Make a list of 10 new terms it introduces. Without reference to the text, test your understanding of each by expressing its meaning in your own words. Include an example of how the term is used whenever possible.

Using Subject Area Dictionaries

Many academic fields have specialized dictionaries that list most of the important words used in that discipline. These dictionaries list specialized meanings for words and suggest how and when to use the words. The field of nursing, for instance, has *Taber's Cyclopedic Medical Dictionary.* Other subject area dictionaries include *A Dictionary of Anthropology, The New Grove Dictionary of Music and Musicians,* and *A Dictionary of Economics.*

Find out whether there is a subject area dictionary for the disciplines you are studying. Most such dictionaries are available only in hardback and are likely to be expensive. However, many students find them worth the initial investment. Most libraries have copies of specialized dictionaries in the reference section.

EXERCISE 12-4

Directions:

For each of the courses you are taking, find out if there is a subject area dictionary available. If so, record its title.

MAPPING RELATED TERMINOLOGY

In most disciplines, you will be learning related groups of terms rather than separate, isolated words. For example, in a criminal justice course, you will learn a cluster of terms that describe the judicial process. In business marketing, you learn terms that describe the marketing management: market diversification, market-focus objective, opportunity forecasts, and so forth. Mapping is an effective method to use when learning such related sets or clusters of words. Mapping, as discussed in Chapter 10, involves drawing a chart or diagram that maps or shows the connection between various terms.

A map can organize terminology to be learned by grouping related terms together and making them more meaningful by showing connections and relationships. Figure 12-1 shows a map that might be useful in organizing the terminology introduced in the first chapter of a physics text. It relates the various states and physical properties of matter. This map makes it easy to visualize how matter is classified and to understand the various external and internal properties used to describe matter.

Mapping can help you avoid the pitfall described earlier of using

Figure 12-1
A Map of New Terminology

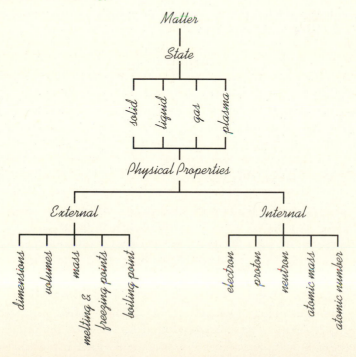

terms but not really understanding their meaning. Mapping forces you to think—to analyze how terms are related; by thinking, you are actively learning.

EXERCISE 12-5

Directions:

Read the following paragraph from the first chapter of a business advertising text and draw a map relating key terms introduced.

Economists take a somewhat different approach, looking at marketing in terms of benefits to buyers. They suggest that consumers buy goods because they feel the goods will provide satisfaction, or utility. Economists identify four types of utility. *Form utility* is created when a producer manufactures, mines and refines, or grows and harvests a product. In addition to form utility you also buy *place utility:* you pay for the product being in a local store instead of in the producer's warehouse. You also buy *time utility:* you pay retailers to have swimwear and Christmas gifts in stock when you want to buy. Finally, you buy *possession utility:* you pay, as part of a sales, lease, or rental transaction, to have possession of a product transferred to you. Because the last three utilities are provided by marketing, marketing might be defined in terms of buyer benefits as the creation of time, place, and possession utilities.[2]

EXERCISE 12-6

Directions:

Select a section of the first chapter from one of your textbooks and draw a map relating the key terms introduced in that section.

LEARNING CORE PREFIXES, ROOTS, AND SUFFIXES

Many words in the English language are made up of word parts called prefixes, roots, and suffixes, or beginnings, middles, and endings of words. These word parts have specific meanings and when added together can provide strong clues to the meanings of a particular word. The terminology in a particular academic discipline often uses a core of common prefixes, roots, and suffixes. For example, in the field of human anatomy and physiology, the prefix *endo* means "inner," and the root *derma* refers to "skin." Thus the word *endoderm* refers to the inner layer of cells in the skin. Numerous other words are formed using this root in conjunction with a suffix:

❏ ❏ ❏
Thinking Critically . . . About Vocabulary

As you learn new terminology for each of your courses, make sure you understand each new term. Use the following suggestions:

1. Learn definitions in your *own* words, not those of the textbook author.
2. Test yourself by explaining a new term to a friend or classmate.
3. Explain to yourself the differences between similar terms.
4. Try to think of examples or situations in which the term can be used.
5. Use newly learned terms in your speech, notetaking, and writing.
6. Learn terms as related sets of information, rather than individual pieces of information. Use mapping (p. 267) to help you organize sets of information.

❏ ❏ ❏

Root	Suffix	Example	Meaning
derma (skin)	*-itis* (inflammation)	*dermatitis*	Inflammation of skin
	-logy (study of)	*dermatology*	Branch of medicine that deals with the skin
	-osis (abnormal or diseased condition)	*dermatosis*	Skin disease

❏ ❏ ❏

As you are learning new terminology for each course, make a point of noticing recurring prefixes, roots, and suffixes. Compile a list of these and their meanings, along with several examples of each. You will find these common word parts useful in learning other new terms that contain them. A sample list for the field of psychology follows:

❏ ❏ ❏

Prefixes	Meaning	Example
psych(o)	Mind or mental processes	*psychoanalysis*
neur(o)	Pertaining to nerves or nervous system	*neurosis*
super	Above, over, outside	*superego*

Roots	Meaning	Example
somat(o)	Pertaining to the body	psychosomatic illness
-phobia	Intense fear	claustrophobia
patho	Indicates disease or suffering	pathological

Suffixes	Meaning	Example
-osis	Disorder or abnormal condition	neurosis
-ic	Pertaining to	neurotic
-ism	Indicates theory or principle of	behaviorism

❏ ❏ ❏

For courses involving scientific measurement, be sure to learn prefixes that refer to the metric system. A partial list follows:

❏ ❏ ❏

Prefix	Meaning
micro	millionth
milli	thousandth
centi	hundredth
deci	tenth
deca	ten
hecto	hundred
kilo	thousand
mega	million
giga	billion

❏ ❏ ❏

EXERCISE 12-7

Directions:

For one of your courses, identify five commonly used prefixes, roots, and suffixes. If you have difficulty, review the glossary of the text to discover commonly used word parts.

DEVELOPING A COURSE MASTER FILE

For each course you are taking, set up a master file in which you include new terminology to be learned and a list of essential prefixes, roots, and suffixes you have identified as important. Also include lists of frequently used signs, abbreviations, symbols, and their meanings. In the sciences, numerous symbols are used in formulas. Some students resist making a special effort to learn the symbols; they assume that they will learn them eventually. This is a mistake because, until you do learn them, you will feel uncomfortable with the course, as if you are on the outside looking in rather than actively participating. You will save yourself time and avoid frequent interruptions if you learn them right away rather than having to refer to the text for translations of every sign or symbol.

You can construct and organize your master file in a number of ways:

Index cards. Using a separate card for each entry, write the term (or symbol, abbreviation, etc.) on the front and the meaning on the back. Create separate packets of cards for prefixes, roots, and suffixes, new terms, abbreviations, and so forth.

Notebook sections. Divide a small (6" x 9") spiral notebook into sections and create running lists of terms and meanings.

Computer files. The computer's word processing capabilities allow you to add to, rearrange, and delete items easily. Using the cut-and-paste or copy functions, you can group similar terms for more effective study. A biology student, for example, grouped terms together according to the following categories: energy and life cells, biological processes, reproduction, biological systems, brain and behavior, and environmental structure issues.

An abbreviated version of a course master file for a nursing course in which students were studying laboratory assessment of blood is shown in Table 12-1.

Because each course deals with very different subject matter, your course master file will differ for each course you are taking. Table 12-2 lists tips for individualizing your course file to suit the requirements of particular academic disciplines. Check with your college's learning assistance center; it may offer lists of common prefixes and roots.

EXERCISE 12-8

Directions:

Begin preparing a master file for one of your courses. Use both your text and corresponding lecture notes. Begin with the first chapter, and list new terms, prefixes, roots, and suffixes as well as symbols and abbreviations.

Table 12-1
SAMPLE COURSE MASTER FILE

New Terminology
plasma—blood from which cellular material has been removed
platelets—photoplasmic disks; promote coagulation
bilirubin—orange-yellowish pigmentation in bile carried to the liver by the blood

Prefixes, Roots, and Suffixes

Prefixes	Meaning	Example
trans-	Across	*transfusion*
electro-	Indicates electricity	*electrophoresis*
hyper-	Abnormal, excessive	*hyperthyroidism*

Roots	Meaning	Example
hem-	Blood	*hematology*
thromb-	Clot	*thrombus*
cardi-	Heart	*cardiodynamics*

Suffixes	Meaning	Example
-lysis	Dissolution or decomposition	*hydrolysis*
-lyte	Substance that can be decomposed by a particular process	*electrolyte*
-stasis	Slowing or stoppage	*hemostasis*

Symbols and Abbreviations
CBC Complete blood count
WBC White blood count
RBC Red blood count
HbF Hemoglobin, fetal
ESR Erythrocyte sedimentation rate

Table 12-2
TIPS FOR LEARNING SPECIALIZED VOCABULARY IN VARIOUS FIELDS OF STUDY

Sciences	Learn standard symbols.
	ex: F = force
	W = work
	Learn the metric system.
	ex: *deci* = tenth
	Learn notation systems.
	ex: $HNO_2 \nrightarrow N_2O_2 + H_2O$
	Consult data books and handbooks.
	ex: *Biology Data Book*
	Merck Index
	Handbook of Chemistry & Physics
	Van Nostrand's Scientific Encyclopedia

Table 12-2
TIPS FOR LEARNING SPECIALIZED VOCABULARY IN VARIOUS FIELDS OF STUDY *(continued)*

Mathematics	Learn words as well as the process they imply. ex: *average* (add, then divide) *product* (multiply) Learn symbols. ex: >, <, Σ, $\int$ Learn abbreviations. ex: *quad., vol.* Consult: *Encyclopedia Dictionary of Mathematics*
Literature	Learn terms used to describe various features of literature. ex: *tone, mood, iambic pentameter* Learn terms that describe various styles of writing. ex: *informal, graphic,* and *verbose* Learn terms that refer to particular parts of literary work. ex: *drama, interlude, finale, denouement* Learn terms that refer to techniques. ex: *flashback, monologue, soliloquy* Learn legendary/mythological figures. ex: *Midas, Venus* Consult: *Handbook of Literary Terms* *A Dictionary of World Mythology*
Arts	Learn terms that describe qualities, impressions, techniques. Learn terms that refer to mode of expression. ex: *design, form, structure* Consult: *The Thames and Hudson Dictionary of Art and Artists*
Applied Sciences, Technical Courses, Computer Science	Learn terms that denote process; concentrate on steps in the process. Develop a working knowledge of the terminology; use the terminology in your speaking and writing. Draw diagrams to get the big picture and to show overall relationships. Connect terminology and processes with everyday experience, observable occurrences. Consult: *McGraw-Hill Dictionary of Scientific and Technical Terms*

(continued)

Table 12-2

TIPS FOR LEARNING SPECIALIZED VOCABULARY IN VARIOUS FIELDS OF STUDY (continued)

Business	Learn terms that describe organization. ex: *conglomerate, franchise* Learn abbreviations. ex: *OTC, IBF, APR* Learn processes and procedures. ex: *price control, time study* Consult: *Dictionary of Business, Finance, and Banking*
Social Sciences	Learn words that describe general behaviors. ex: *aggression, assimilation* Learn stages and processes. ex: *oral stage, displacement* Learn laws, principles, theories. ex: *late selection theory, Sapir-Whorf Hypothesis* Learn important researchers, theorists. ex: *Maslow, Keynes* Consult: *International Encyclopedia of the Social Sciences*
History	Learn important historical figures. ex: *Napoleon, Mao Zedong* Learn places of historical significance. ex: *Sparta, Babylonia, Prussia* Consult: *Encyclopedia of World History*

SUMMARY

1. Each academic discipline has its own set of specialized terminology that makes possible accurate and concise description and discussion of its content. A major task in approaching a new field of study is to learn its specialized language.
2. Consistent systems for marking and recording new terminology are important for both class lectures and textbook reading.
3. In reading new terminology, make certain you truly understand each new term by using them in your thinking, speaking, and writing.
4. To learn new terminology, use the following techniques:

   ❏ Use mapping. It will enable you to group related terms and learn them more easily.
   ❏ Learn core prefixes, roots, and suffixes in each field, and use them as a means of recalling words and learning new terms.

❏ Develop a course master file, a system of collecting all new terminology; essential prefixes, roots, and suffixes; as well as frequently used symbols, abbreviations, and their meanings.

CLASS ACTIVITY

Directions:

Each student should bring a textbook to class and designate several chapters he or she has already read. Students should exchange texts, and each student should devise a quiz to test understanding of new terminology. The quiz should resemble Quiz 2 on p. 265. Avoid asking questions such as those included in Quiz 1, p. 265. Once quizzes are prepared, the quiz and textbook are returned to owner, and the owner completes the quiz without reference to the text. Each pair of students evaluates and discusses responses and performance.

FURTHER ANALYSIS

Directions:

Analyze the following situation and answer the questions that follow:

A well-respected biology professor teaches her class from the first day using extensively the terminology of her field. Rarely does she explain or define a term. Some students say they are easily confused. Others complain among themselves, saying, "She assumes we know everything already; if we did, we wouldn't be taking the course!"

1. Do you agree or disagree with their complaints? Why?
2. Why do you think the professor chooses this approach?
3. How does this teaching style facilitate active thinking and learning?
4. What might students in this class do to prepare for the professor's lectures?
5. How should students adjust their lecture notetaking techniques to account for this lecture style?

DISCUSSION

1. What tests or checking methods could you devise to be certain that you *understand* new terminology and have gone beyond memorizing definitions?
2. What system, other than a course master file, have you used to learn specialized terminology? Evaluate its effectiveness.

FURTHER READING

Refer to sources listed in Table 12-2.

Gordon, Helen H. *Wordforms: Context, Strategies, and Practice, Book II.* 2nd ed. Belmont, CA: Wadsworth, 1991.

Hopper, Jane, and JoAnn Carter-Wells. *The Language of Learning: Vocabulary for College Success.* Belmont, CA: Wadsworth, 1994.

13

Study Strategies for Academic Disciplines

Learning Objectives

Discover particular characteristics of each discipline

Adapt your reading and study strategies for each discipline

Anticipate particular thought patterns in each discipline

Adapt lecture notetaking techniques to each discipline

Each academic discipline is a unique system of study; each takes a specialized approach to the study of the world around us. To illustrate, let's choose as an example a popular house pet—the dog—and consider how various disciplines might approach its study.*

❏ An artist might consider the dog as an object of beauty and record its fluid, flexible muscular structure and meaningful facial expressions on canvas.

*Based on an example from Mainon, *Writing in the Arts and Sciences*, pp. 4–5.

❏ A psychologist might study what human needs are fulfilled by owning a dog.

❏ The historian might research the historical importance of dogs— their use as guard dogs in warfare or their role herding sheep.

❏ A zoologist might trace the evolution of the dog and identify its predecessors.

❏ A mathematician might treat the dog as a three-dimensional object comprising planes and angles.

❏ An economist might focus on the supply and demand of dogs and the amount of business that is generated (kennels, supplies, dog food).

❏ A biologist would categorize the dog as *Canis familiaris*.

❏ A physiologist would be concerned with the animal's bodily functions (breathing, heart rate, temperature).

Each academic discipline, then, approaches a given object or event with a different focus or perspective. Each has its own special purposes and interests that define the scope of the discipline. You will find that each discipline has its own methodology for studying topics with which it is concerned. Because each discipline is unique, each requires somewhat different study and learning strategies.

The purpose of this chapter is to show you how to modify and adapt your learning, thinking, and study strategies to five general academic areas: the social sciences, the life and physical sciences, mathematics, literature and arts, and career fields. For each of these disciplines, unique approaches and characteristics are discussed, and then techniques for adapting textbook reading and lecture notetaking strategies are described.

APPROACHING NEW FIELDS OF STUDY

In your first few years of college, you are likely to encounter disciplines with which you have had no prior experience. Anthropology, political science, or organic chemistry may be new to you. In the beginning, these new fields of study may seem unfamiliar or foreign. One student described this feeling as "being on the outside looking in," watching other students participate in the class but unable to do so himself. At first, you may feel lost, confused, or frustrated in such courses. These feelings may result from unfamiliarity with the specialized language of the discipline, not knowing what types of learning and thinking are expected, and unfamiliarity with conventions, approaches, and methodology of the discipline.

When approaching a new field of study, try the following:

Spend more time than usual reading and studying. You are doing more than reading and studying: You are learning how to learn as well.

Learn as much as possible until you discover more about what is expected. You will need as much information as is available to begin to fit information into patterns.

Since you do not know how you will eventually organize and use it, process the same information in several different ways. For example, in an anthropology course, you might learn events and discoveries chronologically (according to occurrence in time) as well as comparatively (according to similarities and differences among various discoveries). In an accounting course, you might organize information by procedure as well as by controlling principles.

Use several methods of learning. Since you are not sure which will be most effective for the types of learning and thinking that are required, try several methods at once. For example, you might underline textbook information (to promote factual recall) as well as write outlines and summaries (to interpret and consolidate ideas). You might also draw diagrams that map the relations between concepts and ideas. (These learning strategies are discussed in detail in Chapter 10).

Ask questions. For example

- ❏ What is the logical progression or development of ideas?
- ❏ Are there any cause and effect relationships operating?
- ❏ What are the practical applications of this information?

Look for similarities between the new subject matter and other academic fields that are familiar to you. If similarities exist, you may be able to modify or adapt existing learning approaches and strategies to fit your new field of study.

Establish an overview of the field. Spend time studying the table of contents of your textbook; it provides an outline of the course. Look for patterns, progression of ideas, and recurring themes, approaches, or problems.

Obtain additional reference materials, if necessary. Some college texts delve into a subject immediately, providing only a brief introduction or overview in the first chapter. If your text does this, spend an hour or so in the library getting a more comprehensive overview of the field.

- ❏ Read or skim several encyclopedia entries in your field of study, taking notes if necessary.
- ❏ Check the card catalog to see how the subject is divided.

❏ Locate two or three introductory texts in the field. Study the table of contents of each and skim the first chapter.

THE SOCIAL SCIENCES AND HISTORY

The social sciences are concerned with the study of people, their development, and how they function together and interact. Included are psychology, anthropology, sociology, political science, and economics. They deal with political, economic, social, cultural, and behavioral aspects of human beings. The term "science" is appropriate because each discipline concentrates on defining problems; observing, gathering, and interpreting information; and reporting measurable results. Some social science courses are required in most degree programs.

What to Expect

Courses in the social sciences tend to have the following characteristics:

❏ They are highly factual. Especially in introductory courses, an instructor's first task is to acquaint you with what is already known—principles, rules, and facts—so that you can subsequently use them in approaching new problems and unique situations.

❏ They introduce a vast number of new terms. Although each academic field has a language of its own, each social science has developed an extensive set of terminology to make broad or largely subjective topics as objective and quantifiable as possible.

❏ They require large amounts of reading. Expect to read several textbook chapters per week. Additionally, your instructor may assign supplementary readings on a regular basis.

❏ They make use of graphics (maps, charts, tables, graphs).

❏ They are research oriented. Many texts describe or report research studies as supporting evidence. In introductory courses, the outcome of the research and what it proves or suggests are usually most important.

❏ They emphasize theories, and often the social scientists who developed them.

How to Read and Study the Social Sciences

Since social science texts tend to be highly factual, it is easy to get lost in detail and to lose sight of the general topics with which the discipline is concerned. Use the following guidelines when reading social science materials:

- ❏ Since large amounts of reading are usually required, be sure to keep up with assignments, reading a chapter section or two each day.
- ❏ Be certain to develop a course master file to record and learn new terminology (refer to Chapter 12).
- ❏ Plan time in your schedule for locating and reading supplementary reading assignments. Often these are on reserve in the library. Be certain to take summary notes on the material.
- ❏ Maintain a focus on large ideas: concepts, trends, and patterns. Previewing before and reviewing after reading will help establish this focus.

What Thought Patterns to Anticipate

Three thought patterns predominate in the social sciences: listing, comparison and contrast, and cause and effect. Table 13-1 describes their uses and includes several examples from specific disciplines.

Taking Lecture Notes

Use the following suggestions to improve your notetaking in social science courses:

Take notes. Regardless of whether the lecture supplements or covers material identical to your textbook, take thorough, complete notes. Recording information you have already read or will read in your text will reinforce your learning. Later, after checking the corresponding text closely, you may shorten and reorganize your notes to best fit with text material.

Summarize cases or examples. Especially in sociology, psychology, and anthropology classes, a lecturer may use case studies (descriptions of a particular person, action, or problem) to illustrate a concept presented in the text. In your notes, try to summarize the key information of the case study, recording enough facts to bring the example to mind again as you review.

Summarize films or tapes. Films and videotapes are often used to illustrate concepts, theories, and problems in psychology, sociology, and anthropology classes. While detailed notes are unnecessary, be sure to jot down the main points the film or tape makes as well as your impressions and reactions.

Edit your notes. In history lecturers, editing your notes is particularly essential. Often an instructor will discuss numerous events, people, and

Table 13-1
THOUGHT PATTERNS IN THE SOCIAL SCIENCES

Pattern	Uses	Examples
Listing	To present facts, illustrations, findings or examples; to list research	Sociology Types of white collar crime Examples of institutional racism Characteristics of aerospace/defense industries Environmental abuses
Comparison and contrast	To evaluate two sides of an issue; to compare and contrast theories, groups, behaviors, events	Political science A comparison of ethnic groups' political power A study of various urban development strategies A discussion of types of consumer representation groups
Cause and effect	To study behavior and motivation; to examine connections among events, actions, behaviors	Psychology Sources of stress and how the body reacts to it The effects of drug therapy on schizophrenia The underlying causes of aggressive behavior Means of controlling and treating phobias

laws simultaneously. Other instructors seem to switch between historical periods, discussing various trends or issues. As you edit, try to indicate chronological sequence of events. Also, try to collect all facts about a particular person, event, or issue in one place.

EXERCISE 13-1

Directions:
Analyze the following situation and answer the questions.

A psychology student has been assigned a 1,000-word paper on the founders of the field of psychology.

1. Analyze the purpose of the assignment.
2. How should the student approach the assignment?
3. Is research necessary? If so, what sources might he or she begin with?
4. What thought pattern(s) could he or she use to organize the paper?

THE LIFE AND PHYSICAL SCIENCES

Life sciences refer to the study of living organisms: anatomy and physiology, zoology, botany, and biology. The physical sciences are concerned with the function, structure, and composition of energy, matter, and substance in our environment and include physics, chemistry, and physical geology. Sometimes called the natural sciences, both types are primarily concerned with two questions: "Why?" and "How?" Scientists constantly ask these two questions and conduct experiments and research to provide the answers.

To work effectively in a science course, adopt a scientific way of thinking. The usual concerns, such as "What is important to learn?" and "How much supporting information do I need to learn?" may be of only secondary importance. Instead, to be most successful, you must adopt a scientific mindset—you need to become comfortable with asking literal questions and seeking answers, or analyzing problems and seeking solutions or explanations.

To benefit most from your learning, ask practical questions. For example, if you are a nursing student studying organic chemistry, the question you must always keep in the back of your mind is "How does what I am learning apply to the field of nursing?"

Some students of science become too involved with fact and detail and fail to step back and look at the larger picture. Often, they fail to recognize connections and relationships between the subject matter at hand and its applications to various concerns and professions.

What to Expect

Scientific and technical material, both in lecture and in textbooks, has special characteristics.

Unfamiliar Subject Matter

While the social sciences present new concepts and principles, they often deal with subjects with which we are familiar and with which we function daily. Social groups, physical and emotional needs, and aspects of culture are examples. Scientific topics, on the other hand, are less familiar to most of us. For example, few of us have a background of everyday experience with molecular structure, mutant genes, or radioactive isotapes.

Because of the new, unfamiliar nature of scientific material, you must be willing to commit more time to its study than you would to other material—perhaps even twice as much. Even excellent students, to whom reading, studying, and learning have always come easily, find it difficult to admit that scientific study requires greater time, effort, and perseverance. Consequently, when learning does not occur as easily as in other subjects, they become frustrated and say that they cannot learn science or that the sciences are too difficult.

Active Participation Is Required

Most rigorous scientific courses require a weekly laboratory in addition to class lectures. Here the purpose is to test, apply, experiment with, or demonstrate the principles presented in lecture. Many students who are new or uncommitted to scientific study fail to recognize the importance of laboratory sessions. Consequently, they fail to approach the course with the expected practical, testing, questioning attitude.

Factual Density

The pure sciences are even more factual than the social sciences. Introductory science courses leave little room for interpretation, debate, opinion, or conjecture. Texts and lectures appear formal, straightforward, and regimented (and to some students who thrive on interaction and controversy—uninteresting).

How to Read and Study Scientific Material

Use the following suggestions in reading and studying scientific material:

Preview assignments. Because scientific material is often unfamiliar, previewing the chapter before you give it a thorough reading is essential. Also preview the problems at the end of the chapter. Reading through these problems will provide clues about important principles emphasized in the chapter. Preview the vocabulary list to identify terms you will need to learn.

Do not skip anything. Unlike with other, more familiar subjects, you cannot afford to skip anything.

Never try to read quickly or settle for getting the gist of meaning. Facts and details are important, as are the connections among them.

Read carefully and thoughtfully. Some students find it effective to read each section of a chapter at least twice: The first reading is intended to acquaint them with key ideas; the second reading is to fill in the details and grasp specific, detailed concepts.

Be alert for gaps in information. Because information in a science course is presented sequentially and understanding depends on mastering earlier information, you may find that you lack background or specific information on a topic. It is your responsibility, if you should identify such a gap, to fill it through reading, researching, using a scientific encyclopedia, or checking with your instructor.

Focus on applications. Though science courses contain a great deal of abstract theory and fact, they are also very concerned with applications. The end-of-chapter problems often focus on use and application of information learned.

Make everyday connections. To make the subject matter less abstract and easier to learn, try to relate facts, ideas, and principles to things with which you are familiar. In a human anatomy and physiology course, for example, when studying the bones in the skeletal system, try to feel your own bones. In chemistry, when studying various types of solutions, think of everyday liquids that are representative of each type.

Ask questions. Do not look for facts—look for answers. Keep in mind constantly the questions Why? How? and Under what conditions? For each occurrence, be sure you understand how and why it happens.

Learn the notation system. Each field uses its own version of shorthand, a series of signs, symbols, and characters that have become standard abbreviations or notations. To work within a given field, then, a first step is to learn its notation system. Make these notations a part of your course master file (see Chapter 12).

Translate formulas into words. Most scientific fields express key relationships in abbreviated formulas. To be certain that you understand the relationship, try to express it in your own words. This will establish verbal connections and make storage and retrieval easier.

Develop a vocabulary master file. The vocabulary of the sciences is exact and precise. In many of the sciences, learning depends on mastering a great deal of new terminology. Fortunately, the sciences rely more heavily on a common base of prefixes, roots, and suffixes than do most other disciplines. It is especially worthwhile, then, to develop a master file of word parts and learn them as soon as possible.

What Thought Patterns to Anticipate

The three most commonly used thought patterns in scientific courses are cause and effect, process, and problem-solution. As you will see below, these three patterns often intertwine. Uses and examples of these patterns are shown in Table 13-2.

Taking Lecture Notes

Use the following guidelines to polish your lecture notetaking in the sciences:

Don't get lost in detail. Lecturers in the life and natural sciences may involve experiments, demonstrations, or solving sample problems. For these activities, it is easy to get lost in recording details, thus losing sight of the principles each is intended to emphasize. Do not try to record all details of each step in a demonstration or experiment; instead, focus on organization and procedures with an intent to identify the overall purpose. For sample problems, frequently solved on the chalkboard, record what the instructor writes, leaving plenty of blank space. Then, as you edit your notes after the lecture, try to describe and fill in what occurred at each step.

Make quick sketches. Diagrams and charts are often used as illustrations. When these are presented, draw a quick sketch, not a careful copy. You can redraw it later during editing, or a similar drawing may appear in your text. Concentrate on the process or point the diagram is intended to show. Label the steps if possible; if time is insufficient, simply number the steps in the process. Later, as you edit your lecture notes, be certain to write out the steps.

Outline or summarize notes briefly. Since notes in the sciences tend to be highly factual, write a brief summary or outline of your notes each day. This will help you to regain a perspective on key ideas and will force you to organize the detail into meaningful groupings.

Use scientific notation. Learn the scientific notation system and use it as you take notes. It is a shorthand system that will speed up your notetaking significantly. At first, to help yourself get started, keep a list of common symbols and abbreviations close at hand for fast reference. As you edit your notes, build the habit of using symbols: Look for places where you could have used a sign or symbol instead of a word, and make connections.

When You Are Having Difficulty

If the sciences are typically a difficult field of study for you, or if you suddenly find yourself not doing well in a science course, try the following survival tactics:

Make changes in your learning strategies. Let's suppose you are a nonscience major taking your one or two required science courses; you

Table 13-2
THOUGHT PATTERNS IN THE SCIENCES

Pattern	*Uses*	*Examples*
Cause and effect	Explain why natural phenomena occur	Biology An explanation of why trees shed their leaves A discussion of why plant cells divide (mitosis) The conditions under which plant fossil formation occurs An explanation of why domesticated plants were important in formulating the theory of natural selection
Process	Describe how events occur; present steps in experimental procedures	Anatomy and physiology How the liver functions How white blood cells function in the immune system Control of organ function by the endocrine system Transmittal of genetic code from parents to child
Problem-solution	Solve practical problems; study currently unexplained phenomena	Physics How sound waves transfer energy How refraction of light produces mirages Practical problems, such as calculating the work done by a woman who lifts a 13 kg suitcase 5 m upward, or estimating the time needed for an 850 W coffee maker to prepare 10 cups of coffee when the water used is 55° F.

may feel as strange as if you were in a foreign country. As a first step to working with "foreign" fields of study, you *must* revise and alter your approaches and strategies. Many students mistakenly think they will get by in their one or two required science courses using the same reading, study, and thinking strategies that work in other fields. Plan on making the changes already described in this section. You cannot be even minimally successful unless you make them.

Learn from classmates. Talk with and observe the strategies of students who are doing well in the course. You are likely to pick up new and useful procedures.

Learn the metric system. If the metric system is used, and you have not learned it, spend the time and effort to learn it. It is essential to most scientific fields.

Double your study time. If you are having trouble with a course, first (if you have not done so already) make a commitment to spend more time and work harder. Use this added time to revise and try out new strategies. Never spend more time using a strategy that is not working.

Purchase a review book, student practice manual, or other learning aid and work with it regularly.

Pull the course together:

❑ Review your notes and text assignments; discover how they work together and where they seem to be headed.

❑ As you review, make lists of topics you do understand and those you do not.

❑ Decide whether you are experiencing difficulty due to gaps in your scientific background. Ask yourself whether the instructor assumes you know things when you do not. If so, consider obtaining a tutor. Check with your college's learning assistance center on the availability of tutorial services.

❑ Ask for help from either your classmates or your instructor.

EXERCISE 13-2

Directions:
Analyze the following situation and answer the questions below.

An English major is taking a required chemistry course to fulfill his general education requirements. A weekly three-hour laboratory is required, for which he must perform a series of experiments and submit a two-page report. The student complains about the lab: If he can find out the results of each experiment by looking them up in a book or by reading his text, he wants to know, why spend the three hours performing experiments for which the results are already known? He also complains about the lab and its required format, since it allows no creativity or self-expression.

1. What could you explain to this student to overcome his objections?
2. What does he fail to understand about science?
3. Evaluate the quality of his thinking about his chemistry course.

MATHEMATICS

Mathematics is a very strict, regimented study that follows a prescribed order of events. Problems are solved using specified step-by-step procedures. Theorems are derived in a tightly logical, sequential order. Much of what you learn is dependent on skills that preceded it. Mathematics, then, is cumulative—skills are built upon one another. For example, you cannot solve bank interest problems in financial accounting if you do not know how to work with percentages.

What to Expect

Mathematics is a discipline that requires regular, consistent, day-to-day study. Here are a few things you should expect in a mathematics course:

Expect every class to count. Class attendance and participation are essential for learning math. Even if there is a "cut" policy, don't cut class. Because math learning is sequential, if you miss one specific skill, that gap in your understanding and competence may cause problems all semester.

Expect regular homework assignments. Whether or not an instructor collects or grades homework, be sure to complete all assignments when they are due. Practice is an essential element in all mathematics courses. Never let yourself get behind or skip assignments. Because today's assignment will be used in the next section or chapter, skipping an assignment will create a gap in your knowledge and interfere with your ability to complete future assignments.

Expect to work independently. Some introductory-level mathematics texts are "programmed," or self-instructional. You are expected to work through the chapter and then complete an in-class quiz demonstrating your mastery of the topic. Other texts are more traditional but also expect you to work on end-of-chapter problems on your own.

Accuracy and precision are important. Many students, accustomed to flexible approaches to learning, have difficulty adjusting to the precise nature of mathematics. In particular, they are disturbed that "close does not count" and that knowledge of technique is not sufficient; rather, the technique must be precisely and accurately applied in order to be considered correct. Develop the habit of checking your work and focusing on accuracy.

How to Read and Study Mathematics Texts

Use the following guidelines for reading and studying mathematics:

Plan on spending more time. Studying a mathematics textbook takes more time than reading textbooks in most other disciplines. As is also true of life and physical sciences, mathematics is concise and factually dense. Nearly everything is important.

Focus on process and procedure. Be certain to understand *why* and *how* various procedures are used.

Pay attention to sample problems. Usually, a textbook section that explains a procedure step by step is followed by a sample problem. The best way to read a section is to read a sentence or two and then refer to the sample problem to see how the information is applied. Then return to the text and read the explanation of the next step, and then refer to the sample problem again. The process of alternating between text and problem may seem confusing at first, but remember that your purpose is to see *how* the problem illustrates the process being described. Then practice solving the problem without referring to the text.

Learn to read mathematical language. Mathematics, through use of notations, symbols, and formulas, expresses complicated relationships in a very brief but concise form. For example, the mathematical equation $c^2 = a^2 + b^2$ says that the square of the hypotenuse of a right triangle is equal to the sum of the squares of the two remaining sides. A large amount of information is packed into the smallest unit of mathematical language.

Study daily. Never let your work pile up until the weekend. The principle of distributed learning (see p. 52) is especially important in mathematics.

Become adept at solving problems. Quizzes and exams are made up almost exclusively of problems to solve. Here are a few tips to follow in solving mathematical problems:

❏ Be certain you understand what the problem is saying and what it is asking for. Try to express the problem in your own words.

❑ Identify the relevant information that is provided to solve the problem. (Some math problems may provide irrelevant or distracting information that is not useful in solving the problem). Underline or circle essential information.

❑ Recall the formulas you have learned that relate to the problem at hand and select which you will work with.

❑ If you do not know or are unsure of how to solve a problem, look for similarities between it and sample problems you have studied.

❑ Be sure to check your work. Many students are frustrated when they lose points, or sometimes full credit, due to arithmetic errors.

Study and practice variations of problems. Explore the different forms in which a problem can be expressed, and identify variations of the same type of problem.

What Thought Patterns to Anticipate

Three thought patterns predominate in the study of mathematics: process, problem-solution, and comparison and contrast, as shown in Table 13-3.

Table 13-3
THOUGHT PATTERNS IN MATHEMATICS

Pattern	Uses	Examples
Process	Describing steps to follow in solving problems or proving theorems	Algebra Solving quadratic equations
Problem-solution	Solving sample problems; homework problems	Business math Computing the interest on a $2,000 car loan at 13.5% add-on rate with monthly payments
Comparison and contrast	Recognizing how new problems are different from sample problems, how problem types differ; determining what operations are used in several types of problems	Basic mathematics Similarities between ratios and percentages

Taking Class Notes

Mathematics instructors seldom present formal lectures. Instead, they work through and explain procedures and problems. Here are a few suggestions for improving your notetaking skills in mathematics classes:

Focus on concepts and procedures. Concentrate on understanding the concept or procedure the instructor is explaining, or the rationale he or she is giving. Then, once you understand it, write it down, either during the lecture or later, as you edit your notes.

Record sample problems. As you edit your notes, try to identify and describe the steps followed in the problems.

Know the text before class. Many instructors follow the textbook closely; consequently, it is useful to become familiar with the chapter before attending class. If you know, for example, that the instructor is working with a sample problem from the textbook, then you can make notes in the margin of your text.

Ask questions. Most instructors are open to and encourage students to ask questions. Do not hesitate to ask a question; often several other people in the class had the same question, but were reluctant to ask it.

EXERCISE 13-3

Directions:
Analyze the following situation and decide what advice you would offer this student.

A theater arts student is failing a required mathematics course. He has identified two difficulties.

1. He has trouble thinking in signs and symbols; the symbols and notations remain foreign and unfamiliar despite repeated attempts to memorize them.
2. Although he knows how to solve sample problems and those done in class, he cannot solve similar problems when they appear on an exam.

LITERATURE AND THE ARTS

Literature and the arts concentrate on the search for reasons, values, and interpretation in all areas of human interest and experience. Often, their focus is on subjective evaluation and interpretation of ideas expressed through literary or artistic works. Arts and humanities cover the full range of human experience. Many vehicles of expression are used to interpret the broad variety of topics covered: music, sculpture, painting, essays, poems, novels, and the body of information known as *criticism* that discusses, interprets, and evaluates each.

What to Expect

Courses in the arts and humanities are unique in the following ways:

They do not focus on a given body of information, sets of theories, facts, and principles to learn. This is unsettling to students who are accustomed to a defined, structured set of information to be learned. Instead, the focus is on ideas or their expression through various literacy or artistic modes.

Most art and humanities courses require and depend heavily on writing skills. Analyses, interpretations, critiques, or reviews of critical essays (essays written about a given literary or artistic work) are often required and are the primary means of evaluation.

Often, there is no right answer or single correct interpretation. A literary work or philosophical theory can be interpreted in numerous ways. The interpretation, however, must be reasoned, logical, and consistent.

The instructor's own values, opinions, and perspective on life are necessarily revealed as he or she interprets and discusses a particular work. Many students find this disturbing and mistakenly assume that they are forced to accept a given set of beliefs and attitudes. Actually, you are never forced to accept—but merely to understand and react to—a given philosophy.

To analyze and interpret art and literature, you must activate your feelings and imagination as well as your critical reasoning skills. You must also define your values and hold them up for comparison with those expressed in various works and those of your instructor and your classmates.

How to Read and Analyze Literature

You will encounter two basic types of reading in the field of literature and criticism. *Original works* refer to a literary piece itself: poems, articles, essays, philosophical treatises, short stories, plays, and novels. *Criticism* refers to all that has been written *about* a given original work and its author (book reviews, essays, biographies). In most introductory courses, the primary emphasis is reading and interpreting original works. However, completing a paper or assignment sometimes requires you to consult secondary sources, to read what someone else thinks of the work you are studying. The suggestions listed below apply to reading original works.

Read slowly, carefully, and more than once.   Read a work the first time simply to establish its overall content and literal meaning: What is it about, or who is doing what, when, and where? Establish the main characters, basic plot, and setting. On your second reading, focus on interpretation. Find the writer's message and think about your reactions to the work.

Annotate as you read.   Jot down your reactions, hunches, insights, feelings, and questions. Mark or underline sections you feel are important—insightful statements by characters, or sections that provide clues to meaning. Circle repeated words or images, mark where characters are described, and look for unusual techniques or style. Table 13-4 lists features that often provide important clue to meaning.

Table 13-4
LITERARY CLUES TO MEANING

Features of Language
Symbolism (objects or events that can be interpreted on several different
 levels)
Descriptive words (words that create a mental picture)
Emotionally charged words
Words and phrases with multiple meanings
Similes and metaphors (words that define by drawing a comparison)
Unusual or striking words
Repetition of words or phrases
Sarcastic or ironic statements (those that say one thing but mean another)
Characterization
What the characters say about their own thoughts, actions, motives
What the characters say about actions, motives of others (their perceptions
 of other characters)
What the characters actually do (compare this to what they say they do—
 often a character is self-deceived or naïve)
Contradictions or inconsistencies
How the writer describes the characters (detect his or her attitude toward
 them)
Organization and Structure
How the work begins, including clues about what will happen next (fore-
 shadowing)
The setting and how it changes
The mood (feeling) the writer creates
How the mood and setting compare the characters' actions
Complications or conflicts that arise
Resolution of these conflicts
Who is telling the story (narrator) and what he or she knows or does not
 know about the characters and their motives and actions
Whether the narrator is objective or biased

Look for themes and patterns. After you have read and annotated, inventory your annotations, looking for themes and patterns. Try to discover how ideas work together to suggest themes. Here are some possible themes in literature:

- ❑ Questions, issues, problems raised by the story: moral, political, philosophical, religious
- ❑ Abstract ideas: love, death, heroism, escapism
- ❑ Conflicting situations: appearance versus reality, freedom versus restraint, poverty versus wealth
- ❑ Common literary topics: self-realization, the inescapability of death, fall from innocence, search for the meaning of life

What Thought Patterns to Anticipate

In original works, the predominant thought patterns include chronological order, process, comparison and contrast, and cause and effect, as shown in Table 13-5.

How to Study and Analyze Art

Art is primarily a visual form of expression (with the exception of music). As is true in the study of literature, there are two main sources of study: the original work and criticism that discusses form, process, and style.

As you study and analyze original art forms, keep the following guidelines in mind:[1]

- ❑ Establish a first impression of and reaction to the work.
- ❑ Learn what background information is available. (Where and when was it created? What is known about the artist? Where was the work originally shown?)
- ❑ Identify, if possible, the purpose of the work. Is it intended to portray a person, show respect, display a dilemma, make a religious statement, express feelings?
- ❑ Study the title and determine how it relates to the work.
- ❑ Examine the subject matter and the characteristics of the medium used and evaluate the techniques. In drawing and painting, for example, you would consider such factors as composition (color, lines, shape), depth, and scale (relative size).
- ❑ After carefully studying the work, ask yourself three questions:
    What is the artist trying to accomplish?
    Why did he or she do what was done? This type of question will force you to examine each feature of the work closely.

❏ ❏ ❏
Thinking Critically . . . About Literature

Literature often makes use of imaginative or creative language to express meaning. Therefore, you must think critically and creatively in order to grasp the full meaning intended by the writer. Here is a brief review of the types of creative expressions used in literature:

1. **Descriptive language.** Descriptive language uses words that create a sensory impression or response. It is intended to help you create a mental picture of what the writer is describing. For example, to describe a stormy evening, a poet may write this:

   Under the thunder-dark cloud, the storm mounts, flashes, and resounds. These words give you a vivid picture of the storm and help you imagine its strength. When reading descriptive language, read slowly, allowing time for sensory impressions to register and for you to react to them.

2. **Connotative language.** Connotative language suggests meanings beyond its primary, dictionary meaning. For example, the words *crowd, mob, gang,* and *audience* all mean a group of assembled people, but their connotative meanings are quite different. A crowd implies large numbers, a mob implies unruly or disorganized behavior, and so forth. Writers select words with particular connotative meanings to create a particular feeling or evoke a particular response. Be sure to critically analyze a writer's use of connotative language to determine what effect he or she intends.

3. **Figurative language.** Figurative language is a way of describing something that makes sense on an imaginative or creative level but not on a literal or factual level. For example, the poetic lines

   A sea/
   Harsher than granite

do not mean than the sea was a rock. Instead, they suggest that the sea shares some characteristics of granite: hardness, coldness, immutability. Two common types of figurative expressions are *similes* and *metaphors.* A simile makes a direct comparison by using the words "like" or "as" (her lips were as red as a rose). A metaphor makes a comparison by directly equating the two objects (her lips were a rose).

Examples: In Michelangelo's *The Creation of Adam,* why is the creator's arm stretched toward Adam's? Why is the creator's body diagonal? Why is Adam's left leg supporting his arm? What is my response to this work and why did I feel that

Table 13-5
THOUGHT PATTERNS IN LITERATURE AND THE ARTS

Patterns	Uses	Examples
Chronological order	Sequence of events in fictional works; noting the development of various artistic or literary periods	Sequence of events in Crane's "The Open Boat"
Process	Studying the process through which writer or artist achieved his or her effect	Development of character in Thurber's "The Catbird Seat"
Comparison and contrast	Studying two or more artists, works, writers, or schools of thought	Comparing Steinbeck's and Hawthorne's use of symbolism
Cause and effect	Examining character motivation, studying effects of various literary and artistic techniques	Evaluating Hemingway's use of tone

way? *Examples:* Why do I feel sorry for the child in the photograph? Why does the portrait seem depressing? Why does that landscape seem inviting and relaxing?

How to Read Criticism

As mentioned earlier, criticism refers to written materials that discuss, interpret, and evaluate a particular work. Some students erroneously assume that criticism is negative or limited to finding fault with a work. Actually, its primary purpose is to analyze and interpret. Criticism may include both positive and negative aspects. Film and book reviews are examples of criticism. Criticism also includes scholarly works that carefully research or examine a particular aspect, theme, or approach. Often, in order to complete a term paper, you will be required to consult several critical sources. In using these sources, follow these guidelines:

❏ Read and study the original work carefully and thoroughly before you consult critical sources.

❏ Make a preliminary interpretation of the work before reading criticism. Decide what you think the work means and why it was produced. Record these ideas in note form. If you consult sources before forming your own impressions, your judgment will be colored by what you read, and you will have difficulty sorting your ideas from those you encountered as you read.

❏ Recognize that not all critics agree; you may encounter three critics who present three different interpretations of Leonardo's Mona Lisa.

❏ Although it is perfectly acceptable to revise your own interpretations based on your reading, do not immediately discard your own interpretation as soon as you encounter one that differs.

❏ Make notes on your readings, recording only key points.

Taking Lecture Notes

Lectures in literature and fine art classes are primarily intended to guide and direct you in your interpretation of original works. Instructors provide essential background information and instruct you in the various themes, conventions, and characteristics of the particular art form. When taking notes, use the following suggestions:

❏ Make notes directly on the page where the poem, story, or art re-production is printed. When an instructor discusses and inter-prets a poem, for example, the easiest way to record notes is to jot them in the margin text to the line or section of the poem to which they refer.

❏ After the lecture, try to summarize the instructor's main points; include the outstanding features of the work, various literary or artistic devices used, and predominant theme(s) identified.

EXERCISE 13-4

Directions:
Analyze the following situation and answer the questions below.

An engineering student is taking a required composition and literature course. He dislikes the course because he feels it has noth-ing to do with his major, and the readings do not address current is-sues. He feels uncomfortable in the course because he is not sure what he should learn. He has not submitted several papers, each of which required him to explore a dominant theme in a specific liter-ary work. He read the work several times but cannot identify any-thing to write about.

1. What does this student fail to understand about literature?
2. What should he do to feel more comfortable and confident about the course?
3. What steps should the student take to solve his problem writing assigned papers?

CAREER FIELDS

Career fields include many applied, currently popular fields such as computer science, allied health, computer-assisted drafting, accounting, business administration, nursing, and technologies/engineering. Career fields are usually highly technical and specialized. They most closely resemble the life and physical sciences, and much of the advice given in the section on life and physical sciences (pp. 283–289) applies here. This section will present *only* information to supplement that contained in the earlier section.

What to Expect

Career fields differ from pure sciences primarily in focus. While the emphasis in life and physical sciences is knowledge and theoretical problem solving, most career fields are concerned with direct, practical application of knowledge and skill. Expect the following:

- ❏ An emphasis on process and procedure
- ❏ More practical applications, in both textbook and lecture, of material taught
- ❏ Labs, practicums, clinical, or on-site work experience as an integral part of the course
- ❏ Grading and evaluation to be performance based. Your grade in an introductory accounting course, for example, will be based on your ability to balance a ledger
- ❏ Exactness and precision. Develop systems of methodically performing tasks so you do not miss or overlook steps

How to Study Career Fields

In studying career fields, use the following suggestions:

Learn the language of the field. Be certain to learn the specialized terminology and incorporate it into your own speech and writing. To communicate effectively on the job, you will need to speak the language of your field.

Maintain a practical focus. Whenever you learn new information or procedures, ask, "How and when will I use this information?"

Note applications of what you are learning. Since exams often test your ability to apply and use what is learned, as you read, make marginal notes indicating situations or circumstances in which the information would be useful.

Table 13-6
THOUGHT PATTERNS IN THE CAREER FIELDS

Pattern	*Uses*	*Examples*

Process	Learning and describing procedures	Nursing
		    Obtaining a radial pulse
		    Passing a nasogastric tube

Problem-solution	Practical applications; clinical or field situations	Computer science
		    Modifying a program to suit job specifications
		    Detecting a bug

What Thought Patterns to Anticipate

Process and problem-solution are the two predominant thought patterns evident in many career fields, as shown in Table 13-6.

Taking Lecture Notes

Use the following suggestions to take notes most effectively:

❏ Lectures often involve practical demonstrations. Focus on the demonstration itself, not on taking notes. Afterward, record the purpose of the demonstration and the points it was intended to emphasize.
❏ Emphasize process and procedure in your notes.
❏ Pay attention to clues your instructor provides about the use and application of information presented.

EXERCISE 13-5

Directions:
Analyze the following situation and answer the questions.

A nursing student is earning A or high B grades in Nursing I and required courses in English composition, anatomy and physiology, and psychology. However, she is failing a clinical practicum that focuses on basic procedures of patient care. She is evaluated in this course by performing procedures, such as taking a blood sample from models in the clinic under close scrutiny by her clinical instructor. Although she memorizes each procedure, step by step, she can't recall them in practical situations. She says she gets nervous and freezes up on clinical evaluations.

1. How should this student revise her learning strategies for the clinical course?
2. What can she do to avoid freezing up on evaluations?

SUMMARY

1. Each academic discipline takes a unique approach to the study of the world around us. Therefore, you must adapt your study and learning strategies to suit it.
2. This chapter presents an approach to each of five general academic disciplines:

   ❏ social sciences
   ❏ life and physical sciences
   ❏ mathematics
   ❏ literature and arts
   ❏ career fields

3. For each discipline, the chapter describes what to expect and offers suggestions for reading and studying subject matter in the field.
4. Common thought patterns are discussed, and suggestions for taking lecture notes are included for each discipline.

CLASS ACTIVITY

Directions:

Groups of four to six students should each select one of the following topics and identify how various academic disciplines might approach and study it:

Topics: 1. Cloning
         2. Television commercials
         3. Senior citizens

FURTHER ANALYSIS

Directions:

Analyze the following situations and answer the questions:

   A business major is taking a public speaking course. The primary course requirements include a midterm and final and seven required speeches. Textbook chapters are assigned and discussed in class, and guidelines for each type of speech are distributed well in advance. The class and instructor critique each speech. This student is having difficulty organizing a systematic approach to learning and study. She claims the speeches involve on-the-spot performance and require little actual study, and she is unable to anticipate what type of exam questions may be asked. Other students in the class claim the course is an "easy A," but she doesn't agree.

1. What suggestions would you offer on how to succeed in this course?
2. What strategies would you recommend for taking class notes?
3. What thought patterns might the student anticipate and use?
4. How should this student prepare for each speech?

DISCUSSION

1. Suppose you are interested in the topic of video games. How many different ways might you approach and analyze the topic? Consider how various disciplines might approach it.
2. At a certain college, a course titled Seminar in Interdisciplinary Studies is a first-semester requirement for all incoming students. The course is taught by four professors, from the departments of philosophy, physics, fine arts, and sociology. The course is intended to explore relationships among traditional liberal arts disciplines. What would be your reaction to taking such a course? Of what value do you think it would be? What study and learning strategies might a course of this type require?
3. Suppose you are fulfilling a physical education requirement by taking a course in bowling. What general academic discipline area do you think the course most closely resembles? Justify your answer.
4. A student is studying a modern language, Spanish, for the first time. What should she expect; how should she approach the course; what thought patterns might help her learn the material?

FURTHER READING

Abrams, M. H. A *Glossary of Literary Terms.* 6th ed. New York: Holt, 1988.

Barnet, Sylvan. *A Short Guide to Writing About Art.* 4th ed. Boston: Little, Brown, 1992.

Maxwell, Martha. *Improving Student Learning Skills.* San Francisco: Jossey-Bass, 1979. "How to Study Chemistry" and "How to Study Physics," 422–442.

McWhorter, Kathleen T. *Academic Reading.* 2d ed. Glenview, IL: Scott, Foresman, 1993.

Tobias, Sheila. *Overcoming Math Anxiety.* New York: Norton, 1994.

Exams: Thinking Under Pressure

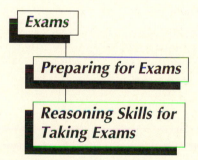

Exams

Preparing for Exams

Reasoning Skills for Taking Exams

14

❑ ❑ ❑ ━━━━━━━━━━━━━━━━━━━━━━━━━━━

Preparing for Exams

Learning Objectives

Organize your review

Approach study thematically

Develop strategies for specific types of exams and for
specific disciplines

Quizzes, midterm examinations, and finals are important aspects
of most college courses. Practically, they are often the basis on
which grades are awarded. However, they are also valuable thinking and
learning experiences. Quizzes or frequent tests force you to keep up with
reading and assignments and provide regular feedback on the quality of
your learning. Longer examinations require you to consolidate and integrate concepts and information. Final exams force you to step back and
retrace the direction of the course, noticing overall trends and patterns
and integrating your learning.

Many students spend a great deal of time preparing for an exam, yet
never seem to earn top grades. Some report that they spend more time
studying than students who do earn the highest grades. Grades, however,
have little to do with the *amount* of time spent studying. What is important is *how* study time is spent. The strategies and techniques you use to
prepare for an exam primarily determine the quality of your learning. The

purpose of this chapter is to show you how to prepare for exams, earning the largest dividends for the time you spend.

ORGANIZING YOUR REVIEW

The following suggestions will help you to approach your study in an organized, systematic manner.

Organize Your Time

The amount of time you will need to spend is determined by your familiarity with the material and the amount of material the exam covers. In general, the longer the interval between exams, the longer you will need to spend in preparation. Organize your review sessions, using the following suggestions:

Review at least one week in advance of the exam. Set aside specific times for daily review. If the exam is in a difficult or troublesome subject, schedule extra study time.

Spend time organizing your review. Make a list of all chapters, notes, and instructors' handouts that need to be reviewed. Divide the material by topic, planning what you will review during each session (see Thematic Study, pp. 309–310).

Review again the night before the exam. Reserve time the night before the examination for a final, complete review. Do not study new material during the session. Instead, review the most difficult material, testing your recall from memory of important facts or information for possible essay questions.

Attend the Class Before the Exam

Be sure to attend the class prior to the exam. Cutting class to spend the time studying, although tempting, is a mistake. During this class, the instructor may give a brief review of the material to be covered or offer last-minute review suggestions. Have you heard instructors make statements such as, "Be sure to look over . . . " or "Pay particular attention to . . . " prior to exams? Listen carefully to the instructor's answers to students' questions: these answers may provide clues about what the exam will emphasize.

Find out whether the examination will be objective, essay, or a combination of both. Also check your notes from the first several classes; some instructors describe their exams as part of their course introduction. If your instructor does not specify the type of exam, ask during or after class.

Find out as much as possible about what the examination will cover. Usually, your instructor will either announce the exam topics or specify the time span that the exam will cover. Some instructors expect you to recall text and lecture material; others expect you to summarize using their perspective on a particular subject; still others encourage you to think, discuss, recall, and disagree with the ideas and information they have presented. You can usually tell what to expect from quizzes and how classes have been conducted.

Attend Review Classes

For final exams, particularly in mathematics or the sciences, professors occasionally offer optional review sessions. Be sure to attend these sessions: Time spent there is likely to be more productive than time spent studying alone.

EXERCISE 14-1

Directions:
Plan a review schedule for an upcoming exam. Include material you will study and when you will study it.

Identify What to Study

In preparing for an exam, use all sources of information, as shown in Table 14-1.

Assess Your Preparedness

Once you have collected and briefly looked over the materials listed in Table 14-1, you can establish how well prepared you are and how much review and study time are necessary. If you are not caught up in your reading, underlining, and homework assignments, make a list of what you have to do. Using this list, decide how to spend the first portion of your remaining study time. Try to get caught up as quickly as possible; double or triple your efforts to do so. Keep in mind that this is work you should have completed by now and, at this point, it is diminishing the time you have left for review.

❑ ❑ ❑
Thinking Critically . . . About Group Study

Studying with friends or classmates is an option that you should weigh seriously. Some students find it highly effective; others report that it is time-consuming and does not produce results. After reading the following advantages and disadvantages, decide whether group study suits your learning style and study demands.

Advantages. Group study forces you to become actively involved with the course content. Talking about, reacting to, and discussing the material aid learning.

One of the best ways to learn something is to explain it to someone else. Explaining an idea forces you to think and test your own understanding. The repetition of explaining something you understand also strengthens your learning. Group study exposes you to other students' perceptions of what is important, how the material is related, and how it can be best learned.

Disadvantages. Unless everyone is serious, group study sessions can often turn into social events where very little study occurs. Moreover, studying with the wrong people can produce negative attitudes that will work against you. (The "None of us understand this and we can't all fail" attitude is dangerous.) By studying with someone who has not read the material carefully or attended class regularly, you will waste time reviewing basic definitions and facts that you already know, instead of focusing on more challenging topics.

Also try to identify your strengths and weaknesses. Identify topics for which you feel unprepared and lack confidence as well as those that you have mastered thoroughly. For example, a student taking Western Civilization identified several topics in history that she felt were her weakest: the Protestant Reformation, exploration and colonization, and absolutism. Then she concentrated on these periods, organizing and consolidating events and trends for each.

EXERCISE 14-2

Directions:
For an upcoming exam, assess how well you are prepared by making a list of topics about which you feel confident and another list of those that will require further study.

Table 14-1
REVIEW STRATEGIES

Type of Material	Suggestions for Review
Textbook chapters	Reread underlining and marking.
	Review chapter summary.
	Use your outlines, notes, summaries, or maps.
Lecture notes	Reread and mark important information.
	Use recall clues to self-test.
Supplementary assignments	Review purpose and relationship to course content.
	Review underlining or summary notes.
Previous tests and quizzes	Mark all items you missed and look for a pattern of error.
	Identify types of questions you miss.
	Identify topics you need to study further.
Instructor's handouts and class assignments	Note purpose of each item and to which lecture they correspond.
	Identify key points emphasized.

THEMATIC STUDY

Most students approach their study and review for exams in convenient but arbitrary units. During a study session, they may review a specific number of pages or a given number of lecture notes. While this approach is systematic, it is not the most conducive to learning. A more meaningful approach is to integrate text and lecture material using a method called *thematic study.*

In thematic study, you focus on topics, or themes, rather than on an arbitrarily chosen number of pages or chapters. It involves pulling together all available material on a given topic and learning it as an organized body of information. In essence, thematic study means studying by topic. For instance, for a macroeconomics test, a student's topics included aggregate demand and aggregate supply, real and nominal GNP, and indexes to measure price changes.

Why Thematic Study Is Effective

Thematic study forces you to think in the following ways:

❏ It forces you to decide what topics are important, to sift and sort and make decisions about course content.

❏ It forces you to integrate information, recognize similarities, and reconcile differences in approach and focus between text and lecture.

❏ It forces you to organize the information from a variety of sources into a meaningful set.

❏ It forces you to practice the skills that you are required to use when you take exams. Exams require you to draw upon information from all sources. Thematic study forces you to do this in advance; consequently, you are better prepared when you take an exam.

Selecting Themes

The key to selecting worthwhile, important themes is your ability to grasp an overview of the course and understand how and where specific pieces of information fit the big picture. To get an overview of the course, try the following suggestions:

Think about how and why the material was covered in the order it was presented. How does one class lecture relate to the next? To what larger theme are the lectures connected? For class lectures, check the course outline or syllabus that was distributed at the beginning of the course. Since it lists major topics and suggests the order in which they will be covered, your syllabus will be useful in discovering patterns.

Focus on the progression of ideas in the textbook. Study the table of contents to see the connection between chapters you have read. Often chapters are grouped into sections based on similar content.

Study relationships. Ask yourself: "To what is the information presented in this chapter leading?" "How does this chapter relate to the next?" Suppose in psychology you had studied a chapter on personality traits; next, you were assigned a chapter on abnormal and deviant behavior. In this situation, the chapter on personality establishes the standard or norm by which abnormal and deviant behavior are determined.

Do not let facts and details camouflage important questions, issues, and problems. Remember to ask yourself What does this mean? How is this information useful? How can this be applied to various situations? Once you have identified the literal content, stop, react, and evaluate its use, value, and application.

Identify predominant thought patterns. Evident in both text and lecture material are patterns that point directly to key topics. For instance, in chemistry, a student identified problem-solution as a key pattern; then he made a list of types of problems and systematically reviewed and practiced solving each type.

EXERCISE 14-3

Directions:

Assume you were to have an examination based on the first four chapters in this book. List the major topics you would review during thematic study.

EXERCISE 14-4

Directions:

For an upcoming exam in one of your courses, identify several topics for thematic study.

How to Prepare Study Sheets

The study sheet system is a way of organizing and summarizing complex information by preparing mini-outlines on each topic. It is most useful for reviewing material that is interrelated and needs to be learned as a whole rather than as separate facts. Several types of information should be reviewed on study sheets:

- ❑ Theories and principles
- ❑ Complex events with multiple causes and effects
- ❑ Controversial issues—pros and cons
- ❑ Summaries of philosophical issues
- ❑ Trends in ideas or data
- ❑ Groups of related facts

The sample study sheet in Figure 14-1 was made by a student preparing for an exam in a communications media course. You will notice that the study sheet organizes the advantages and disadvantages of the various types of media advertising and presents them in a form that invites easy comparison of the various media forms.

To prepare a study sheet, first select the information to be learned. Then outline the information, using as few words as possible. Group together important points, from both your text and lecture notes, that relate to each topic. Try to use one or more thought patterns as a means of organization.

Figure 14-1
A Sample Study Sheet

Forms of Media Advertising

Media form	Advantages	Disadvantages
1. Newspapers	- widely read - regional flexibility - offer use of inserts	- little buyer selectivity
2. Magazines	- better appearance than newspapers - longer life - people do reread	- advance commitment required - may have to buy entire national circulation
3. TV	- reaches 95% of households - can produce favorable product images - can choose stations to carry the ad	- commercial clutter (must compete with other ads)
4. Radio	- inexpensive - can afford high level of repetition - geographic selectivity - can change ads frequently and easily	- short lived (can't reread) - people don't listen to the ads
5. Outdoor Advertising	- large amount of repetition - low cost per exposure	- copy must be short

The computer is an excellent aid to thematic study. If, as suggested in Chapter 10, you are able to type both your textbook and lecture notes into a computer file, then the preparation of study sheets is easily done. Using the word processor's copy function, you can compile information from various sets of text and lecture notes on a given topic.

EXERCISE 14-5

Directions:

Prepare a study sheet for one of the themes you identified in Exercise 14-3.

Review Strategies

Once you have developed study sheets, the next step is to develop effective review strategies. Many students review by rereading and rereading their notes and text underlining. Rereading is a passive, inactive approach that seldom prepares you well for any exam. Instead, review for an exam should be a dress rehearsal for the exam itself. Think of a theater company preparing to perform a play. In rehearsal they simulate, as closely as possible, the conditions of their actual performance. Likewise, in preparing for an exam you should simulate the actual exam situation. You must, in effect, test yourself by asking questions and answering them. Since the exam is written, it is helpful to *write,* not just to mentally construct answers.

Asking the Right Questions

As you review, be sure to ask questions at each level of thinking: knowledge, comprehension, application, analysis, synthesis, and evaluation. Refer to Chapter 1 for a review of each of these levels. Refer to Table 14-2 for sample questions you could ask at each level if you were preparing for an exam on the media advertising material covered in Figure 14-1.

Table 14-2
SAMPLE QUESTIONS BASED ON STUDY SHEET IN FIGURE 14-1

Level of Thinking	Sample Questions
Knowledge and comprehension	What percentage of households does TV reach? Which media offer regional flexibility?
Application	What types of products could be most effectively advertised in each media form?
Analysis	Why don't people listen to the ads on the radio?
Synthesis	What are the similarities between radio and newspaper advertising?
Evaluation	How did the author decide what is low cost?

Knowledge and Comprehension Questions. These levels require recall of facts; remembering dates, names, definitions, and formulae falls into these categories. The five "W" questions—Who? What? Where? When? and Why? are useful to ask.

Application Questions. This level of thinking requires you to use or apply information. The two following questions best test this level:

In what practical situations would this information be useful?

What does this have to do with what I already know about the subject?

Analysis Questions. Analysis involves seeing relationships. Ask questions that test your ability to take ideas apart, discover cause-effect relationships, and discover how things work.

Synthesis Questions. This level involves pulling ideas together. Ask questions that force you to look at similarities and differences.

Evaluation Questions. This level involves making judgments and assessing value or worth. Ask questions that challenge sources, accuracy, long-term value, importance, and so forth.

How To Test Yourself.

To test yourself, follow these steps.

- ❏ Review each study sheet several times, asking questions at the various levels of thinking.
- ❏ As you find information that is difficult, unclear, or unfamiliar, mark it for later reference and further study.
- ❏ Jot appropriate questions in the margin or on the back of the study sheet. You may wish to refer to these as your predict questions for essay exams (see p. 317).
- ❏ Write answers to each of your questions. The process of formulating a written response clarifies your thinking and helps you learn the information.
- ❏ Critique your answers. First verify the correctness and completeness of factual information. Then analyze and think about your response. Did you really answer the questions? What related information might you have included? What are the implications of what you have said?
- ❏ Review both questions and answers periodically.

Some students find it useful to write their questions using a computer. Each question is entered in a test preparation file, and answers are typed on a separate line below. Some information can be copied from lecture and/or textual note files to save time. Review of questions and answers is simple using the scroll function. You can position each question at the bottom of the screen, without the answer showing. Then test your recall by writing the answer (on paper) or through mental review. Finally, to check your recall, scroll ahead to review the answer.

EXERCISE 14-6

Directions:
Choose a textbook chapter on which you are currently working. Write questions at each level for several main topics covered.

STRATEGIES FOR PARTICULAR TYPES OF EXAMS

While basic study and review strategies are the same for all types of examinations, there are specific techniques to use as you prepare for objective exams, essay exams, quantitative exams, open-book exams, take-home exams, and final exams.

Preparing for Objective Exams

Objective exams are those that require a brief right or wrong answer. These include multiple choice, true/false, matching, and fill-in-the-blank.

Objective tests often require mastery of a great deal of factual data—information at the knowledge and comprehension levels. Often, too, test items require you to apply, analyze, synthesize, and evaluate these facts. An effective way to prepare for an exam in which a large amount of factual learning is required is to use an index card system.

Using Index Cards

Step 1. Using 3 × 5 inch index cards (or small sheets of paper), write names of terms, laws, principles, or concepts on the front of the card and facts and details about them on the back. To review the significance of important events in a history course, for example, write the event on the front of one card, its importance on the back. To learn definitions, record the word on the front and its meaning on the back. The sample index cards shown in Figure 14-2 were prepared for an economics examination.
Step 2. To study each of these cards, look at the front and try to recall what is written on the back. Then, turn the card over to see if you were correct. As you work, sort them into two stacks—those you know and those you cannot remember.

Step 3. Go back through the stack that you did not know, study each, and retest yourself, again sorting the cards into two stacks. Continue with this procedure until you are satisfied that you have learned all the information. Review the index cards several times a day on each of the three or four days before the exam. On the day of the exam, do a final, once-through review so that the information is fresh in your mind. Several sample index cards are shown in Figure 14-2.

This index card system has several advantages. Writing helps you learn, so preparing the cards is also a learning process. You spent time learning what you do not know and avoid wasting time reviewing already learned material. Cards are more effective than lists of material. If you study a list of items, you run the risk of learning them in a fixed order. When a single item appears out of order on the exam, you may not remember it. Sorting and occasionally shuffling your index cards eliminate

Figure 14-2
Sample Index Cards

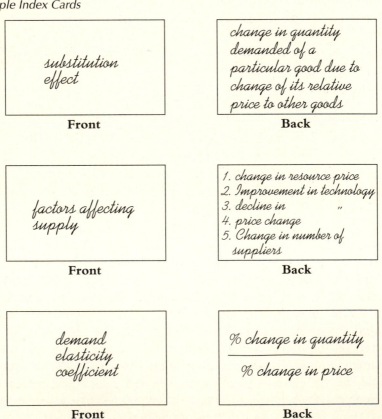

this problem. You can carry cards in a pocket or purse and study them in spare moments.

EXERCISE 14-7

Directions:

Choose a course in which you expect to take an objective examination. Prepare a set of index cards for one chapter you have studied.

Preparing for Essay Examinations

Essay examinations demand complete recall; you begin with a blank sheet of paper on which you must answer the question. Reviewing for an essay exam is a process of concentrated thematic study.

Predict possible questions. You have already learned how to identify important themes or topics. The next step is to formulate actual questions that might be asked about each theme. Predicting essay questions is a process of analyzing the relationships that exist within the material (see Chapter 7) and writing questions that concern these relationships. Some professors provide strong clues about essay questions, or they indicate general topics to review. As you predict questions, be sure to include all course material; avoid trying to second-guess the instructor as to the content of the exam.

Write rough draft answers. Once you have identified possible exam questions, the next step is to practice answering them. Do not take the time to write out full, complete sentences. Instead collect and organize the information you would include in your answer and record it in brief note or outline form, listing the information you would include. Figure 14-3 shows a sample essay question and a rough draft answer.

Use key word outlines. As a convenient way to remember what your draft answer includes, make a key word outline of your answer. For each time in your draft, identify a key word that will trigger your memory of that idea. Then list and learn these key words. Together, these words form a mini-outline of topics and ideas to include in an essay on this topic. A key word outline is shown in Figure 14-4.

Predicting and answering possible examination questions is an effective technique for several reasons. Predicting forces you to analyze the material, not just review it. Drafting answers forces you to express ideas in written form. Through writing you will realize relationships, organize your thoughts, and discover the best way to present them.

Figure 14-3
Sample Essay Question and Answer

Question: Discuss the organized social life of monkeys and apes.

Rough draft response:

Social Structure developed for following advantages:

   group can spot predators & rally a defense

   foraging for food is more efficient if done in groups

   access to opposite sex is assured for reproduction

   groups permit socialization and learning from elders

Social structure organized according to following principles

   infants and young are dependent on mother

      longer than most animals

      allows for learned behavior to occur

      "   " juvenile play - imp't for

         social bonds as adults

   adults hold social rank in group

      males dominate

      hierarchy often more significant among

         males than females

Sexual bonding occurs among mating adults

      breeding occurs only during specific seasons

      males are aware of estrous cycle of female

   grooming - acceptable form of social contact

      functions 1. remove parasites

         2. establish and maintain

            social relationships

You will save time while taking the exam. If you have already collected and organized your thoughts, then you can use the time those processes would have taken to prepare a more complete, carefully written answer.

The computer is a useful tool for predicting and answering essay exam questions. The word processing function enables you to rearrange information, thereby experimenting with various means of organizing and consolidating information. The various typographic features (boldface print, italics, underlining) enable you to add visually striking (and easy to

Figure 14-4
Sample Key word Outline

Advantage
   Defense
   Food
   Reproduction
   Learning
Principles
   Dependency
   Social Rank
   Sexual Bonding
   Grooming

remember) points of emphasis. For example, you might underline key points or place key words in boldface print.

EXERCISE 14-8

Directions:
Select a course in which you expect to have an essay examination or an essay question on your next exam. Predict and record possible essay questions. Then choose one question and prepare a rough draft answer and key word outline.

Preparing for Open-Book Exams

Open-book exams are those that allow you to refer to your textbook or lecture notes during the exam. At first, this type of exam may seem easy, almost a giveaway. Some students make the mistake of doing little or no preparation. Actually, an open-book exam is often an essay exam in which the instructor will assess your ability to interpret, evaluate, react to, or apply a given body of information. The focus is on your ability to think about and use available information.

Organization of information is the key to preparing for open-book exams. Time is usually limited and often a key factor in taking an open-book exam. If you have to waste time on an exam searching for a piece of information, it can affect the quality of your answer. Study sheets (see pp.

311–313) are effective because they draw together and organize information by topic. One useful addition to your study sheets is page references, both from your texts and lecture notes, allowing you to check your source for information on a particular topic, if needed.

Preparing for Take-Home Exams

Take-home exams are a variation of the open-book exam. However, instead of requiring you to complete the exam within a specific class time, the instructor allows you to leave the classroom and work on it for a specified period of time, usually several days. Usually, more extensive, complete answers are expected. Some instructors may expect research as well. A more carefully written, concise, and clear response is expected than for in-class writing. Be sure at the time the exam is distributed to clarify, as best you can, what is expected in terms of length, sources to be used, and format. If the exam consists of only one question, the take-home exam closely resembles the assignment of a paper in terms of what is expected (see Chapter 16 for suggestions on writing papers).

Preparing for Problem-Solution Exams

Exams in mathematics and in some of the sciences, such as chemistry and physics, consist primarily or exclusively of problems to solve. Here are a few suggestions on how to prepare for such exams:

- ❏ Organize problems by types, and outline strategies for solving each type. Anticipate possible variations on each type.
- ❏ Prepare study sheets that include formulas and principles. Also include conversions and constants.
- ❏ Review by practicing solving problems—not by reading through sample problems and their solutions.
- ❏ Identify types of problems with which you have had trouble either on homework assignments or on quizzes, and spend extra time with these. Try to identify at what stage or step in the solution process your difficulty occurs.
- ❏ Give yourself a practice exam, selecting items from homework or previous quizzes. Complete the exam within the same time limit you expect to take the actual exam.

Preparing for Final Exams

Final exams differ from other types of exams in two respects: They are longer and more comprehensive, covering a larger body of material.

What is more important, however, is that they often emphasize the integration of course content. To prepare for final exams, use the following suggestions:

Begin your study well in advance. Finals all occur roughly within a one-week time period, usually immediately following the last class of the term.

Condense all course materials. Prepare a master study sheet from your individual study sheets, drawing together and relating various topics.

Focus on large ideas. Concentrate on concepts, trends, historical perspectives, principles, methods, patterns, and long-range effects—instead of individual facts. Try to identify themes that run through much or most of the course content. The theme of self-identity, for example, may pervade a Native American history course; a theme of revolution and change may be the focus of a course on eighteenth-century American literature.

Review outlines of course content. Refer once again to your course syllabus or outline and your textbook's table of contents to reestablish an overview of the course. In preparing for a final exam, recall the "big picture" in order to avoid the mistake of becoming lost or overwhelmed by detail.

Anticipate essay questions. If your final will include essays, try to predict and answer these questions. Essays on finals often are targeted to areas of major emphasis. As a starting point, ask yourself these questions:

> What key ideas, themes, or processes has the professor been discussing all semester?
>
> Where does everything seem to be leading?
>
> What long-lasting, beneficial ideas, processes, or principles have we learned?
>
> To what topics has the professor devoted considerable time in class lectures or discussions?

Review previous exams and quizzes. Identify topics and areas of weakness for more intensive review. Look for patterns, trends, types of questions, and areas of emphasis.

EXERCISE 14-9

Directions:
Using all the material you have covered up to this point in one of your courses, predict several essay questions that might appear on a final examination in that course.

STRATEGIES FOR SPECIFIC ACADEMIC DISCIPLINES

A key to becoming a top student is to study for each exam differently. Since each course, each instructor, each lecture is different, each exam will also be different and require slightly different types of preparation. An examination in a literature course is quite unlike an examination in business management; an exam in mathematics is very different from one in political science. Table 14-3 offers suggestions for preparing for examinations in various academic disciplines. As you read this table, keep in mind that these strategies are general guidelines, not rules to follow. They may not always work, depending on the specific course, how the professor conducts it, and the types of exams given.

EXERCISE 14-10

Directions:
List the courses in which you are currently enrolled. For each course, predict the next type of exam you will have and the major topics it will cover. Then describe how you will approach each, emphasizing how you will modify your approach to suit the subject matter.

SUMMARY

1. Quizzes, tests, and exams are valuable thinking and learning experiences. The strategies and techniques you use to prepare primarily determine the quality of your learning.
2. A well-organized review is essential to effective learning. It involves

   ❏ organizing your time
   ❏ deciding how you study
   ❏ selecting what to study

3. Thematic study, an approach that integrates textbook and lecture material, focuses on topics or themes. Using thematic study involves reorganizing material on study sheets and using them to self-test.
4. Self-testing concentrates on five levels of questioning:

   ❏ knowledge and comprehension

Table 14-3

TIPS ON STUDYING FOR EXAMS IN VARIOUS ACADEMIC DISCIPLINES

Academic Discipline	Emphasis/Focus of Study
Mathematics	Practice solving problems.
	Identify troublesome problem types and concentrate on them.
	Try to anticipate variations on general problem types.
	Memorize formulas.
Sciences	Make lists of themes and principles covered; consider various situations in which these may be applied.
	Identify types of problems you expect to be covered and practice solving them.
	In the life sciences, be certain to learn and understand classifications.
Career fields	Focus on applications: How is the information to be used?
	Anticipate questions that apply information by hypothetical situations or case studies.
	Learn procedures and processes and distinguish when each is appropriate.
Literature and the arts	Focus on trends and patterns demonstrated through series of works.
	Be certain to learn full names of works and correct spelling of authors' or artists' names.
	Compare and contrast various works and authors or artists.
	Expect most exams to require essay answers.
	Note characteristics and features of particular works as well as themes, significant issues.
Social sciences	Exams often contain both objective and essay questions.
	Objective exams test basic knowledge of theories, principles, concepts; essay questions may be on applications or a case study.
	Learn specialized vocabulary.
	Focus on relationships: comparisons and contrasts, cause and effects, sequences.

❏ application
❏ analysis
❏ synthesis
❏ evaluation

5. A separate set of study techniques suits each type of exam:

❏ objective
❏ essay
❏ quantitative
❏ open-book
❏ take-home
❏ final exams

6. Different academic disciplines require different strategies for study and review.

CLASS ACTIVITY

Directions:

Each student should bring a copy of a quiz or exam he or she has already taken in another course. If possible, select one that includes an essay question. Also bring your textbook and lecture notes that correspond. (If your instructors do not allow you to keep completed exams, try to recall and jot down an essay question from one of your exams.) Small groups of students (three or four per group) should examine textbook chapters and corresponding lecture notes on which the exam was based, without looking at the exam. For each set of materials it reviews, each group should do the following.

1. Identify topics for thematic study (based on table of contents, prereading of textbook chapters, and skimming of lectures notes).
2. Discuss what type(s) of exams seem appropriate for the material.
3. List topics, definitions, and types of problems that would make good exam questions.
4. Predict possible essay questions, if appropriate.
5. For each of the steps above, the person who took the examination may verify, confirm, or reject the group's response by referring to the actual exam.

FURTHER ANALYSIS

A freshman student is carrying a normal load of four courses: English composition, calculus, psychology, and first-year accounting. He works part-time at a nearby convenience store. Throughout the semester he has maintained a low C average in each course. He owes his barely average grades to a verbal-auditory learning style that enables him to take good lecture notes and to a good memory of what was said in class, which allowed him to pass hour-long exams. He has done little with the textbook assignments except to read each once quickly, spending about two hours a week on each course.

Now it is the week before final exams. In calculus, he knows the exam will be composed entirely of problems to solve. In psychology, he expects multiple choice and short answer questions and one essay question. In English, he will have a take-home final, and in accounting, he expects some multiple choice but more emphasis on practical problems. He realizes that he can no longer recall each lecture, especially those from the first half of the course, and that he cannot rely on memory to handle final exams.

Eight days remain until finals begin, and the student is scheduled to work 20 hours at his job. He thinks he is best prepared for calculus and least prepared for psychology.

1. What serious changes should the student consider making to his daily schedule?
2. What study and review schedule would you recommend to give him the best chance of passing each of his courses?
3. What study and review strategies would you recommend for *each* course?

DISCUSSION

1. Explain why you agree or disagree with the following strategy for preparing for an exam: "Learn everything that the professor particularly emphasized, and become familiar with the remainder as best you can."
2. You should have a fairly good idea of the grade you will earn on an exam before you take it. Agree or disagree.
3. Describe a situation in which you found group study particularly effective or particularly ineffective?

4. What types of exams do you handle best? Which are most difficult? Explain these differences in reference to your learning style (see Chapter 6).
5. How do you know when you are well prepared for an exam?
6. How can you improve your performance on exams?

FOR FURTHER READING

Pauk, Walter, and J. Millman, *How to Take Tests.* New York: McGraw, 1969.

Wark, David M., and Rona F. Flippo. "Preparing for and Taking Tests." in *Teaching Reading and Study Strategies,* Rona F. Flippo and David C. Caverly, eds. Newark, DE: International Reading Association, 1991. 294–338.

15

Reasoning Skills for Taking Exams

Learning Objectives

Approach exams with an advantage

Develop reasoning skills for objective exams

Learn techniques for writing effective essay exam answers

Control test anxiety

Answering examination questions, both essay and objective types, demands keen thinking and reasoning skills. These skills often distinguish top students from hard working, above average ones, or the A students from the B students. This chapter is intended to show you how to approach exams as tasks of thinking and reasoning. If you follow the suggestions offered, your performance on examinations should improve, and you will approach exams more confidently, aware of the skills each type of exam question requires. Rate your present level of skill in taking exams by completing the questionnaire shown in Figure 15-1.

Figure 15-1
Rate Your Test-Taking Strategies

Directions:
Respond to each of the following statements by checking "Always," "Usually," or "Never."

	Always	Usually	Never
1. Do you preview your entire exam paper before beginning?	❏	❏	❏
2. Do you allocate and keep track of time while taking the exam?	❏	❏	❏
3. Do you review the exam once you've finished?	❏	❏	❏
4. Do you avoid changing answers frequently unless you are certain that your first answer is wrong?	❏	❏	❏
5. Do you always read all of the choices on a multiple choice exam before choosing the answer?	❏	❏	❏
6. Do you use the point value of short answer questions as a guide to how much information to provide?	❏	❏	❏
7. Do you read the directions before beginning the exam?	❏	❏	❏
8. Do you prepare a brief outline before writing an essay question answer?	❏	❏	❏
9. Are your essay exam answers neat, organized, and grammatically correct?	❏	❏	❏
10. Do you look for clues in essay questions that suggest how to organize your answer?	❏	❏	❏

STARTING WITH AN ADVANTAGE

One key to success on any type of examination is to approach it in a confident, organized, and systematic manner. Unless you feel as if you have the situation under your control, you will probably not do well on the exam, regardless of how much you have prepared or how well you think and reason. Here are several useful tips to give you an important advantage.

Time Your Arrival Carefully

Arrive at the examination room a few minutes early, in time to get a seat and get organized before the instructor arrives. If you are late, you may miss instructions and feel rushed as you begin the exam. If you arrive too early (15 minutes ahead), you risk anxiety induced by panic-stricken students who are questioning each other, trading last-minute memory tricks, and worrying about how difficult the exam will be.

Sit in the Front of the Room

The most practical place to sit in an exam is in the front. There, you often receive the test first and get a head start. Also, it is easier to concentrate and avoid distractions at the front of the room. At the back, you are exposed to distractions such as a student dropping papers, someone whispering, or the person in front who is already two pages ahead of you.

Preview the Exam

Before you start to answer any of the questions, quickly page through the exam, noticing the directions, the length, the type of questions, the general topics covered, and the number of points the questions are worth. Previewing provides an overview of the whole exams and helps to eliminate the panic.

Plan Your Time

After previewing, you will know the numbers and types of questions included. The next step is to estimate how much time you should spend on each part of the exam, using the point distribution as your guide. If, for example, an exam has 30 multiple choice questions worth 1 point each and 2 essay questions worth a total of 70 points, you should spent twice as much time on the essay questions as on the multiple choice items. If the point distribution is not indicated on the test booklet, ask the instructor. As you plan your time, allow three to four minutes at the end of the exam to read through what you have done, answering questions you skipped and making any necessary corrections or changes. To keep track of time, always wear a watch.

If you are taking an exam with the question and point distribution shown below, how would you divide your time? Assume the total exam time is 50 minutes.

❏ ❏ ❏

Type of question	Number of questions	Total points
Multiple choice	25	25
True/False	20	20
Essay	1	55

❏ ❏ ❏

You probably should divide your time as indicated.

❏ ❏ ❏

Previewing	1–2 minutes
Multiple choice	10 minutes
True/False	10 minutes
Essay	25 minutes
Review	3–4 minutes

❏ ❏ ❏

Avoid Reading Too Much into the Question

Most instructors word their questions so that what is expected is clear. A common mistake students make is to read more into the question than is asked for. To avoid this error, read the question several times, paying attention to how it is worded. If you are uncertain of what is asked for, try to relate the question to the course content, specifically the material you have studied. Do not anticipate hidden meanings or trick questions.

EXERCISE 15-1

Directions:

For each of the exams described below, estimate approximately how you would divide your time:

1. Time limit: 75 minutes

Type of question	Number of questions	Total points	Minutes
Multiple choice	20	40	—
Matching	10	10	—
Essay	2	50	—

2. Time limit: 40 minutes

Type of question	Number of questions	Total points	
True/False	15	30	—
Fill-in-the-blanks	10	30	—
Short answer	10	40	—

REASONING SKILLS FOR OBJECTIVE EXAMS

The most common types of objective exam questions are multiple choice and true/false, although some instructors include matching and fill-in-the-blank items as well.

General Suggestions

Before we examine particular types of objective exams, here are a few general suggestions to follow in approaching all types of objective exams: **Read the directions.** Before answering any questions, read the directions. Often, an instructor may want the correct answer marked in a particular way (underlined rather than circled). The directions may contain crucial information that you must be aware of in order to answer the questions correctly. In the items below, if you did not read directions and assumed the test questions were of the usual type, you could lose a considerable number of points.

> *True/False Directions:* Read each statement. If the statement is true, mark a T in the blank to the left of the item. If the statement is false, add and/or subtract words that will make the statement correct.

Multiple Choice Directions: Circle all the choices that correctly complete the statement.

Leave nothing blank. Before turning in your exam, check through it to be sure you have answered every question. If you have no idea about the correct answer to a question, guess. You might be right! On a true/false test, your chances of being correct are 50 percent; on a four-choice multiple choice question, the odds are 25 percent. The odds improve if you can eliminate one or two of the choices.

Students frequently turn in tests with some items unanswered because they leave difficult questions blank, planning to return to them later. Then, in the rush to finish, they forget them. To avoid this problem, when you are uncertain, choose what looks like the best answer, and mark the question number with an X or checkmark; the, if you have time at the end of the exam, give it further thought. If you run out of time, you will have an answer marked.

Look for clues. If you encounter a difficult question, choose what seems to be the best answer, mark the question so that you can return to it, and keep the item in mind as you go through the rest of the exam. Sometimes you will see some piece of information later in the exam that reminds you of a fact or idea. For example, a psychology student could not recall a definition of behaviorism for a short-answer question. Later on the examination, a multiple choice item mentioned the psychologist Skinner. The student remembered that Skinner was a behaviorist and knew enough about him to reason out an answer to the short-answer item. At other times, you may notice a piece of information that, if true, contradicts an answer you had already chosen.

Don't change answers without a good reason. When reviewing your answers during an exam, don't make a change unless you have a reason for doing so. If a later test item forces your recall of information for a previous item, change your answer.

True/False Tests: Making Judgments

True/false tests require you to make judgments, based on your knowledge and information about the subject, about the correctness of each item. The following suggestions will help you make more accurate judgments and reason the answer with a higher degree of accuracy:

Watch for qualifying words and phrases. Watch for words that qualify or change the meaning of a statement; often just one word makes it true or false. Consider for a moment a simplified example:

❑ All students are engineering majors.
❑ Some students are engineering majors.

Of course, the first statement is false, whereas the second is true. In each statement, only one word determined whether the statement was true or false. While the words and statements are much more complicated on most true/false exams, you will find that one word often determines whether a statement is true or false.

Examples:

❑ *All* paragraphs must have a stated main idea.
❑ Spelling, punctuation, and handwriting *always* affect the grade given to an essay answer.
❑ When taking notes on a lecture, try to write down *everything* the speaker says.

In each of the examples, the word in italics modifies—or limits—the truth of each statement. When reading a true/false question, look carefully for limiting words such as *all, absolutely, some, none, never, completely, only always, usually, frequently, most of the time.* Close attention to these words may earn you several points on an exam.

Read two-part statements carefully. Occasionally, you may find a statement with two or more parts. In answering these items, remember that both or all parts of the statement must be true in order for it to be correctly marked "True." If part of the statement is true and another part is false, as in the following example, then mark the statement "False."

> The World Health Organization (WHO) has been successful in its campaign to eliminate smallpox and malaria.

While it is true that WHO has been successful in eliminating smallpox, malaria is still a world health problem and has not been eliminated. Since only part of this statement is true, it should be marked "False."

EXERCISE 15-2

Directions:
Read each of the following statements and underline the portion that is not true:

1. Although thinking is a single-dimensional skill, most students can improve their thinking skills.

2. Patterns are difficult to recognize in most college lectures, but it is important to record as many key points as possible.
3. Problem solving and decision making are similar processes; each depends on the other for success.
4. Because textbooks are highly structured, it is usually possible to learn efficiently by rereading.

Look for negative and double-negative statements. Test items that use negative words or word parts can be confusing. Words such as *no, none, never, not, cannot* and prefixes such as *in-, dis-, un-, il-,* or *ir-* are easy to miss and always alter the meaning of the statement. Make it a habit to underline or circle negative words as you are reading examination questions.

Statements like the following that contain two negatives are even more confusing:

> It is not unreasonable to expect that Vietnam veterans continue to be angry about their exposure to Agent Orange.

In reading such statements, remember that two negatives balance or cancel each other out. So *not unreasonable* can be interpreted to mean "reasonable."

Making you best guess. When all else fails and you are unable to reason out the answer to an item, use these three last-resort rules of thumb.

Absolute statements tend to be false. Since very few things are always true, with no exceptions, your best guess is to mark statements that contain words such as *always, all, never,* or *none* as false.

Mark any item that contains unfamiliar terminology or facts as false. If you have studied the material thoroughly, trust that you would recognize as true anything that was a part of the course content.

When all else fails, it is usually better to guess true than false. It is more difficult for an instructor to write plausible false statements than true statements. As a result, many exams have more true items than false.

EXERCISE 15-3

Directions:
The following true/false items are based on content presented in this text. Read each item; then locate and underline the word(s) or phrase(s) which, if changed or deleted, could change the truth or falsity of the statement. Indicate whether the statement is true or false by marking T for true and F for false.

1. Decision making is primarily a process of discovering alternatives.
2. A table never displays more than two sets of data.
3. Critical thinking is often defined as the careful, deliberate evaluation of ideas and information for the singular purpose of establishing their importance.
4. Most students avoid taking responsibility for their grades by shifting the blame to others.
5. Previewing rarely enables you to focus your attention on a reading assignment.
6. Process and procedure are usually important in mathematics courses.
7. A study sheet is most useful for reviewing material that is interrelated.
8. Falling behind on reading assignments is often a sign of academic difficulty.
9. Active learning is primarily a discrimination task.
10. Retrieval of information from memory depends exclusively upon its relevance and meaningfulness.

Matching Tests: Discovering Relationships

Matching tests require you to select items in one column that can be paired with items in a second column. The key to working with matching tests is to discover the overall pattern or relationship between the two columns. Begin by glancing through both columns before answering anything to get an overview of the subject and the topics the test covers. Are you asked to match dates with events, terms with meanings, people with accomplishments, causes with effects? In the following excerpt, from a literature test, determine the relationship that exists:

Column 1	Column 2
1. Imagery	a. "One short sleep past, we wake eternally and Death shall be no more; Death, thou shalt die."—Donne
2. Simile	b. "We force their [children's] growth as if they were chicks in a poultry factory.—Toynbee
3. Personification	c. "And many a rose-carnation feeds with summer spice the humming air."—Tennyson

Use the following suggestions to answer matching items:

Answer the items you are sure of first, lightly crossing off items as they are used.

Don't choose the first answer that seems correct; items later in the list may be better choices.

If the first column consists of short words or phrases and the second is lengthy definitions or descriptions, save time by reverse matching; that is, look for the word or phrase in Column 1 that fits each item in Column 2.

Short-Answer Tests: Listing Information

Short-answer tests require you to write a brief answer, usually in list or brief sentence form, such as asked by the following example:

List three events that increased the U.S. involvement in the Vietnam War.

In answering short answer questions, keep the following in mind:

Use the point distribution as a clue to how many pieces of information to list. For a nine-point item asking you to describe the characteristics of a totalitarian government, give at least three ideas.

Plan what you will say before starting to write.

Use the amount of space provided, especially if it varies for different items, as a clue to how much should be written.

If you are asked to list three causes or to describe four events, number your answer so each point is clear and easy to identify.

Write your answer in sentence form. Unless you are specifically directed to "list."

Fill-in-the-Blank Tests: Factual Recall

Test questions that ask you to fill in a missing word or phrase within a sentence require recall of information rather than recognition of the correct answer. Therefore, it is important to look for clues that will trigger your recall. Here are a few suggestions:

Look for key words in the sentence. Use them to determine what subject matter and topic are covered in the item. Here is a sample item: Kohlberg devised a _____ to chart the course of "moral development." In this item you should focus on "Kohlberg," "chart," and "moral development."

Decide what type of information is required. Is it a date, name, place, new term? In the above item, a name or title is needed.

Use the grammatical structure of the sentence to determine the type of word called for. Is it a noun, verb, or qualifier? In the above item you must supply a noun. The correct answer is "stage theory."

Multiple Choice Tests: Recognizing Correct Answers

Multiple choice is the most frequently used type of exam and often the most difficult to answer. The following suggestions should improve your success in taking this type of exam:

Read all choices first, considering each. Do not stop with second or third choices, even if you are certain that you have found the correct answer. Remember, on most multiple choice tests your job is to pick the *best* answer, and the last choice may be a better answer than any of the first three.

Read combination choices. Some multiple choice tests include choices that are combinations of previously listed choices, as in the following item:

> The mesodermal tissue layer contains cells that will become
> a. skin, sensory organs, and nervous systems
> b. skin, sensory organs, and blood vessels
> c. bones and muscle
> d. stomach, liver, and pancreas
> e. a and c
> f. b, c, and d
> g. a, c, and d

The addition of choices that are combinations of the previous choices tends to make items even more confusing. Treat each choice, when combine with the stem, as a true or false statement. As you consider each choice, mark it true or false. If you find more than one true statement, then select the choice that contains the letters of all the true statements you identified.

Use logic and common sense. Even if you are unfamiliar with the subject matter, you can sometimes reason out the correct answer. The following test item is taken from a history exam on Japanese-American relations after World War II:

Prejudice and discrimination are
a. harmful to our society because they waste our economic, political, and social resources
b. helpful because they ensure us against attack from within
c. harmful because they create negative images of the United States in foreign countries
d. helpful because they keep the majority pure and united against minorities

Through logic and common sense, it is possible to eliminate choices *b* and *d*. Prejudice and discrimination are seldom, if ever, regarded as positive, desirable, or helpful since they are inconsistent with democratic ideals. Having narrowed your answer to two choices, *a* or *c*, you can see that choice *a* offers a stronger, more substantial reason why prejudice and discrimination are harmful. The attitude of other countries toward the United States is not as serious as a waste of economic, political, and social resources.

Examine closely items that are very similar. First, try to express each in your own words, and then, analyze how they differ. Often this process will enable you to recognize the right answer.

Look for the level of qualifying words. As note for true/false tests, qualifying words are important. Since many statements, ideas, principles, and rules have exceptions, be careful in selecting items that contain such words as *best, always, all, no, never, none, entirely, completely,* all of which suggest that a condition exists without exception. Items containing words that provide for some level of exception, or qualification, are more likely to be correct. Here are a few examples of such words: *often, usually, less, seldom, few, more,* and *most*.

In the following example, notice the use of the italicized qualifying words:

In most societies
a. values are *highly* consistent
b. people *often* believe and act on values that are contradictory
c. *all* legitimate organizations support values of the majority
d. values of equality *never* exist alongside prejudice and discrimination

In this question, items *c* and *d* contain the words *all* and *never,* suggesting that those statements are true without exception. Thus, if you did not know the answer to this question based on content, you could eliminate items *c* and *d* on the basis of the level of qualifiers.

Some multiple choice questions require application of knowledge or information. You may be asked to analyze a hypothetical situation or to use what you have learned to solve a problem. In answering questions of this type, start by crossing out unnecessary information that can distract you. In the following example, distracting information has been eliminated.

~~Carrie is~~ comfortable ~~in her new home~~ in New Orleans. When she ~~gets dressed up and~~ leaves her home and goes to the supermarket ~~to buy the week's groceries,~~ she gets nervous and angry and feels that something is going to happen to her. She feels the same way when walking ~~her four-year-old~~ son Jason in the park ~~or playground.~~

Carrie is suffering from
- a. shyness
- b. a phobia
- c. a personality disorder
- d. hypertension

Jot down the essence. If a question concerns steps in a process or order of events or any other information that is easily confused, ignore the choices and use the margin or scrap paper to jot down the information as you can recall it. Then select the choice that matches what you wrote.

Avoid the unfamiliar. Avoid choosing answers that are unfamiliar or that you do not understand. A choice that looks complicated or uses difficult words is not necessarily correct. If you have studied carefully, a choice that is unfamiliar to you is probably incorrect.

Choose the long answers. As a last resort, when you do not know the answer and are unable to eliminate any of the choices as wrong, guess by picking the one that seems most complete and contains the most information. This is a good choice because instructors are usually careful to make the correct answer complete. Thus, the answer often becomes long or detailed.

Make educated guesses. In most instances, you can eliminate one or more of the choices as obviously wrong. Even if you can eliminate only one choice, you have increased your odds on a four-choice items from one in four to one in three. If you can eliminate two choices, you have increased your odds to one in two, or 50 percent. Don't hesitate to play the odds and make a guess—you may gain points.

EXERCISE 15-4

Directions:

The following multiple choice items appeared on an exam in psychology. Study each item and use your reasoning skills to eliminate items that seem incorrect and then, making an educated guess, select the best answer:

1. Modern psychological researchers maintain that the mind as well as behavior can be scientifically examined primarily by
   a. observing behavior and making inferences about mental functioning
   b. observing mental activity and making inferences about behavior
   c. making inferences about behavior
   d. direct observation of behavior

2. Jane Goodall has studied the behavior of chimpanzees in their own habitat. She exemplifies a school of psychology that is concerned with
   a. theories
   b. mental processes
   c. the individual's potential for growth
   d. naturalistic behavior

3. If a psychologist were personally to witness the effects of a tornado upon the residents of a small town, what technique would he or she be using?
   a. experimentation
   b. correlational research
   c. observation
   d. none of the above

4. A case study is a(n)
   a. observation of an event
   b. comparison of similar events
   c. study of changes and their effects
   d. intense investigation of a particular occurrence

5. Events that we are aware of at a given time make up the
   a. unconscious
   b. subconscious
   c. consciousness
   d. triconscious

6. Unlocking a combination padlock
   a. always involves language skills
   b. always involves motor skills

  c. never involves imaginal skills
  d. seldom involves memory skills

WRITING EFFECTIVE ESSAY EXAMS

To many students, essay exams present a greater challenge than objective exams. However, they also provide a greater opportunity to demonstrate your learning and to distinguish yourself as an excellent student. Your essays reveal a great deal about your level of mastery of the course content as well as your ability to organize, synthesize, and apply it. Essay exams measure your ability to think about the subject and communicate those thoughts in written form.

Writing effective essay answers involves four stages: (1) organizing your approach, (2) analyzing the question, (3) constructing your answer, and (4) writing your answer.

Organizing Your Approach

Here are a few suggestions to help you approach essay exams in an organized, systematic manner:

Read the directions. Before reading any of the essay questions, be certain to read the general directions first. They may tell you how many questions to answer, how to structure your answer, what the point distribution is, or what the minimum or maximum length for your answer should be.

When you have to make a choice. When the directions specify a choice of questions to answer, select those on which you will be able to score the most points. Some essay questions are more difficult than others; some require specific, exact information, while others call for a reasoned, logical interpretation or evaluation. Take time to make a careful choice. A few moments spent at the beginning may well save you the time it takes to switch from one question to another should you realize midway that you are not able to prepare an adequate response.

Answer the easiest question first. Assuming the questions are of equal point value, answer the easiest question first. Knowing you are doing well will build your self-confidence and help you to approach the remainder of the exam with a positive attitude. You will be able to complete the easiest question fairly quickly, leaving the remainder of time to be divided among the more difficult questions.

Make notes as you read. As you read a question the first time, you may begin automatically to formulate an answer. Jot down a few key words that will bring these thoughts back when you are ready to organize your answer.

Analyze the question. Well-written essay questions define the topic and provide clues about what to include, what thought patterns to use, how to organize your answer, and what types or kinds of information to include, as shown in the following item.

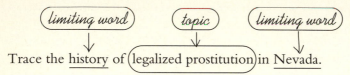

Trace the <u>history</u> of (legalized prostitution) in <u>Nevada</u>.

Here the topic, legalized prostitution, is clearly defined, and it is limited or restricted in two ways: (1) you are concerned only with its history—not its status today, or its effects; and (2) you are concerned only with the state of Nevada.

Here are a few more examples: the topics have been circled and the restricting or limiting words have been underlined.

List several categories (of speeches) and describe their <u>primary functions and uses.</u>
<u>Describe</u> the basic <u>differences</u> between the <u>reproductive cycles of</u> (angiosperms and gymnosperms.)
<u>Compare</u> the <u>purpose and function</u> of analytical (reports and research reports.)

Develop the habit of looking for and marking or circling these key words as you analyze essay questions.

Watch for questions with several parts. Students often fail to answer all parts of an essay question. Most likely, they become involved with answering the first part and forget to complete the remaining parts. Questions with several parts come in two forms. The most obvious form is as follows:

For the U.S. invasion of Panama, discuss the (a) causes, (b) immediate effects, and (c) long-range political implications.

A less obvious form that does not stand out as a several-part question is shown below:

Discuss <u>how</u> the (Equal Rights Amendment) was developed and <u>why</u> its passage has aroused controversy.

When you find a question of this type, circle the topic and underline the limiting words (as in the example) to serve as a reminder.

Use thought patterns as clues to content and organization. Essay questions contain one or more clue words that indicate the predominant thought pattern(s) to use in constructing, organizing, and writing your answer. These words specify what approach you are to take in answering the question. They indicate whether you are to make comparisons, summarize, explain, or answer in some other way. Here is a sample essay question:

Identify and compare the three stages of African literature.

The topic of this essay question, African literature, is limited to a consideration of its three stages. The clue words "identify" and "compare" specify what type of response is called for. They tell you *what* to say about the stages of African literature. First you are to identify—that is, name and briefly describe—each stage. Then you are to compare the three stages, describing their similarities. The most commonly used clue words, and the thought patterns they often suggest, are summarized in Table 15-1.

EXERCISE 15-5

Directions:

Read each of the following essay questions. In each question, underline the topic, circle the limiting word(s), and identify the thought pattern(s) the question suggests.

1. Discuss the long-term effects of the trend toward a smaller, more self-contained family structure.
2. Trace the development of monopolies in the late nineteenth and early twentieth centuries in America.
3. Explain one effect of the Industrial Revolution upon each of three of the following:
   a. transportation
   b. capitalism
   c. socialism
   d. population growth
   e. scientific research
4. Discuss the reason why, although tropical plants have very large leaves and most desert plants have very small leaves, cactus grows equally well in both habitats.
5. Describe the events leading up to the War of 1812.
6. Compare and contrast the purposes and procedures in text book marking and lecture notetaking.
7. Briefly describe a complete approach to reading and studying a textbook chapter that will enable you to handle a test on that material successfully.

8. List four factors that influence memory or recall ability, and explain how each can be used to make study more efficient.
9. Summarize the techniques a speaker or lecturer may use to emphasize the important concepts and ideas in his lecture.
10. Explain the value and purpose of the previewing technique, and list the steps involved in prereading a textbook chapter.

Table 15-1
ESSAY EXAM QUESTIONS

Thought pattern	Clue word	Example	Information to include
Chronological	Trace	Trace the history of the foreign exchange market.	Describe the development or progress of a particular trend, event, or process in chronological order.
Process	Describe	Describe how an advertisement is produced and prepared.	Tell how something happened, including how, who, where, why.
Comparison	Compare	Compare the causes of air pollution with those of water pollution.	Show how items are similar as well as different; include details or examples.
Contrast	Contrast (differentiate)	Contrast the health care systems in the United States with those in England.	Show how the items are different; include details or examples.
Cause and effect	Prove	Prove that ice is a better cooling agent than air when both are at the same temperature.	Give reasons or evidence, or establish that a concept or theory is correct, logical, or valid.
	Justify	Justify former President Carter's attempt to rescue hostages in Iran.	Give reasons that support an action, event, or policy.

Table 15-1
ESSAY EXAM QUESTIONS *(continued)*

Thought pattern	*Clue word*	*Example*	*Information to include*
	Criticize	Criticize the current environmental controls to combat air pollution.	Make judgments about quality or worth; include both positive and negative aspects, explaining or giving reasons for your judgments.
	Evaluate	Evaluate the strategies our society has used to treat mental illness.	React to the topic in a logical way. Discuss the merit, strengths, weaknesses, advantages, or limitations of the topic, explaining your reasons.
Listing	Discuss	Discuss the effectiveness of drug rehabilitation programs.	Consider important characteristics and main points.
	Enumerate (list)	Enumerate the reasons for U.S. involvement in the Persian Gulf War.	List or discuss one by one.
	State (illustrate)	State Boyle's Law and illustrate its use.	Explain, using examples that demonstrate or clarify a point or idea.
	Summarize	Summarize the arguments for and against offering sex education courses in public schools.	Cover the major points in brief form; use a sentence and paragraph form.
Definition	Define	Define thermal pollution and include several examples.	Give an accurate meaning of the term with enough detail to show that you really understand it.
Classification	Diagram	Diagram the stamen and pistil of a lily.	Make a drawing and label its parts.

Constructing Your Answer

As soon as they have finished analyzing the question, many students begin immediately to write the answer. A far better technique is to take a few moments to think about, plan, and organize your ideas.

Outline. Make a brief word or phrase outline of the ideas you want to include in your answer.

Rearrange the outline. Study your word outline and rearrange its order. You may want to put major topics and important ideas first and less important points toward the end. Or you may decide to organize your answer chronologically, discussing events early in time near the beginning of the essay and mentioning more recent events near the end. The topic you are discussing will largely determine the order of presentation.

If the point value of the essay is given, use that information as a clue to how many separate points or ideas may be expected. For example, for an essay worth 25 points, five major points may be expected.

If you are having difficulty recalling needed information or if you should suddenly "go blank," try a technique called brainstorming. Basically, it involves writing a list of everything and anything you can think of related to the topic. Then review your list; you are likely to find some ideas you can use in your answer.

Writing Your Answer

The appearance, organization, and correctness of your essay influence your grade. Numerous experiments have been done; most indicate that well-organized, correctly written papers receive nearly one letter grade higher than papers that express the same content but do so in a poorly organized, error-filled manner. Use the suggestions in Table 15-2 to present a correctly written paper. A sample essay answer is shown in Figure 15-2.

If Your Run Out of Time

Despite careful planning, you may run out of time before you can finish writing one of the essays. If this happens, try to jot down the major ideas that you would discuss fully if you had time. Often your instructor will give you partial credit for this type of response, especially if you mention that you ran out of time.

Figure 15-2
A Sample Essay Question and Answer

ESSAY QUESTION

Crime is a human act that violates criminal law. Identify the various categories of crime. Describe and provide an example of each.

ANSWER

There are five categories of crime. Each violates one or more aspect of criminal law. The first category, Index Crime, are those identified by the Federal Bureau of Investigation and includes criminal homicide, rape, robbery, burglary, aggravated assault, larceny, auto theft, and arson.

The second type of crime is white-collar crime. These crimes may be committed by corporations or individuals, usually within the course of daily business. The criminals are often affluent and respectable citizens. Some examples are embezzlement and income tax evasion.

A third type of crime is professional crime. Professional crimes are committed by criminals who pursue crime as a day-to-day occupation. They often use skilled techniques and are respected by other criminals. Shoplifters, safecrackers, or cargo highjackers are examples of professional criminals.

Organized crime is a fourth type of crime. Organized crime involves the sale of illegal goods and services and is conducted by criminals who organize into networks. Organized crime is often transmitted through generations and does not depend on particular individuals for its continuation. Organized crime often involves political corruption. Examples of organized crime are gambling, narcotics sales, and loan sharking.

A fifth type of crime is victimless crime. These crimes involve willing participants; there is no victim other than the offender. Examples include drug use, prostitution, and public drunkenness.

If You Don't Know the Answer

Despite careful preparation, you may be unable to answer a particular question. If this should happen, do not leave a blank page; write something. Attempt to answer the question—you may even hit upon some partially correct information. However, the main reason for writing something is to give the instructor the opportunity to give you at least a few points for trying. If you leave a completely blank page, your instructor has

Table 15-2
TIPS AND TECHNIQUES FOR PRESENTING ESSAY ANSWERS

Tips	*Techniques*
Use correct paragraph form.	Explain one idea per paragraph.
Begin you answer with a thesis statement.	Write a sentence that states what the entire essay will discuss.
Make your main points easy to find.	State each main point in a separate paragraph; use headings; number ideas; use blank space to divide ideas.
Include sufficient explanation.	Provide several supporting details for each main idea.
Avoid opinions and judgments.	Include only factual information unless otherwise requested.
Make your answer readable.	Use ink; use 8$\frac{1}{2}$ x 11 inch paper; number your pages; write on one side; leave margins and spaces between lines.
Proofread your answer.	Read through your answer to check only grammar, spelling, and punctuation.

no choice but to give you zero points. Usually losing full credit on one essay automatically eliminates one's chances of getting a high passing grade.

CONTROLLING TEST ANXIETY

Do you get nervous and anxious just before an exam begins? If so, your response is perfectly normal; most students feel some anxiety before an exam. In fact, research indicates that some anxiety is beneficial and improves your performance by sharpening your attention and keeping you alert.

Research also shows that very high levels of anxiety can interfere with performance on a test. Some students become highly nervous and emotional and lose their concentrations. Their minds seem to go blank, and they are unable to recall material they have learned. They also report physical symptoms: Their hearts pound, it is difficult to swallow, they break out in a cold sweat.

Test anxiety is a very complicated psychological response to a threatening situation. It may be deep rooted and related to other problems and past experiences. The following suggestions are intended to help ease your test anxiety. If these suggestions do not help, the next step is to discuss the problem with a counselor.

❑ ❑ ❑
Thinking Critically . . . About Returned Exams

Most students do not pay enough attention to returned exams. If you usually file away returned exams for future reference once you have noted your grade, STOP. You can learn a lot by analyzing a returned exam. Use the following suggestions:

1. **Analyze where you lost your points.** Make a list of topics on which you lost points. Do you see a pattern? Can you identify one or more topics or chapters that were particularly troublesome? If so, review that material now, and make a note to review it again before your final exam.

2. **Analyze the questions you missed.** If the exam had several parts, where did you lose the most points (essay or multiple choice, for example)? Adjust your study and review strategies accordingly, using the suggestions in the previous chapter.

3. **Analyze the level of thinking (see chapter 1, p. 17) required in the questions you missed.** Did you miss knowledge and comprehension questions? If so, you will need to spend more time on factual recall. If you missed questions that require analysis, then you should adjust your study plan to include more thought and reflection. If you missed questions that require synthesis, then you should devise study strategies that force you to pull information together. If you missed application questions, spend more time looking at practical uses and applications of course content. If you missed evaluation questions, ask more critical questions about course content.

Be Sure Test Anxiety Is Not an Excuse

Many students say they have test anxiety when the truth is that they have not studied and reviewed carefully or thoroughly. The first question, then, that you must answer honestly is this: Are you really *unprepared* for the exam and therefore justifiably anxious?

Get Used to Test Situations

Psychologists who have studied anxiety use processes called "systematic desensitization" and "simulation" to reduce test anxiety. Basically, these processes allow you to become less sensitive or disturbed by tests by putting yourself in test like conditions. Although these are complicated processes used by trained therapists, here are a few ways you can use them to reduce your own test anxiety:

Become familiar with the building and room in which the test is given. Visit the room when it is empty and take a seat. Visualize yourself taking a test there.

Develop practice or review tests. Treat them as real tests and do them in situations as similar as possible to real test conditions.

Practice working with time limits. Set an alarm clock and work only until it rings.

Take as many tests as possible, even though you dislike them. Always take advantage of practice tests and in-chapter exercises. Buy a review book for the course you are taking, or a workbook that accompanies your text. Treat each section as an exam and have someone else correct your work.

Control Negative Thinking

Major factors that contribute to test anxiety are worry, self-doubt, and negative thinking. Just before and during an exam, anxious students often think such things as "I won't do well," "I'm going to fail," "What will my friends think of me when I get a failing grade?" This type of thinking is a predisposition for failure; you are telling yourself that you expect to fail. By doing this, you are blocking your chances for success. One solution to this problem is to send yourself positive rather than negative messages. Say to yourself, "I have studied hard and I deserve to pass" or "I know that I know the material" or "I know I can do it!"

Compose Yourself Before the Test Begins

Before you begin the test, take 30 minutes or so to calm yourself, to slow down, and to focus your attention. Take several deep breaths, close your eyes, and visualize yourself calmly working through the test.

SUMMARY

1. Exams require you to think and reason about course content.
2. The chapter begins by offering tips for approaching the exam confidently, in a systematic manner.
3. Objective exams may include

   ❏ true/false

❑ matching
❑ short answer
❑ multiple choice items

4. General strategies for taking objective exams as well as specific suggestions for approaching each type are given.
5. Essay exams require you to organize and express ideas that demonstrate your mastery of course content.
6. Writing effective essay exams is a four-step process:

❑ organizing your approach
❑ analyzing the question
❑ constructing your answer
❑ writing your answer

7. Numerous strategies are offered for each stage, and thought patterns are discussed as aids in determining both content and organization.

CLASS ACTIVITY

Directions:

Each class member should write a response to the following essay question. Then, form groups of four or five students and follow each step listed below:

Problem solving is a vital and important skill. Describe the problem-solving process and illustrate its use in a particular academic situation.

1. Group members should read and evaluate each other's answers. Specifically, they should rate each answer and award it a grade of A, B, C, or D on each of the following criteria:
   a. Correct and complete information (refer to Chapter 4)
   b. Sufficient detail and explanation
   c. Clear organization of class
   d. Effectiveness of thesis statement
   e. Grammatical correctness and readability
2. Group members should defend, compare, contrast, and discuss each other's ratings.

FURTHER ANALYSIS

Directions:

Given below is an essay question and one student's response to that question. The question was worth 30 points on an examination totaling 100 points; total test time was 75 minutes. Read and analyze the question and the essay answer and then respond to each question listed below:

Discuss each stage of the memory process, and identify and explain several strategies for improving the effectiveness of each stage.

Essay Answer

Memory is important in everyone's life because it is the means by which we store and remember information. Psychologists have identified three stages: encoding, storage, and retrieval. In the encoding stage you put facts and ideas into a code, usually words, and file it away in your memory. Encoding can be improved by defining your purpose for learning and using various sensory modes. Storage involves keeping information in your permanent long-term memory.

The effectiveness of storage can be improved by immediate review of material you have just read or heard. Organizing or recording the information is also useful because it allows you to store the information in chunks. Developing retrieval clues is also an effective storage strategy.

Retrieval, the third stage of the memory process, is the ability to get back information that is in storage. You can improve retrieval by practice, by learning beyond mastery, and through elaboration.

1. Evaluate the accuracy of the information presented by referring to Chapter 5.
2. Evaluate the effectiveness of the writer's thesis statement.
3. Comment on the writer's organization.
4. Did the writer include sufficient explanation and detail?
5. What additional information might the writer have included?
6. What specific suggestions would you make to help this student improve his skill in answering essay questions?

DISCUSSION

1. Some students find one type of examination question easier to handle than others. What factors could explain these differences?
2. If a student is 10 minutes late for a class in which an hourly exam is being given, what should he or she do?

3. Some colleges operate on the honor system: A student is obligated to report another student whom he or she observes cheating on an exam. Students who fail to report cheating are also considered guilty. What is the policy on your campus for students who have been found cheating on exams? Agree or disagree with this policy.
4. Suppose that you wake up the morning of an important exam feeling queasy and feverish. You realize you have caught the flu. What should you do?

FURTHER READING

Boyd, R. T. C. *Improving Your Test-Taking Skills.* Washington, DC: American Institute for Research, 1988.

Bragdon, Allen D. Can You Pass These Tests? New York: Harper, 1987.

Flippo, Rona F. Testwise: *Strategies for Success in Taking Tests.* Belmont, CA: David S. Lake, 1988.

Hembree, R. "Correlates, Causes, Effects, and Treatment of Test Anxiety." *Review of Educational Research* 58 (1988):47–77.

Pena-Paez, Alberto, and John R. Surber. "Effect of Study Strategy Skill Level on Test Performance." *English Quarterly* 23 (1990):31–39.

PART

□ □ □

6

Writing: A Vehicle for Thinking

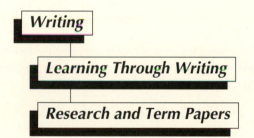

Writing

Learning Through Writing

Research and Term Papers

16

□ □ □

Learning Through Writing: Reports, Projects, and Class Assignments

Learning Objectives

Use writing as an aid to learning and thinking

Understand the stages in the writing process

Approach various types of writing assignments effectively

Writing is an important intellectual activity; it is both a means of thinking and learning and a means of communication. Some form of writing is required in most college courses and in most careers, as well. As a general rule, the further you progress in your education, the more writing you will be expected to do. Advanced courses in a discipline require more writing than introductory ones. Junior and senior courses, as you concentrate on a major, involve more writing than freshman and sophomore courses. Similarly, graduate and professional study require more writing than undergraduate coursework.

Throughout college, then, you will face a wide variety of writing tasks, including essay examinations, critiques, themes, laboratory reports, critical essays, and term papers. The primary purpose of each of these writing tasks is to focus and direct you thinking—to lead or guide you to uncover new ideas, detect relationships, question old ideas, and evaluate both old and new ideas. The purpose of this chapter is to establish the role of writing within the thinking and learning process and to provide strategies for approaching the diverse types of writing that college demands.

WRITING AS A THINKING AND LEARNING STRATEGY

Many students mistakenly think of writing as a mechanical process, focusing on features of correctness, grammar, and spelling. Actually, these features are only functional rules that provide a vehicle for the expression of ideas. Most importantly, writing is a learning and thinking strategy. Nearly all learning and study strategies involve some type of writing:

❏ ❏ ❏

Learning/Study Strategy	*Type of Writing Involved*
Time management	Organizing lists, planning schedules
Specialized terminology	Course master file
Textbook reading/review	Underlining, annotation
Class lectures	Notes, recall clues
Organizing course content	Outlining, mapping, summarizing
Taking exams	Making notes, study sheets, outlining essay answers

❏ ❏ ❏

Writing, then, is an essential part of learning; it enables you to condense, organize, and synthesize information.

Writing is also a vital thinking strategy.

It is a means of clarifying your ideas. When you write about a topic, you are forced to sift through what you know it, to evaluate its worth or appropriateness, and to see how the various ideas connect. Through this process you may decide you do not know enough and realize that research is necessary.

Writing is an effective way of generating new ideas. As you will see later in this chapter, writing tends to bring ideas forward. In a sense, writing brings out ideas from a sub- or half-conscious level to full consciousness. Writing is a composing process, a means of creating a new and unique web of meanings.

Writing is a means of testing how clearly you understand ideas. To express an idea in your own words, you must understand it fully.

Writing is a means of organizing ideas. Whether you are writing on a familiar topic or have done considerable research to explore an unfamiliar one, your mind is overloaded with information. It is nearly impossible for you mind alone to organize the large volume of material. Writing, then, ables you to see how facts and ideas fit together—to discover connections and relationships.

Writing gives shape and form to thought. Writing about a topic allows you to examine it from various angles or study it in different ways.

ANALYZING WRITING ASSIGNMENTS

To earn the best grade possible, as well as to learn as much as possible from an assignment, you must analyze its purpose. Once you understand what it is intended to accomplish, you will be able to plan and develop strategies to complete it. In general, all assignments are intended to guide your learning and thinking. Try to identify the specific thinking skills each assignment demands. Is the assignment intended to

enable you to apply a process?
evaluate a controversial issue?
focus on solutions?
compare policies, events, or theories?

The most valuable clues to the purpose of an assignment are provided by your professor at the time the assignment is announced. Here are a few suggestions:

Listen carefully and make notes on what is said. Carefully record the assignment, using your professor's wording. While the exact wording may seem unimportant at first, it often contains important clues. For example, whether a professor directs you to write a *detailed* analysis or a *careful* analysis of a collateral reading assignment makes a difference. A detailed analysis is to be very specific, while a careful analysis is to be thorough and well thought out.

Notice when the assignment is given. Often the assignment is given in conjunction with a discussion of the material to which it relates. Review your notes for clues.

Ask questions (and encourage other students to do so as well). The more your professor talks about the assignment, the more you will learn about what is expected.

Identify the intended audience. Your approach should vary accordingly. Often the audience is your instructor.

Connect assignments with course topics. Most assignments are given within the context of course content. They relate to, explain, or explore a major topic of study within the course. An important part of successfully completing an assignment is to connect it with its corresponding course content.

EXERCISE 16-1

Directions:
Analyze the purpose of each of the following assignments.

Course	Assignment
1. Economics	A football team is by definition a team production process. Determine three ways that the coaches of a college team monitor and control individual players' performances on the football team.[1]
2. Data processing	Two of the problems with very large programs are that they are very difficult to

❏ ❏ ❏
Thinking Critically . . . About Writing Assignments

When you analyze an assignment, try to discover the level of thinking it requires (see Chapter 1, p. 17). Assignments require various levels of thinking, and an awareness of what is required will help you produce a better paper. For example

❏ An assignment to submit a synopsis of an assigned journal article requires you to condense factual information. Hence, knowledge and comprehension are important. Thus, you should concentrate on presenting facts clearly and correctly in an organized fashion.

❏ An assignment that asks you to react to a quotation requires analysis and evaluation, so you should write a well-thought-out analysis and carefully evaluate it in relations to course content.

❏ A question that asks you to write a chemical equation for an event, such as the burning of rocket fuel in oxygen, requires you to apply information you have learned, so be sure to recall the relevant principles.

❏ If an assignment asks you to compare three essays and then write one of your own on the same topic while incorporating some of the ideas expressed in the original three, synthesis is required. Focus on creating a unique but accurate essay that contains some of your own ideas as well as some from the assigned essays.

get right in the first place and then are very difficult to make changes to. How would you tackle the equivalent problems for a telephone directory? Assume that the correct names, addresses and phone numbers for the directory are stored on individual index cards and that changes come in during the year on similar cards.[2]

3. Physics

Your instructor describes the following situation and asks you to comment on it: Two classmates are discussing the design of a roller coaster. One classmate says that each summit must be lower than the previous one. Your other classmate says this is nonsense, for as long as the first one is the highest, it doesn't matter what height the others are. What do you say?[3]

THE STAGES OF THE WRITING PROCESS

When beginning to work on a paper or assignment, many students just pick up a pen and start writing. Usually this is not the best way to begin. In writing as in reading, strategies you use *before* you begin writing as well as *after* you have written the paper can help ensure that you have produced an acceptable, well-written product. The steps or stages that most good writers go through in writing a paper are prewriting, organizing, writing, revising, and proofreading.

Prewriting

You might think of prewriting as a process similar to previewing. Previewing (see Chapter 5) focuses your attention on the material so that you anticipate its content and organization. In writing, you need to anticipate and plan content and organization and let your ideas take shape. Here are a few tips:

Getting organized

When and where you write are important. Choose a time of day when you are at peak concentration and a place that is free of distractions. Have plenty of paper, pens, pencils, and a dictionary available. Begin by reviewing your assignment. Reread either your instructor's statement or your notes, if the assignment was given orally.

Once you are familiar with the nature and scope of the assignment, establish a time schedule for its completion. Never try to complete a paper in one evening. You need time to let the paper rest; then come back to it later to reconsider what you have written with a different perspective and with a critical eye.

Developing Ideas About the Assignment

Before you begin to write, jot down your ideas and generate new ones. There are numerous ways to generate ideas, several of which are described below. Experiment with each until you find one that seems to work for you. Let us suppose your assignment in an interpersonal communications class is to write an essay discussing the persuasive appeal of magazine advertising. To generate ideas, you might use the following techniques:

Brainstorming. It works like this: Take a piece of paper and start making a list of anything that comes into your mind about magazine advertising. As you do this, you might look at several typical advertisements. Do not be concerned about whether you are writing in complete sentences or whether the ideas make sense or connect to one another. Keep writing continuously for a set period of time, four to five minutes or so. When you have finished, reread what you have written. You will be surprised at the number of ideas you have discovered. Underline or rewrite those ideas that seem worth including in your paper. Figure 16-1 shows an excerpt from one student's brainstorming session.

Figure 16-1
Brainstorming

Costs of writing ads-
types of people who write ads
reasons why people read ads
effects of colors
design
layout
sex appeal
eye catching
seasonal appeal
holiday appeal
humor in ads
use of celebrities
status
emotional appeals-love
thrift

❑ ❑ ❑

Thought Pattern	*Sample Question*
Sequence/Order	Through what process is an advertisement written?
Comparison and Contrast	In what respects are all advertisements similar? What distinguishing features make some ads more effective or appealing than others?
Cause and Effect	Why do advertisements appeal to readers? How do ads influence buyer behavior?
Listing	List the features of an advertisement that contribute to its persuasive appeal.
Classification Problem-Solution	What types of persuasive appeals are made? Is it ethical for advertisements to influence the wants and needs of small children who lack the ability to recognize persuasive advertising?

❑ ❑ ❑

Questioning. Working under a time limit, usually five minutes or less, make a list of all the questions you can think of about the topic. Include anything that could possibly be asked about the topic. When you have finished, reread the questions, and, as you did for brainstorming, identify those which, when answered, would be worth including in your paper. Use of this technique is shown in Figure 16-2.

Patterning. Again working under a time limit, analyze the topic using the six key thought patterns used throughout this text. Patterning involves asking questions from each of these perspectives, thus providing you with six different ways of looking at the topic. The sample questions that follow are those you might ask about the persuasive appeal of magazine advertising.

Figure 16-2
Questioning

> How expensive are ads to write? Who writes them? Who decides who they appeal to and what appeal will be used? Do they affect everybody the same way? Cost to run an ad in the NY Times? v.s. local paper? How do advertisers decide what magazines to run ads in? Do people really read ads? Are there subliminal messages in ads? Will a magazine print any ad submitted?

EXERCISE 16-2

Directions:
Choose one of the topics listed below. Write about that topic for five minutes, using the technique of brainstorming.

1. An end-of-chapter discussion question from one of your texts
2. A possible essay exam question for one of your courses
3. The title of a textbook chapter that you have not read

EXERCISE 16-3

Directions:
Choose one of the topics given below. Write as many questions as you can think of about the topic. Limit your time to five minutes.

1. Unemployment
2. The value of a college education
3. Soap operas

EXERCISE 16-4

Directions:
Choose one of the topics given below. Use patterning to generate questions about the topic. Limit your time to five minutes.

1. Sports in America
2. Violence and television
3. Animal rights

Organizing and Outlining

Once you have identified some ideas to include in your paper, the next step is to organize them. This involves arranging the ideas in an order that will result in an understandable and well-written paper. One effective way to organize your ideas is to make an informal outline, or list of topics in the order you will discuss them. Writing an outline will force you to discover the relationship of ideas to one another. To accomplish this, use the following steps:

Make a list of the ideas you plan to include.

Read through the list, looking for ideas that are similar or those that should follow one another.

Group ideas together so that they are listed in a logical order. Use one or more thought patterns.

As you work through these steps, you will likely generate new ideas as well. Add them to your list or outline.

EXERCISE 16-5

Directions:

Select one of the topics you worked with in the previous exercises in this chapter. Organize your ideas generated from that activity into a brief outline.

Formulating a Thesis

A thesis is the organizing and controlling idea of your paper. It is a statement that the remainder of your paper supports and explains.

Here are a few examples of thesis statements for a one-page paper on the topic of fad diets:

❏ Fad diets can be dangerous if they deprive the body of essential vitamins and minerals.

❏ Fad diets reflect our culture's search and desire for easy and fast solutions to problems.

❏ Fad diets that rely on excessive quantities of one type of food are often unsuccessful for long-term weight loss.

At times your thesis may be clear and obvious. If so, then you are ready to move on to preparing a draft. Other times, however, a thesis may not be at all obvious. Here are a few suggestions to help you arrive at a thesis:

Allow time for incubation to occur. Have you ever awakened in the morning with the solution to a problem you were not able to solve the night before? Or has a solution suddenly come to you when you were not even thinking of the problem? These occurrences can be explained by a process known as *incubation*. It means that your preconscious or subconscious mind continues to work on a problem even after you have stopped consciously thinking about it. Therefore, be sure to allow yourself enough time for incubation to occur. Take frequent breaks; let an assignment sit overnight before you complete it. Definitely do not try to complete a major assignment in one evening.

Look for connections. Can you see trends or patterns in the ideas you have generated? What do they point toward, suggest, or support?

Write lists of all possible thesis statements. Do not try to make them complete or correct at this point. Then explore each carefully.

Look at parts of various statements. Could they be combined?

Predict topics. What would each possible thesis statement allow you to write about; and what topics would it exclude?

List titles. If you have difficulty writing a thesis, write a list of possible titles for your paper instead. Titles, because they are brief, force you to capture what your paper is about.

Discuss your ideas. Don't overlook the value of talking with others. The process of explaining your paper to a friend will help you come upon a workable thesis.

Brainstorm or research some more. If all your efforts still do not produce a thesis, consider the possibility of further brainstorming or research to collect new information.

Once you have chosen a thesis statement, rework your informal outline to most effectively support your thesis. Reorganize your ideas and eliminate those that do not directly relate to the thesis. Add more information, if necessary.

EXERCISE 16-6

Directions:
Using the outline you wrote for Exercise 16-5, write a thesis statement.

Writing a Draft

Once you have organized your ideas and have formed a tentative thesis, you are ready to begin writing a first draft of your paper. Here are a few suggestions:

Always plan on revising your work. Your first draft should never be your final copy.

As you begin, be concerned only with getting your ideas down on paper. Do not be concerned with exact word choice or with correct punctuation. You can check and correct those details later.

Using your outline as a guide, discuss the ideas in the order in which they appear in the outline.

Be sure to explain each idea completely. A common fault instructors find with student papers is that they do not include enough detail. Try to include, where appropriate, examples, reasons, descriptions, or other supporting information.

As you write, you may think of other ideas to discuss later; jot these ideas in the margin for further reference.

The physical act of writing—moving a pen across the page or typing—forces you to be actively involved with the task and commands your concentration and attention. Often, this physical activity alone is insufficient; you seem to run out of ideas, or what you write does not seem to be expressing what you want to say. When this occurs, get up and move around; increase your level of physical activity by taking a walk or running an errand.

If you have to stop writing before a draft is finished, be sure to stop at a point from which you will be able to begin working again easily. Never stop at a point where you do not know what to say next; resuming writing will be difficult and frustrating. Instead, stop at a place where you know what will come next; jot down a word or two as a reminder.

EXERCISE 16-7

Directions:

Using your outline and thesis statement written in the two previous exercises, write a first draft of a 1–2 page paper.

Revising

Revision is the step that can make a good paper better or an unacceptable paper acceptable. Revision involves rereading, rewriting, and making changes to improve both the content and organization of your paper. Use the following tips:

Do not revise as soon as you have finished writing. Instead, arrange for a lapse of time between writing and revision. The lapse of time gives you the distance and objectivity you do not have immediately upon completing your draft.

If you have trouble evaluating your paper, ask a friend to read and criticize it. Also, ask him or her to summarize what your paper said. This will allow you to see if you have expressed your ideas clearly and accurately.

To evaluate your own paper, try asking yourself the following questions:

❏ Are the ideas expressed clearly?
❏ Do the ideas tie together to form a unified piece of writing?
❏ Could the paragraphs be rearranged to be more effective?
❏ Is each major idea supported with facts and details?
❏ Is additional information needed?
❏ Do transitional sentences lead from one idea to another?

Check the balance of the paper. Are ideas equally weighted, or do you spend too much time on one idea?

Check the beginning and ending. Does you paper have a clear and interesting introduction? Does it draw to a close or just stop?

Look for words and phrases that carry little meaning. Revise them so they express clear, vivid ideas.

EXERCISE 16-8

Directions:
Revise the draft you wrote in Exercise 16-7.

Proofreading

Once you have prepared the final copy of your paper, be sure to read it to detect any errors in spelling, punctuation, grammar, and usage. At this point, try to ignore the flow of ideas and concentrate on checking each sentence for errors. To locate spelling errors, try reading the paper backward, word for word.

Although you may not think it is fair, your paper's physical appearance and grammatical correctness often influence its grade. It pays to make sure your work is free of error.

EXERCISE 16-9

Directions:
Proofread the paper you wrote in the previous exercise.

USING COMPUTERS AND WORD PROCESSING

Using a computer's word processing capability can save you time in the preparation of a paper of any length. The word processing software allows you to revise and edit without retying or rewriting the entire paper. For example, in a handwritten or typed paper, if you realized you need to add a sentence, you would need to rewrite or retype the entire page. Using the word processing software, you can insert the sentence, then reprint the page in a relatively short time. Here are a few other examples of tasks that can be performed easily using a word processor:

❏ add, delete, or move a word or sentence
❏ add or delete punctuation
❏ correct a misspelling
❏ change the order of paragraphs
❏ automatically number pages
❏ change margins to fit more or fewer words per page

In addition to revising and editing, the word processor is also useful in outlining and first draft stages of writing as well. By rearranging your outline (rather than rewriting), you can experiment with several means of organizing your paper. The word processor enables you to move back and forth within your paper, adding, deleting, or rearranging, details and ideas.

Most word processing software is easy to use. Directions appear on the screen, a "help menu" can be accessed by pressing a key, and printed reference cards often are provided. Here is some advice for beginning to learn word processing:

If you do not know how to type, take a course in basic keyboarding, or use a self-instructional software program designed to teach you basics about the keyboard.

If your college offers a workshop on learning word processing, be sure to take it.

The first word processing program you learn to use will take time. However, the time you invest will be well spent. You will save hours each semester using the word processor to write your papers.

Try to learn to use the word processor with another student. You will find you can help each other, and learning will be more fun.

While you are learning, be certain to save what you have typed frequently. In case you make a mistake or there is a power outage, you will not lose everything you have typed.

Special Features

Some word processing programs have additional features that offer valuable assistance to student writers.

❏ Spelling checker. The computer scans your document, identifies words you have misspelled, and provides you with the correct spelling.

❏ Electronic thesaurus. The computer provides a list of synonyms for a specified word. This feature enables you to replace an overused word or to include a more descriptive or precise word than you originally used.

Graphics

Separate graphics software programs will enable you to create professional-quality charts, graphs, tables, and diagrams. Graphics enhance the appearance of your paper and are particularly useful if an oral presentation of your paper is required.

Tutorial Software

Software is often available in the college learning lab or writing center that provides review and practice of various features of writing such as punctuation, sentence structure, subject-verb agreement, pronoun agreement, and so forth. If you are having a problem with a particular aspect of writing, working through the self-instructional software will help you become aware of and correct the problem.

APPROACHING ASSIGNMENTS IN ACADEMIC DISCIPLINES

Each academic discipline is unique in the types and styles of writing it requires. Your ability to diversify and adapt your writing skills to fit the requirements and conventions of each discipline may mean the difference between successful and mediocre performance in your courses as well as later, in your chosen career.

Many students think incorrectly that there are only two basic types of papers: opinion and research. They think that either they must collect facts from other sources or they must discuss their own attitudes, opinions, and beliefs about a given topic. Actually, college papers are seldom purely research (reporting of facts) are rarely call exclusively for unqualified opinion. Instead, most require reasoning, thinking, evaluation, and reaction. Often, research is necessary, followed by focused, reasoned reaction and interpretation.

This section of the chapter focuses on four common types of writing required in various academic disciplines. Each is approached as a guided thinking task. The research paper will be discussed in the next chapter.

Themes or Compositions

Most commonly assigned in English courses, themes or compositions require you to present or discuss your own ideas on a particular topic. Often this type of assignment is simply called a "paper." Usually, the instructor specifies the topic or general subject area and may or may not require a specific approach or focus. One instructor might simply ask you to write a paper on any form of censorship, while another may provide a stronger focus: to discuss pornography and censorship. Often the paper's length is suggested in number of either words or pages.

In composition classes, the emphasis is on process as well as content. You might, for example, be asked to write a description of a person with whom you are well acquainted. This assignment is intended to guide you in the process of descriptive writing, and the instructor is interested in the techniques you use as well as what you say. When writing themes and compositions, keep these suggestions in mind:

The purpose of the assignment is particularly important. If the purpose of a paper is to apply the principles of narrative writing, be sure your paper is consistent with and demonstrates those principles.

Although you may be writing from your own experience without reference to research, you must still be accurate in your facts and specific.

If asked about an unfamiliar topic, spend an hour or so in the library reading about the topic. Once you have explored the topic, you will feel more confident in writing about it.

Critical Essays

In the arts, humanities, and social sciences, you will often be asked to write critical essays that require you to think, react to, reason, and write about particular authors, artistic or literary works, theories, or events. The list below identifies typical types of writing assignments and provides an example of each. As you read the list, notice once again that thought patterns are evident.

❏ ❏ ❏

Type of Assignment	*Example*
Compare two authors, two poems, two solutions to an issue or dilemma.	Dickens and Thoreau hold very different world views. Summarize, then contrast, the two views using specific references to their works.
Analyze two competing viewpoints.	If the United States were to become involved in another war in Southeast Asia, what international and domestic problems can you anticipate for China and for the United States?
Speculate on probable outcomes.	How might Charles Dickens react to reading Vonnegut's *Slaughter house Five?*
Comment on the validity, morality, or value of an issue, work, or decision.	Discuss and react to the Supreme Court decision on prayer in public education.
Answer a debatable question.	Can a person deaf from birth understand the concept of music?

❏ ❏ ❏

In working with critical essays, use the following tips:

Every assignment requires thinking and reasoning; do not limit your paper to statements of opinion. You are expected, even if it is not directly stated in the assignment, to support, explain, and justify your ideas.

Do not hesitate to be creative; often the development of creative thinking is one of the purposes of the assignment.

Brainstorming, one of the prewriting techniques, is particularly useful as a means of generating ideas.

Be certain to relate the assignment, as clearly as possible, to course content, referring to topics studied that pertain to the assignment. For example, in answering the question about another Southeast Asian war, you might use information on the Vietnam War and its problems as a base of discussion.

Reviews and Critiques

In a variety of courses, you may be asked to write a review or to critique an artistic or literary work, performance, demonstration, film, video, scholarly paper, journal article, or piece of professional work (such as a ledger prepared by an accountant). A few sample assignments are listed below:

❏ Review the following computer program and identify its weaknesses.
❏ Study the nursing objectives written for Patient X and comment on their appropriateness.
❏ Critique the film *Lawrence of Arabia* from the perspective of historical accuracy.

In a review or critique, you are expected to focus on the successful features as well as the weaknesses or problems in the work, unless otherwise directed. It is to be an evaluation of the work, similar to movie reviews that appear weekly in most newspapers. You should also include, usually at the beginning, a brief summary or description of the work at hand. Here are a few additional suggestions:

If you are lacking background information, or the work seems unfamiliar, take some time for reading or research. If it is a poem you are to critique, find out about the poet, the time during which he or she wrote, and common themes, concerns, or issues of the poet.

Take notes as you read, watch, or study the work.

Plan on rereading and closely studying the work several times, if possible.

Depending on the length of the assignment, select three to six key points or aspects of the work you want to cover. Do not plan on reviewing every feature of the work.

Discuss the work with other students, especially one-time performances and demonstrations that you cannot review. Others may have approached the work with a different perspective or interpretation; you can broaden your viewpoint by considering alternate interpretations.

Laboratory Reports

Laboratory reports are a very specialized type of writing required in technical courses and in the life and physical sciences. Most of these courses have a required weekly laboratory session during which time you learn procedures, conduct experiments, and verify existing principles. Most professors require a written report for each lab conducted. In this report, you are expected to detail your purposes, procedures, materials, observations, results, and conclusions. For many introductory level courses, a commercially printed laboratory workbook or manual is required. If so, the format and contents of your lab report are often clearly specified. If no such manual is used, your professor will most likely provide a standard format to be used.

To write effective laboratory reports, use the following guidelines:

Usually lab reports are divided into sections, and sometimes, subsections, using an outline format. The report itself, however, should be written in complete-sentence form.

Use direct, straightforward, precise language. Avoid elaborate descriptions; be as concise as possible.

Take careful notes as you conduct the experiment. You will need detailed information for your results section.

Draft your report as soon as possible after completing the lab, while the details are still fresh in your mind.

Be sure to differentiate clearly between results and conclusions. Results refer to what happened during the experiment, while conclusions are interpretations of results, their significance, importance, and application.

Consistent presentation of format is important in the sciences. The placement of titles, dates, and numbering of pages are details considered important. Scientists, of which your professor is one, are accustomed to exact, consistent, precise records that make data easy to analyze and that eliminate error and misinterpretation. To make the best possible impression, spend time with your report's format. Present data in table form, numbered and titled. Clearly label each section.

SUMMARY

1. While writing is commonly thought of as a form of communication, this chapter emphasizes writing as a means of thinking and learning.

2. Writing is an essential part of learning; it enables you to

   ❏ organize and clarify ideas
   ❏ generate new ideas
   ❏ give shape and form to thought

3. Instructors often use written assignments to guide and direct your learning.

4. In completing written assignments, it is important to analyze their purpose and to identify the tasks they involve.
5. Many writing assignments require you to synthesize information, thereby creating a new and original work. Thought patterns are an effective means of synthesizing information.
6. Writing is a six-stage process involving

❏ prewriting
❏ organizing and outlining
❏ formulating a thesis
❏ writing a draft
❏ revising
❏ proofreading

7. Different types of written assignments are given in various academic disciplines. The types include:

❏ themes
❏ critical essays
❏ review and critiques
❏ laboratory reports

CLASS ACTIVITY

Directions:
Complete each of the following steps:

1. Each student should locate two or three popular magazines and use and exchange them to complete the following assignment:
   Review a selection of men's, women's, and general circulation magazines. Study the advertisements—photos, drawings, and text—and write a brief, one-page paper describing the attitudes they project toward male and female sex roles. Include specific examples to support your ideas.
2. After each student has completed the assignment, students working in pairs or small groups should answer the following questions:
   a. What was the purpose of the assignments?
   b. What number of magazines did you decide was sufficient to review?
   c. What type of notes did you take, and how were they organized?

    d. What thought pattern(s) were useful in completing this assignment?

    e. Describe the stages of the writing process that you used.

3. Students should exchange, read, and evaluate each other's papers. Evaluate (a) the thesis statement, (b) supporting information, and (c) organization.

FURTHER ANALYSIS

Directions:
Analyze the following situation and answer the questions.

A sociology class studying institutional racism was asked to write a one-page paper in response to the following:

> At predominantly white campuses across the country, it is common to see minority students clustered among their racial peers. For example, all-black tables in cafeterias are not uncommon. How does one account for this informal segregation? Is it desirable or undesirable? How so?

One student had difficulty with the assignment and felt it asked her to make a decision about an issue that she had not observed on her campus. She started to write the paper, but found she had little to say. Finally, she wrote the following thesis statement.

> Students should be able to sit wherever and with whom they choose, whether they are black and white.

1. Do you think the student had understood the purpose of the assignment? Explain your answer.
2. Offer suggestions that may have helped her approach the assignment more effectively?
3. What strategies might she have used to generate ideas?
4. Evaluate her thesis statement by predicting how well it fulfills the assignment.

DISCUSSION

1. Over the past month, what uses have you made of writing *outside* of school? Make a list of these situations. What conclusions can you draw about how you use writing?

2. Analyze your own approach to writing by considering what factors make it easy or difficult. (Consider such factors as time, place, type of assignment.)
3. Some experienced writers compose using a typewriter or word processor. Other claim only handwriting seems to focus and direct their thinking. Discuss the relative merits of each to write papers.

FURTHER READING

Axelrod, Rise B., and Charles R. Cooper. *Reading Critically, Writing Well.* 3rd ed. New York: St. Martin's, 1993.

Behrens, Laurence, and Leonard J. Rosen. *Writing and Reading Across the Curriculum.* 4th ed. New York: HarperCollins, 1993.

17

Research and Term Papers

Learning Objectives

Approach various types of term papers

Take advantage of available library resources

Develop a systematic procedure for writing research
papers

Term papers, also called research papers, represent an essential
part of college learning. Some students dread, even avoid,
courses in which a term paper is assigned because it involves a considerable commitment of time and effort. Although term papers are hard work,
they do provide numerous advantages and excellent opportunities that
more than compensate for the effort required.

Term papers allow you to distinguish yourself—to demonstrate your
diligence, hard work, thinking and organizational skills, creativity, and
talent. They enable you to display your skills to your best advantage and
capture your professor's recognition or attention.

Term papers allow you to work as hard as you want to. Unlike an
examination, which occurs within a specific time frame, with limited
preparation and writing time, a term paper is open-ended, without rigid
time constraints.

Term papers are excellent opportunities for students who are not good test-takers, those who do not think best in pressured or highly structured situations.

Term papers provide the opportunity to look ahead in an academic discipline, to go beyond the basics and explore advanced study in the field. By researching a topic, you learn a great deal about the field: how topics are examined, how research is conducted, and how new ideas are explored. Students who are undecided about their major often find a field of study that interests them through the in-depth study a term paper requires.

Term papers develops and polish valuable research skills. The ability to research a topic efficiently and thoroughly is a skill you will use throughout life, long after you are finished with formal education. Numerous everyday situations as well as job-related tasks require research. For instance, you may wish to research a certain automobile model's performance before you purchase a new car, learn which features of a house should be inspected before purchase, or learn about an illness or physical problem you face. As you search for a job, you may need to research various companies from which you have received offers; once you accept a job, research is often necessary to remain current in your field.

The purpose of this chapter is to enable you to approach researching and writing term papers in an organized, systematic manner. Various types of term papers will be discussed along with the level of thinking skills they demand. Available library resources and services will be reviewed, and guidelines for writing the paper will be offered.

TYPES OF TERM PAPERS AND LEVELS OF THINKING SKILLS

Before beginning to work on a term paper, you should analyze the task, identifying the types of thinking it demands. There are three basic types of term papers, each of which requires successively higher level thinking skills and more extensive research. These types are described below.

Type 1: Consolidation and Summarization of Information

In entry-level freshman course, such as Introduction to Philosophy or Introductory Psychology, term papers often are assigned to acquaint you with the research process and to familiarize you with available sources of information in the field. In effect, you are learning *how* to research topic, as well as exploring your particular topic. Consequently, these papers demand the least in terms of thinking and creativity. Usually, you are asked to explore one topic and to consolidate, summarize, and record your findings. Here are a few examples of this type of assignment:

Sociology
 Report on several theories of group process or leadership.

American Government
 Choose one of the First-Amendment freedoms and trace its history from its inclusion in the Bill of Rights to modern times.

For these types of papers, focus on investigating your topic thoroughly and completely, uncovering all aspects, features, and characteristics.

Type 2: Analysis and Interpretation

Term papers for intermediate-level courses, those beyond freshman courses but not restricted to majors, often require an in-depth study and analysis of information collected. Research is the basis for reasoning and thinking about a particular topic of study. For example, you may be asked to research and then compare two theories, or to analyze the effects of a historical event, or to evaluate possible solutions to a social problem. (Notice here, again, the predominance of thought patterns).

The key to researching and writing this type of term paper is to focus on the nature of the assignment, in much the same way as you analyze an essay exam question. Determine which thought processes are called for and what types of information you will need to complete the assignment.

Type 3: Original or Creative Research

In advanced, specialized courses, term papers often require you to research a topic and then produce or create original work based on the research. For example, in business law, you might be asked to research the history of breach of contract law, and then to use your knowledge to prepare a brief on a hypothetical case. In a literature course, you might be asked to review several critical analyses of a novel and then develop your own interpretation of its symbolism.

When researching for this type of paper, you will need to keep reaction notes as well as research notes (see pp. 388–391). In your reaction notes, record your impressions, ideas, and criticisms of the research as well as any related ideas that can be of help to you while researching. You will also need to read the research sources in a critical evaluative manner, focusing on what information, approaches, or interpretations seem valid and useful.

EXERCISE: 17–1

Directions:
Study each of the following term paper topics and decide which type of research they require:

1. A comparison of the trade and export policies of the United States and Canada
2. The long-term effects of child abuse
3. A proposal to control computer crime

LIBRARIES: RESOURCES AND SERVICES

Today, libraries and the students who use them are faced with the difficult task of keeping up with the rapid growth in fields of knowledge, often referred to as the information explosion. Each year an estimated 35,000 to 40,000 books are published in the United States alone. Thousands of newspapers, periodicals, and professional journals published daily, weekly, or monthly add significantly to this volume of information. Consequently, libraries are rapidly expanding, changing, reorganizing, and converting to advanced technological or computerized systems of data management. A library, then, is no longer a building in which the college's books are housed; it is a vast array of resources and services. To research a topic efficiently, you must be familiar with the library and the resources and services available.

Learning Your College Library's System

A first step to using your library effectively is to become familiar with its organization and floor plan. Large universities have a library system, with specialized libraries located throughout the campus, as well as a central library. If possible, before you have a research assignment to complete, go to the library and notice how it is organized and what services it provides. If tours are available, take one; the knowledge you gain may save you hours of time when you can least afford to spend it. Some library systems provide videotapes on how to use the library; others offer workshops. If none of the above are available, visit the library, ask for a floor plan, and take your own tour.

To become familiar with your campus library, discover the answers to the following questions:

❏ Where is the reference desk? (Reference librarians are available to help you locate sources, solve research problems, and answer your questions.)

❏ What classification system is used to shelve and catalog books?

❏ How is the card catalog organized or accessed, if on computer? Are there separate files for subject, author, and title cards, or are they alphabetized together?

❏ To which periodicals does your library subscribe? How are back issues stored, and how do you obtain them?

❏ If your library does not own a book or article you need, can you request it through an interlibrary loan system? If so, how?

❏ Does the library have a reserve desk or section where professors may place materials "on reserve" for restricted or limited circulation?

❏ What other services and facilities are offered or housed in the library? (Consider listening rooms, study rooms, and duplicating services.)

Locating and Using Information Sources

There are four main sources of information in most libraries: reference books, circulating books, periodicals, and nonprint materials (tapes, films). The key to conducting thorough research is to learn *how* to find what you need in each of these sources. Fortunately, certain tools and resources make this task easier:

Check the catalog under the general subject heading. Many college libraries have computerized their card catalog, making the information it contains more accessible. If you cannot seem to find any listings under the subject, most likely you are not using the right heading. Check the reference titled *Library of Congress Subject Headings,* which lists appropriate subject headings for various topics.

Check bibliographies. Learn whether any bibliographies (lists of sources on a particular subject) have already been published on your topic. To find out, check the reference book titled *Bibliographic Index,* which provides an annual list of bibliographies arranged by subject heading. Your next step is to determine whether a bibliography listed in the *Index* is available in your library. The bibliography may contain both books and periodical articles that pertain to its subject.

Check indexes of periodicals. While a card catalog lists books available on a given topic, it does not list magazine or journal articles. To locate these, you must use a periodical index in a particular academic discipline. While most students are familiar with and have used the *Readers' Guide to Periodical Literature,* many are not aware of the more specialized ones. Here are a few examples:

Social Sciences Index	*General Science Index*
Education Index	*Environment Index*

These indexes are prepared annually and list topics alphabetically.

Read abstracts. If you find a large number of periodical articles on your topic and wish to learn more about a specific article to decide if it is worthwhile or whether it duplicates information you already have, find out if an abstract (brief summary) is available in a book of abstracts. For example, articles pertaining to topics in psychology are summarized in a reference source titled *Psychological Abstracts.* Abstracts exist for a variety of subject areas. Determine what is available in your field.

Use a computerized search. Many libraries subscribe to one or more computer systems that enable you to request a list of all sources of information on a given topic. A computerized search usually provides titles of books related to your topic and titles, authors, and brief summarizes of articles published on your topic. The search will include all available sources, whether or not your library owns them.

To initiate a computerized search, check with the reference librarian. He or she can explain how to begin. Be sure to ask if there are any costs involved. You will begin by choosing *descriptors,* words the computer will use to search for information on your topic. The success and completeness of a computerized search depend on choosing accurate and comprehensive descriptors. You can also use descriptors to limit your search. You could, for example, request only sources published after 1990.

Ask the librarian for assistance. Especially for your first few research projects, consult with the reference librarian for sources you may have overlooked or research procedures that may save time and effort.

EXERCISE 17–2

Directions:

For your major field of study, prepare a list of the major indexes, reference books, and periodicals. Verify the accuracy of your list by consulting a reference librarian. (If you are an undecided or undeclared major, select a possible field of study.)

GUIDELINES FOR WRITING RESEARCH PAPERS

This section offers general guidelines and presents step-by-step procedures for completing a successful research paper.

Tips for Getting Started

The first college research paper you do is always the most difficult because you are learning or refining a new process as well as doing the paper.

Determine its importance. Find out how important the research paper is by finding out how heavily the paper counts in your final course grade. This information will help you determine how much time and effort you should put into the paper.

Get an early start. Even if the paper is not due until the end of the semester, start working on it as soon as possible. Starting early may enable you to produce a good rather than a just barely acceptable paper. If you have not done a research paper before, you will need time to become familiar with the process.

There are several other advantages to starting early. You will find books and references readily available in the library, while if you wait until everyone is working on their papers, popular sources will be in use or checked out by other students. You will also have time to acquire information you may need from other libraries through interlibrary loan services. Finally, you will have the time to think, to organize, and even to make mistakes and have time to correct them.

Develop a timetable for the completion of your paper, such as the one shown in Figure 17-1.

Consult with your instructor. If you experience difficulty or feel uncertain that you are taking the right approach, ask your professor for advice. Often, through their experience with the subject matter, professors are

Figure 17-1
Sample Weekly Timetable

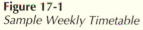

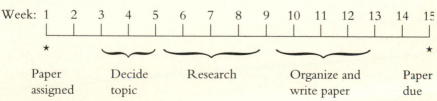

able to suggest alternative approaches to the topic, recommend a particular reference, or suggest a different organization. However, do not consult your professor until you have wrestled with the problem yourself and have come to a standstill. When you do speak with your professor, take your notes, outlines, and drafts and have specific questions in mind.

Consider using a word processor. As discussed in the previous chapter, a computer's word processing capabilities are a real help in producing a paper. When dealing with lengthy papers, as research papers tend to be, the word processor is particularly helpful in organizing, revising, and editing.

Steps in Writing a Term Paper

A term paper is a research report; its purpose is to report as concisely as possible the results of research you conducted, and if called for by the assignment, to interpret, evaluate, and apply those findings. Writing a term paper is best done systematically, following the steps listed below:

1. Narrow and define your topic.
2. Research your topic.
3. Organize your ideas.
4. Develop a thesis statement.
5. Write and revise your paper.
6. Prepare the final copy.

Step 1: Narrow and Define Your Topic

Choosing and narrowing your topic is critical to producing a good paper. If you begin with an unmanageable topic, regardless of how hard you work, you will be unable to produce an acceptable paper. Your task will be much easier if you choose a manageable topic—one for which information is readily accessible and understandable.

The most important consideration in selecting a topic is to choose one that is neither too broad nor too narrow. If you choose a topic that is too broad, it will be impossible for you to cover all its aspects adequately. On the other hand, if it is too specific, you may have difficulty finding enough to write about. For most students, the tendency is to select a topic that is too general.

Suppose you are taking a course in ecology and you have been assigned a five- to seven-page research paper. Your instructor will allow you to choose any topic related to the course of study. You have always been interested in environmental pollution and decide to do your research paper on this subject. Because pollution has many causes, many types, and many effects, both immediate and long term, you realize that the topic of environmental pollution is much too broad. To narrow or limit this topic, you might choose one type of pollution—air pollution, say—and its causes or the effects. Then you might decide to limit your topic to a study of the various types of air-pollution control devices, or their effects. Often it is necessary to narrow your topic two or three times. The process of narrowing a topic might be diagrammed as shown in Figure 17-2.

To narrow your topic, think of ways it could be subdivided. To learn how a subject is divided, check the card catalog in the library under your subject and read the subject headings. Also skim through encyclopedia articles on the topic to learn a little about it. Depending on your subject, you may also wish to consult other texts in the subject area to get a brief overview of the field.

EXERCISE 17–3

Directions:

Assume that one of your professors has assigned a research paper on one of the following subjects. Choose one and narrow it to a topic that is manageable in a 10-page paper. If necessary check the card catalog, an encyclopedia entry, or textbooks in the field.

1. Clothing styles and fashion
2. Test-tube babies
3. Sports
4. Death
5. Pornography

Once you have narrowed your topic, the next step is to define your approach to it. Decide (1) whether you want to prove something about

Figure 17-2
Narrowing a Topic

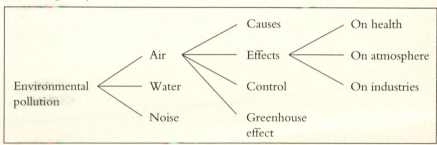

your topic, inform others about it, or explain or analyze it and (2) who your audience is. In some cases, your approach may have already been defined by your instructor when the paper was assigned. The approach you choose will affect directly how you proceed from this point. The sources you consult, the amount of reading you do, and the thesis statement you develop are each shaped by your purpose.

Step 2: Research Your Topic

Once you have narrowed your topic, the next step is to research your topic using logical and systematic search strategies. Use the following procedure:

Choose a Documentation Format

As you use sources, you will need to keep a record of the complete title, author, publisher, place, date, and pages. Before you begin, select the format you will use for the term paper's bibliography and use this format to record sources as you use them. Various documentation styles are available; often a particular style is preferred in a specific academic discipline. Style manuals detail these documentation styles. These include the following:

> *The MLA Handbook for Writers of Research Papers, Thesis, and Dissertations.* New York: Modern Language Association, 1988.
> *Publication Manual of the American Psychological Association,* 4th ed. Washington: APA, 1994.

Organize Notetaking Systems

You will need two systems: one for recording sources used, another for recording notes from these sources. Many researchers find it efficient to list their sources on 3 x 5 inch index cards, permitting fast alphabetization of actual sources used when preparing the bibliography. For each source, in addition to bibliographic information, also record its library call number (this will save you time should you need to locate the source again).

For taking notes, the 5 x 8 inch or 4 x 6 inch cards are best. Use a separate card for each subtopic or aspect of your topic. In the upper right corner, record the author's last name and the pages you used. In the upper left corner, write the subtopic. Be sure to write only on one side of the card. A sample source card and sample notetaking card are shown in Figure 17-3.

Here are a few suggestions for taking good research notes:
Record the information in your own words instead of copying the author's words. By recording the author's wording, you run the risk of

Figure 17-3
Sample Source and Notecards

Environmental Quality,
1994. Washington, D.C.:
Council on Environmental
Quality, p. 33-35

Source card

Effects - CO_2   *Weinstein*
                                                p. 122-135

effects of carbon dioxide release three
burning of fossil fuels
1. Upsets balance between CO_2 & oxygen
2. traps surface heat on earth's surface
3. interferes w/ ability of ocean bacteria to
maintain acidity of sea water.: interfering
with reproduction of bacteria which release
oxygen into atmosphere

Note card

using the author's working in your paper, perhaps without realizing that you have done so. Whenever you use an author's words instead of your own, you are required to use quotation marks and give the author credit by indicating the author and source from which the material was taken. Failure to give credit is known as *plagiarism*. Plagiarism is a form of theft of ideas or words and therefore a serious error, and many institutions penalize students who either knowingly or unknowingly plagiarize.

Try to summarize and condense information. You will find that it is impossible to record all the information appearing and reappearing in various sources. If you have already made a note once, do not spend time writing it again. Occasionally, you may need to check back through your notes to see what you have already recorded. You might, however, want to note the fact that there is common agreement in a number of sources about the information.

Record useful quotes. If you find a statement that strongly supports your thesis, you may want to include it as a quotation in your paper. Copy it down exactly and place it in quotation marks in your notes, along with its page reference.

Preview and Skim Sources. Reading reference material is very different from reading textbooks. Because high recall is not required when reading reference sources, you can afford to skim, scan, and skip large portions of material. Previewing is a valuable means of identifying useful sources. Once you have located a book or article, preview it to determine if it contains useful and sufficient information. Pay particular attention to its index and table of contents.

Get an Overview of Your Topic. Once you have identified your topic, do some preliminary reading to get an overview, a general idea of the basic issues and problems. A good starting point is a general encyclopedia, such as the *Encyclopedia Britannica.* Also check specialized encyclopedias that cover topics only in particular fields such as music, art, or history. As you read, note and record useful reference sources. Also jot down ideas about how to approach, further limit, or organize your topic. Refer to your course textbook for suggested readings or additional sources of information.

Proceed from General to Specific Sources. As you delve deeper into your topic, work with increasingly specific, detailed reference sources. You might progress from a book on the general subject that includes your topic, to a book on your general topic, to a periodical article specifically about your topic, and then to numerous other articles that explore in depth one aspect of your topic, as shown below:

> General book: *The Ecology Action Guide*
> More specific book: *Vanishing Air*
> Periodical article on the topic: "Air Pollution and Human Health"
> Article on one aspect of the topic: "Lung Cancer and Particulate Matter"

Use Sources as References to Additional Sources

Once you begin researching a topic, you will find that one source, through its bibliography, leads to several additional sources, and each of those will also provide further references. Read carefully the introductory pages in scholarly journal articles; writers often provide a valuable review of related research before proceeding with the substance of their article.

Know When Your Research Is Complete

Questions often posed by students are "How do I know when to stop?" or "How will I know when I've adequately explored the topic?" The answer to these questions is fairly simple: You will know you have researched your topic thoroughly when you not longer discover new information in up-to-date sources or when you have accumulated too much information. When numerous sources seem to repeat others, then you can be confident that you have left no aspect of your topic unexplored.

Step 3: Organize Your Ideas

This step sharpens the focus of your paper by establishing a direction and method of organization. Begin by rereading all your research notes and studying different ways to organize them. Identify topics that overlap and others that can be grouped together under a more general subtopic. Next, sort your cards in separate piles according to subtopic. Then, with each pack of cards laid out in front of you, try to arrange them in a logical order or pattern. You might arrange your subtopics chronologically, in order of importance, or by cause and effect. Often your purpose for writing, or the content of the paper, will dictate the order or arrangement. Experiment with several arrangements until you find one that seems best.

❏ ❏ ❏
Thinking Critically . . . About Research Sources

When conducing research for a term paper, be sure to critically evaluate your sources. Not all sources are equally valuable or appropriate. Use the following suggestions to evaluate reference sources:

1. Check the copyright date. Be sure you are using a current source.
2. Be sure to use an authoritative source. The material should be written by someone who is a recognized authority or who is working within his or her field.
3. Choose first-hand accounts of an event or experience rather than second- or third-hand accounts whenever possible.
4. Choose sources that provide the most complete and concrete information.
5. Avoid sources that present biased information and those that include personal opinion and reactions.

Suppose your topic is the effects of air pollution on human health. You have collected information on various specific pollutants, such as hydrocarbons, and the health problems they create. You have also found information on types of diseases and illnesses related to air pollution: lung cancer, cardiovascular disease, and so forth. As you reread your notecards, you realize you can organize your ideas in two ways: according to types of pollutants or according to types of health problems. The organization you choose determines the emphasis, focus, and direction of your paper. To make a decision, consider which you can organize and present more effectively.

Once you have chosen an organization, prepare a tentative general outline, listing the subtopics in order. Now that you can see how the ideas relate to one another, reread your outline and revise it.

Step 4: Develop a Thesis Statement

The next step is to devise a thesis statement that will unify and organize your paper. A thesis statement concisely reveals the focus and purpose of your paper. You might think of a thesis statement as similar to the topic sentence of a paragraph that states what the entire paragraph is about.

Here are a few examples of weak thesis statements followed by several examples of strong, specific thesis statements, each on the topic of air pollution. As you read, notice how they differ.

❏ ❏ ❏

Weak	*Strong.*
Air pollution is at the root of many health problems.	Air pollution has had a dramatic effect on the lives of twentieth-century Americans in terms of smoking regulations, antipollution devices, and industrial control.
Air pollution has affected each of our lives in numerous ways.	Air pollution has been a primary cause of numerous health-related problems, including lung cancer, respiratory disease, increased infant mortality, cardiovascular disease, and death rates among the elderly.
Scientists predict that air pol-	Air pollution may create a

lution may create a green-house effect.	greenhouse effect, severely altering our environment and producing drastic climatic changes.

❏ ❏ ❏

Notice that each strong statement takes a specific focus on the topic and states what aspects of the topic the paper will discuss.

Plan on changing, revising, or narrowing this statement as you proceed through the remaining steps. Right now your thesis statement should express the idea *you think* your paper will explain or discuss. In a sense, the thesis statement further narrows your topic by limiting your paper to a specific focus or approach. Once you have established your thesis, go back to your outline and revise and reorganize, adding subtopics. Tighten your outline so it effectively develops your thesis statement.

EXERCISE 17–4

Directions:

Assume that each of the following is the topic of a research paper. For each, narrow the topic and write a thesis statement that suggests a direction of development or focus for the topic:

1. Cigarette smoking
2. Capital punishment
3. Terrorism
4. Choosing a career
5. AIDS

Step 5: Write and Revise Your Paper

Using your outline as a guide and your note cards to provide the specific facts and information, write a first draft of your paper. It should have a brief introduction of one or two paragraphs, a body, and a conclusion or summary. In the introduction, you should state the thesis of the paper. Before starting it, you might lead up to it by supplying necessary background information or by providing a context.

The body, which is most of the paper, should explain and discuss the thesis statement. Each idea should be directly related to and support the thesis statement. Finally, in the conclusion or summary you should draw together the ideas you presented and bring the paper to a close.

That is, in the last several paragraphs, try to review the major points you presented and connect them, once again, to the thesis statement.

Once you have written a first draft, reread, evaluate, and revise it. As with any other type of paper, revision is a critical step that can make a major difference in quality. Make certain that your thesis is carefully and thoroughly developed and explained. Plan to make several revisions to produce a well-written paper. Refer to Chapter 16, pp. 367–368, for additional revision suggestions.

Step 6: Prepare the Final Copy

It is generally agreed that a typewritten (or word processed) final copy is strongly desirable. Some professors require typewritten copy; most prefer it to handwritten papers. If you have poor, illegible handwriting, your professor may have difficulty reading the paper and may unconsciously react to your paper negatively or critically. A typewritten copy, on the other hand, presents a neat appearance and suggests that you care enough about your work to present it in the best possible form.

An important part of preparing a final copy, regardless of whether it is handwritten or typed, is proofreading. Once you have prepared the final copy, be sure to take the time to read it through and correct spelling, punctuation, and grammar. If you are weak in one or more of these areas and cannot easily recognize your own errors, ask a friend to proofread your paper and mark the errors.

The final steps to completing a research paper are to prepare a list, or bibliography, of all the sources that you used to write the paper, and to prepare any endnotes necessary. Endnotes indicate the sources from which you have taken quotations or which contained unique or specialized information particular to a certain source. You will need to ask your instructor which format he or she prefers or consult a handbook to determine the specialized format endnotes require. Several handbooks are listed as Further Readings at the end of this chapter.

As mentioned earlier, if you keep careful records of sources as you collect data and information for a paper, preparing a bibliography is a relatively simple task. In the bibliography, you simply list alphabetically the sources you used. Depending on your instructor, as well as the subject area with which you are working, different formats may be expected. Although each format requires basically the same information, arrangement of information as well as punctuation may vary. Some instructors may specify a particular format, while others may accept any standard, consistent format. If your instructor prefers a particular format, by all means use it. Otherwise use the *MLA Handbook* for humanities courses and the American Psychological Association (APA) format for social and physical sciences.

SUMMARY

1. Research and term papers provide an opportunity to explore a topic and demonstrate your learning in a low-pressure, creative, and flexible manner.
2. There are three basic types of term papers, each of which requires a different type and level of thinking skills:

   ❑ one requires consolidation and summarization of information
   ❑ a second type requires analysis and interpretations
   ❑ a third involves original or creative research

3. Effective use of libraries is the key to research. It is essential to become familiar with your campus library, its services, and its facilities.
4. A library houses four main sources of information:

   ❑ reference books
   ❑ circulating books
   ❑ periodicals
   ❑ nonprint materials

5. Preparation of a term paper is a six-step process:

   ❑ narrowing and defining your topic
   ❑ researching your topic
   ❑ organizing your ideas
   ❑ developing a thesis statement
   ❑ writing and revising the paper
   ❑ preparing a final copy

CLASS ACTIVITY

Directions:

Form research teams of four students and complete each of the following activities in preparing a term paper:

1. Select a subject from a list below and narrow it to a topic appropriate for a 15- to 20-page research paper:

body language	psychosomatic illnesses
science fiction	reverse discrimination
nuclear disarmament	suicide
Third World countries	popular music

2. Decide upon a documentation format and obtain a style manual that describes it.

3. Working as a team, visit the library. Each person should locate one source that will provide an overview of the topic. Include a general encyclopedia and a subject area encyclopedia. Each team member should review sources located by other members.
4. Working together so as not to duplicate efforts, each member should obtain five specific sources on a particular aspect of the topic and prepare notecards on those sources.
5. The group should review each other's notes, discussing different focuses or directions a paper on this topic might take. Write a thesis statement for each possibility discussed.

FURTHER ANALYSIS

For his freshman composition course, a student is required to write a term paper of about 3,000 words on a current controversial issue. After considering various issues, he chose capital punishment and began his research by consulting the card catalog. Several books on the topic were already checked out; he located and checked out three books. Next he checked the past year's *Readers' Guide to Periodical Literature* and located and photocopied six news magazine articles on recent cases in which executions were carried out. After taking notes from these sources, the student became frustrated. He was unable to develop a working outline or formulate a thesis statement.
Directions:
Explain the student's frustration, evaluate his research strategy, and offer suggestions.

DISCUSSION

1. An economics instructor announced to her class that each student had the option of taking a final examination or writing a 10-page term paper and asked students to be prepared to indicate their preferences at the next class session. What questions would you ask the instructor before making a decision?
2. What course of action would you take if, in the middle of collecting research information, you felt the topic you had chosen was too technical and complicated?
3. A classmate in your Western Civilization class is "remodeling" and "revising" her boyfriend's term paper that he wrote for the same course last year taught by a different instructor. The original paper earned a B grade, so she is confident that with modest

revisions, the paper will earn an A grade. The student justifies her action by saying that she will learn just as much about the topic by reading and revising that paper as if she had written it herself. Evaluate her justification. What does it suggest about this student's attitude toward and strategies for learning?

FURTHER READING

Lester, James D. *Writing Research Papers: A Complete Guide.* 7th ed. New York: HarperCollins, 1993.

Meyer, Michael. *The Little, Brown Guide to Writing Research Papers.* 3rd ed. New York: HarperCollins, 1993.

Winkler, Anthony C., and JoRay McCuen. *Writing the Research Paper.* 3rd ed. New York: Harcourt, 1989.

Self-Assessment Questionnaire

❑ ❑ ❑

General Study and Thinking Skills	Chapter	Always	Sometimes	Never
Is class attendance important to you?	1			
Do you ask questions in class?	1			
Do you approach tasks with an open, active and questioning mind?	1			
Do you analyze tasks by determining what type(s) of thinking they require?	1			
Do you do what is necessary to learn and master the material, even if it is time-consuming?	1			
Are you alert for early warning signals of academic difficulty?	1			
Have you made an effort to become acquainted with your professors and academic advisor?	2			

	Chapter	Always	Sometimes	Never
Are you aware of various sources of academic assistance on your campus?	2			
Have you developed a semester study plan?	3			
Do you study in the same place regularly?	3			
Do you experiment with new learning techniques?	6			
Do you select strategies to complete a task before you begin it?	6			
Do you monitor the effectiveness of your learning?	6			
Do you use techniques to improve your ability to store and retrieve information?	5			
Do you use thought patterns to improve your learning efficiency?	7			
Do you solve problems systematically?	4			
Do you question and evaluate what you read and hear?	4			

Textbook Study

	Chapter	Always	Sometimes	Never
Do you preview assignments before reading them?	6			
Do you attempt to discover the overall plan of a chapter before reading it?	9			
Do you approach graphic materials as visual thought patterns?	9			

	Chapter	Always	Sometimes	Never
For courses with technical and specialized vocabulary, have you developed a course master file?	12			
Have you developed systematic review strategies for reading assignments?	9			
Do you use different learning strategies for various academic disciplines?	13			

Class Lecture

	Chapter	Always	Sometimes	Never
Do you read or preview corresponding textbook assignments before attending lectures?	8			
Have you developed a workable abbreviation system?	8			
Can you anticipate and identify lecturer's thought patterns?	8			
Do your notes reflect the lecture's organization as well as important content?	8			
Do you edit your notes regularly?	8			
Do you adapt your note-taking techniques to suit different lecture styles?	8			
Do you adapt your note-taking techniques for various academic disciplines?	8, 13			

Organizing and Synthesizing Course Content

	Chapter	Always	Sometimes	Never
Do you underline and mark your texts?	10			

	Chapter	Always	Sometimes	Never
Have you developed a system of marginal annotation?	10			
Do you use recall clues?	10			
Do you use outlining to reflect thought patterns?	10			
Have you used summarizaton to condense ideas?	10			
Do you find mapping a useful strategy to organize information?	10			

Preparing for and taking Exams

	Chapter	Always	Sometimes	Never
Do you organize your review by preparing a review plan or timetable?	14			
Have you successfully identified thematic study units?	14			
Do you use study sheets or the index system to prepare for objective exams?	14			
Are you able to predict essay exam questions?	14			
Have you developed strategies for integrating text and lecture material?	14			
Have you developed strategies for taking each type of exam?	15			
Do you preview an exam and plan your time before beginning to answer questions?	15			
Are you able to write an organized, effective essay exam answer?	15			

	Chapter	Always	Sometimes	Never

Writing Skills

Question	Chapter	Always	Sometimes	Never
Do you use writing as a means of thinking and learning?	16			
Do you take time to identify the purpose of an assignment before you begin working on it?	16			
Do you plan and organize ideas before you begin to write an assignment?	16			
Is revision an important part of your writing strategy?	16			
Are you familiar with the resources and service available from the library on your campus?	17			
Do you approach research in a logical, systematic manner?	17			
Do you follow the recommended six-step approach in writing term papers?	17			

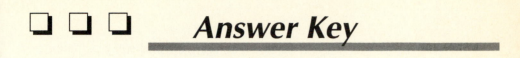

Answer Key

Note:

Answers are not included in this key for those exercises that require lengthy or subjective responses or the underlining and marking of passages, or for class discussion or further analysis exercises. For some exercises, other answers than those given here may be acceptable.

Chapter 1—Learning and Study: Strategies for Success

EXERCISE 1-5

1. Review the purposes of the assignment and evaluate how effectively your paper accomplishes those purposes.
2. Identify why the reading was assigned and how it relates to course content.
3. Establish the purpose of the diagram; write the procedure or concept it illustrates in the margin; understand the relationships among its parts.
4. Predict what the exam will cover and identify necessary materials to review; identify topics or areas of strength and weakness and plan time accordingly.
5. Analyze the context and select the synonym that best conveys your intended meaning; make a note of the word for future reference or study.

6. Identify what principles the lab is intended to demonstrate; identify the purpose of each procedural step.

EXERCISE 1-6

1. Object language is the intended an unintended display of material objects as a form of communication.
2. Object language can include items you own, carry, or use.
3. An example of object language is wearing a pair of expensive, name-brand sneakers.
4. Variable response
5. Variable response
6. Ruesch and Kees's categorization does not include facial expressions. It does not include body movements (such as patting, hugging, etc.) as forms of nonverbal communication.

EXERCISE 1-7

1. Application
2. Application, analysis, synthesis
3. Comprehension
4. Application, analysis
5. Analysis, evaluation
6. Analysis, synthesis, evaluation
7. Analysis, synthesis
8. Comprehension, application, analysis
9. Synthesis
10. Application, analysis, synthesis

Chapter 4—Problem-Solving and Decision-Making Skills

EXERCISE 4-1

1. Forgot note cards; need notecards; solutions: (1) speak with instructor, (2) be absent, (3) go and get them and arrive late, (4) speak without notes
2. Sources unavailable; sources needed; solutions: use another library, change topic
3. Partner is incompatible; want more compatible partner; solutions: request a change, discuss problem with partner, work by yourself

EXERCISE 4-2

1. Problem: supervision of son
   analysis: speak with school principal, seek help from friends and relatives, research cost of babysitter
2. Problem: undecided about curriculum change
4. Analysis: visit career counseling center, research various curriculum choices, study college catalog

EXERCISE 4-3

1. Hire a babysitter; call upon friends, neighbors, or relatives for assistance; pay a senior high escort; take afternoon/evening classes
2. Transfer to a computer-related field; spend a semester as an undeclared major

Chapter 5—Learning and Memory

EXERCISE 5-1

1. Variable response
2. No intent to remember
3. Form three group numbers: Number Seven Theory
4. Selective attention
5. It took more than 20 seconds to walk to another room

EXERCISE 5-2

1. Elaborate rehearsal and recording
2. Elaborate rehearsal and recoding
3. Pictures and diagrams may recode the information presented in the text; they also serve as a form of elaboration
4. The second group recoded the information

EXERCISE 5-3

1. Student did not use recoding; learned by rote memory
2. She used rote learning; information was learned incompletely; she failed to store the information properly; she was unable to retrieve what she had learned; forgetting had occurred
3. a. Motor.
   b. Motor and/or imaginal
   c. maginal and motor

d. Iinguistic and imaginal

e. linguistic

4. You learned it by rote memory in a fixed order.

EXERCISE 5-4

1. Listening or reading about functions and charting procedures; practicing with hypothetical charts; reading an actual patient's chart

2. Listening to song; rote repetition and elaborative rehearsal; repeating or singing the lyrics

3. Listening or reading about parts and functions of ledger; completing practice exercises; balancing sample ledgers

4. Listening or reading about functions and procedures of each key; practices; using computer for specified purpose

EXERCISE 5-5

1. Retroactive interference, if he learned other new numbers the next day; he did not store the information properly so he could retrieve it easily; failure to rehearse the number

2. Elaborative rehearsal; describe robber in words (recode into linguistic code)

3. Proactive interference; old learning of Hebrew may interfere with learning of Spanish. Retroactive interference; he may forget Hebrew words as he learns Spanish ones

4. You could confuse time periods, characteristics, themes, or British and American writers

EXERCISE 5-6

1. Divide into social/economic/emotional or mother/father/children

2. Divide into political, economic, and social or short-, intermediate-, and long-term causes

3. Divide into importance to United States, to Western world, to world economy

4. Divide into short-, immediate-, and long-term problems or air, water, and land problems or divide by cause of problem (e.g., problems caused by water pollution)

EXERCISE 5-7

1. Think of examples of each from everyday speech and/or familiar literature

2. Group according to type or characteristic
3. Elaborate using practical example; group factors into categories
4. Ask questions about each step

EXERCISE 5-8

1. Repetition; use various sensory modes, elaboration; visualization, learn beyond mastery; immediate review
2. Immediate review, visualization, numerous sensory channels, connect with previous learning, retrieval clues, simulate retrieval
3. Numerous sensory channels, recording, elaboration, visualization, connect with previous knowledge
4. Elaboration (practical examples), categorize types (facial, body), retrieval clues, connect with previous knowledge.

Chapter 6—A Systematic Approach to Learning

EXERCISE 6-2

Student A

Situation 1. Draw diagram of courtroom, take notes
Situation 2. Draw map or prepare brief outline
Situation 3. Draw map
Situation 4. Draw a diagram

Student B

Situation 1. Discuss with classmates; think of related trials
Situation 2. Relate to personal experience; discuss with classmates
Situation 3. Think of practical situations that illustrate the differences
Situation 4. Think of situations in which conditioning works or has been applied

Student C

Situation 1. Tape record trial (if allowed); notice issues, principles involved
Situation 2. Write notes and read them aloud; tape record summary notes; look for underlying principles
Situation 3. Tape record your reactions and summary; look for issues and reasons for differences
Situation 4. Look for similarities and differences in forms of conditioning

EXERCISE 6-3

1. A letter requesting a job that has not been advertised
2. Less competition; may arrive just when an opening has occurred
3. May be a waste of time; no opening available
4. Model
5. A folder or record of your credentials

EXERCISE 6-7

1. Check with the reference librarian on availability of reference books that index mythological and biblical characters and terms.
2. Refer to an English handbook.

EXERCISE 6-8

Recall Questions: How has adjusted income changed?
How is income distributed among various age groups?
How is income related to mobility?
How are family characteristics determined by income?
Does poverty increase or decrease during a recession?
What programs alleviate poverty?

Connection Questions: What economic factors caused the historical changes?
What economic factors cause income to be unequally distributed?
How does this information connect to recent lecture topics?

Chapter 7—Patterns of Academic Disciplines

EXERCISE 7-1

1. Chronology
2. Spatial order
3. Process
4. Spatial order
5. Process
6. Chronology
7. Process
8. Order of importance

EXERCISE 7-2

1. Comparison
2. Contrast
3. Contrast

4. Comparison
5. Comparison and contrast

EXERCISE 7-3

Cause	*Effect*
1. Buying decisions	price
2. Data entry system	Difficulty to run
3. Airlines using computerized systems to gain competitive edge	Justice Department investigated
4. Poorly designed systems	Users suffer
5. Time span of nuclear war threats	Forgetting dangers

EXERCISE 7-4

1. Single cause, multiple effects
2. Single cause, single effect
3. Multiple causes, single effect
4. Multiple causes, single effect
5. Multiple causes, multiple effects

EXERCISE 7-5

1. Love, fear, hate
2. Pop, rock, classical, folk
3. Sex, age, racial
4. Civil and military or local, state, and national
5. Drama, poetry, essay, novel

EXERCISE 7-6

2, 4

EXERCISE 7-7

1. A person who participates in amateur or professional sports
2. A behavior intended to mislead or deceive
3. Sounds that produce pleasing or aesthetically worthwhile response
4. An evaluation statement that details your credit history and potential
5. An attitude that regards some people or groups as less valuable to worthwhile than others

EXERCISE 7-8

1, 2, 3, 5

EXERCISE 7-9

1. Cause-effect, listing
2. Listing, classification
3. Cause-effect, chronological order
4. Classification, comparison-contrast
5. Cause-effect, order of importance

EXERCISE 7-10

1. Process
2. Cause-effect
3. Listing, classification
4. Comparison-contrast
5. Process

6. Process
7. Cause-effect
8. Cause-effect, lisitng
9. Comparison-contrast
10. Comparison-contrast, problem solving

EXERCISE 7-11

1. Problem-solution, process
2. Comparison-contrast
3. Cause-effect
4. Comparison-contrast
5. Cause-effect, classification

6. Classification
7. Process, cause-effect
8. Classification
9. Listing
10. Comparison-contrast

Chapter 8—Notetaking for Class Lectures

EXERCISE 8-4

1. Comparison-contrast
2. Process, listing, problem solving
3. Cause-effect, classification
4. Classification, listing
5. Cause-effect

Chapter 9—College Textbooks: Thinking and Learning Strategies

EXERCISE 9-1

This text's rationale, purposes, content overview, special features

EXERCISE 9-4

1. Death, injury, divorce, physical separation
2. Listing, classification, cause-effect
3. Variable response

EXERCISE 9-5

1. Tobacco industry, labor unions, senior citizens
2. Cause-effect, classification, comparison-contrast

EXERCISE 9-6

1. Diversification
2. It is a form of elaboration, providing a realistic example
3. Yes, it shows consequences

EXERCISE 9-8

1. Broader coverage from sick poor to entire community
2. From curative to preventative
3. Chronology, classification

EXERCISE 9-9

1. Positive
2. Independent
3. Inverse

EXERCISE 9-10

1. To show how each of the three branches can influence the others
2. The president appoints the judges
3. The court can declare laws unconstitutional
4. The legislative branch

Chapter 11—Critical Analysis of Course Content

EXERCISE 11-1

Pattern: comparison-contrast
Notetaking: note differences and similarities—evaluate each article using criteria listed. Use a separate sheet for each article

EXERCISE 11-2

1. Fact	6. Opinion
2. Opinion	7. Opinion
3. Fact	8. Fact
4. Opinion	9. Opinion
5. Fact	10. Fact

EXERCISE 11-3

1. Fact
2. Opinion
3. Fact
4. Fact
5. Opinion

EXERCISE 11-5

1. Not a generalization
2. Information on its literacy characteristics and value
3. Facts and statistics on legitimate drug consumption and its profitability
4. Facts about costs of building rentals in various areas of the country
5. Information on creativity and on each example given
6. Research studies on intimacy and verbal communication
7. Not a generalization
8. Not a generalization
9. Not a generalization
10. Statistics on costs of heroin and amount addicts use

EXERCISE 11-6

1. Cosby is a popular well-known figure, and fatherhood is a topic with which nearly everyone has experience as a child
2. McDonald's food and service is popular, and there is no British corporation that can provide equivalent food and services
3. Couples are placing more emphasis on home life and family

EXERCISE 11-7

1. Informed opinion, statistical evidence supporting the reason why it is opposed, examples
2. Informed opinion, examples, historical documentation

3. Statistical data, informed opinion, analogies
4. Personal observation, examples, historical documentation
5. Personal observation, examples

EXERCISE 11-8

1. Room, comfort, world-class
2. Wasted, purposeless
3. Drunken, disgrace, insult
4. Creative genius, far beyond, insights
5. Competitive opportunities, academic excellence unyielding, emphasis, outstanding, commitment, admirable

Chapter 12—Learning Specialized and Technical Vocabulary

QUIZ 1

1. Into a location in the table
2. Phenomenon of some tables being more likely than others
3. One that spreads elements uniformly throughout the table
4. Because they depend on the set of elements that will be encountered in practice
5. Behavior that appears random but that is reproducible

Chapter 13—Study Strategies for Academic Disciplines

EXERCISE 13-1

1. To learn about the beginnings of the field of psychology
2. Choose a focus for the paper (comparison, concentration on contributions, identification with various schools of psychology)
3. Yes, unless the student's text contains detailed information. Encyclopedia, biographical dictionary
4. Comparison-contrast, classification

EXERCISE 13-2

1. The lab is intended to teach process and procedure
2. Science is a means of exploring and solving problems; one needs to be familiar with experimental procedures and learn to record them in order to solve new problems
3. Passive; fails to ask questions and look for purposes

EXERCISE 13-3

1. The student should translate symbols to words
2. The student should verbalize types of problems and their distinguishing characteristics

EXERCISE 13-4

1. Themes in literature are themes that recur throughout life
2. Review the course objectives; talk with his instructor, talk with other students who have taken the course
3. Review class notes, read criticism to get ideas

EXERCISE 13-5

1. Practice performing each procedure on models, if lab is available; make procedure meaningful by concentrating on purpose of each step; avoid rote memorization; use elaboration, visualization
2. Visualize herself completing each procedure; learn beyond mastery through simulated practice

Chapter 15—Reasoning Skills for Taking Exams

EXERCISE 15-1

1. Preview	1–2 minutes
Multiple choice	15 minutes
Matching	5 minutes
Essay	50 minutes
Review	3–4 minutes
2. Previewing	1 minute
True/False	7 minutes
Fill-in-the-blanks	10 minutes
Short answer	20 minutes
Review	2 minutes

EXERCISE 15-2

1. Although . . . skill
2. Patterns . . . lectures
3. Each . . . success
4. It . . . rereading

EXERCISE 15-3

1. Primarily or discovering	F
2. Never	F
3. Often	T
4. Most	F
5. Rarely	F
6. Usually	T
7. Most	T
8. Often	T
9. Primarily	F
10. Exclusively	F

EXERCISE 15-4

1. A	4. D
2. D	5. C
3. C	6. B

EXERCISE 15-5

Topic	Limiting Word	Thought Pattern
1. Trend . . .	long-term effects	cause-effect, listing
2. Monopolies	development, in the nineteenth and twentieth centuries, in America	chronology
3. Industrial Revolution	one effect	cause-effect, listing
4. Cactus growth	reason why	cause-effect, listing
5. War of 1812	events leading up	chronology, cause-effect
6. Textbook marking/lecture notetaking	purposes and procedures	comparison-contrast
7. Textbook chapter	approach to reading and studying	process
8. Lecturer	techniques, important concepts	listing
9. Previewing technique	value, purpose, steps	cause-effect, listing

Chapter 16—Learning Through Writing: Labs, Projects, and Class Assignments

EXERCISE 16-1

1. To discover application of the team production process
2. Application and problem-solving
3. Application of principles of kinetic energy (energy of motion)

Chapter 17—Research and Term Papers

EXERCISE 17-1

1. Analysis and interpretation
2. Consolidation and summarization
3. Original research

EXERCISE 17-4

1. Due to its negatives health effects, cigarette smoking is once again being regarding as a form of deviant behavior
2. Capital punishment is not an effective deterrent to criminal behavior
3. Terrorism is the natural, unavoidable outgrowth of diverse political interests in a world of diminishing resources
4. Career choice is influenced by numerous factors including skill and abilities, attitudes, and life goals
5. AIDS has had a dramatic effect on scientific and medical communities, forcing them to redirect their attention from diverse research interests to a national health issue

References

Sylvan Barnet. *A Short Guide to Writing About Art.* Boston: Little, Brown,1989.

Shirley K. Bell. "Is abortion morally justifiable?" *Nursing Forum,* Vol. XX, No. 3

Louis Berman and J. C. Evans. *Exploring the Cosmos.* 2nd ed. Boston: Little, Brown and Co., 1977.

Robert B. Ekelund and Robert D. Tollison. *Economics.* Boston: Little, Brown and Co., 1986.

J. Ross Eshleman and Barbara G. Cashion. *Sociology: An Introduction.* Boston: Little, Brown and Co., 1985.

Paul G. Hewitt. *Conceptual Physics.* 5th ed. Boston: Little, Brown and Co., 1985.

Walter S. Jones. *The Logic of International Relations.* 5th ed. Boston: Little, Brown and Co., 1985.

Brenda Kemp and Adele Pilitteri. *Fundamentals of Nursing.* Boston: Little, Brown and Co., 1984.

Edward M. Kennedy. "The Need for Handgun Control." *Los Angeles Times,* April 5, 1981.

Robert L. Lineberry. *Government in America.* 3rd ed. Boston: Little, Brown and Co., 1986.

George Miller. "The magic Number. Seven Plus or Minus Two: Some Limits on Our Capacity for Processing Information." *Psychological Review* 63 (1956):81–97.

Kenneth J. Neubeck. *Social Problems: A Critical Approach.* Glenview, IL: Scott, Foresman, 1979.

Robert C. Nickerson. *Fundamentals of Structured COBOL.* Boston: Little, Brown and Co., 1984.

Edward M. Reingold and Wilfred J. Hansen. *Dale Structures.* Boston: Little, Brown and Co., 1983.

Carl E. Rischer and Thomas A. Easton. *Focus on Human Biology.* 2nd ed. New York: HarperCollins, 1995.

Rosemary A. Rosser and Glen L. Nicholson. *Educational Psychology.* Boston: Little, Brown and Co., 1984.

Frederick A. Russ and Charles A. Kirkpatrick. *Marketing.* Boston: Little, Brown and Co., 1982.

Adam Smith. "Fifty Million Handguns." *Esquire,* April, 1981.

H. F. Spitzer. "Studies in Retention." *Journal of Educational Psychology* 30 (1939):641–656.

Roger Starr. "The Case for Nuclear Energy." *New York Times,* Nov. 8, 1981.

Gerald A. Weinberg and Dennis P. Geller. *Computer Information Systems.* Boston: Little, Brown and Co., 1985.

Richard L. Weaver. *Understanding Interpersonal Communication.* 6th ed. New York: HarperCollins, 1993.

419

Endnotes

CHAPTER 1

1. Weaver, p. 283–284
2. Neubeck, p. 247

CHAPTER 5

1. Miller, pp. 81–97
2. Spitzer, pp. 641–656.

CHAPTER 6

1. Ekelund and Tollison, p. XXV.

CHAPTER 7

1. Lineberry, p. 316.
2. Kemp and Pilitteri, p. 194.
3. Nickerson, p. 121.
4. Lineberry, p. 276.
5. Jones, p. 183.
6. Jones, p. 185.
7. Jones, p. 364.
8. Jones, p. 278.
9. Jones, p. 5.
10. Rosser and Nicholson, p. 81.
11. Jones, p. 376.
12. Jones, p. 390.
13. Lineberry, p. 564
14. Lineberry, p. 610.
15. Jones, p. 370.

CHAPTER 10

1. Berman and Evans, p. 145.

CHAPTER 11

1. Lineberry, p. 547.
2. Smith.
3. Smith.
4. Kennedy.
5. Eshleman and Cashion, p. 165.
6. Eshleman and Cashion, p. 313.
7. Bell.
8. Starr, p. 12.

CHAPTER 12

1. Reingold and Hansen, p. 334.
2. Russ and Kirkpatrick, p. 5.

CHAPTER 13

1. Barnet, pp. 21–22.

CHAPTER 16

1. Ekelund and Tollison, p. 156.
2. Weinberg and Geller, p. 178.
3. Hewitt, p. 97.

Credits

Chapter 1, p. 19: From *Understanding Interpersonal Communication,* 6th ed. by Richard L. Weaver II. Copyright © 1993 by HarperCollins College Publishers.

Figure 6-3: From Raymond A. Dumont and John M. Lannon, *Business Communications.* Copyright © 1985 by Raymond A. Dumont and John M. Lannon. Reprinted with permission of Little, Brown and Company.

Figure 9-1: From Sylvan Barnet and Marcia Stubbs, *Practical Guide to Writing,* 4th ed. Copyright © 1983 by Sylvan Barnet and Marcia Stubbs. Reprinted by permission of Little, Brown and Company.

Figures 9-2 and 9-3: From Barbara Schneider Fuhrmann, *Adolescence, Adolescents.* Copyright © 1986 by Barbara Schneider Fuhrmann. Reprinted by permission of Little, Brown and Company.

Figure 9-5: From Clara Shaw Schuster and Shirley Smith Ashburn, *Process of Human Development,* 2nd ed. Copyright © 1986 by Clara Shaw Schuster and Shirley Smith Ashburn. Reprinted by permission of Little, Brown and Company.

Figure 9-6: From Robert L. Lineberry, *Government in Amercia,* 3rd ed. Copyright © 1986 by Robert L. Lineberry. Reprinted by permission of Little, Brown and Company.

Figure 9-7: Robert B. Ekelund and Robert D. Tollison, *Economics.* Copyright © 1986 by Robert B. Ekelund and Robert D. Tollison. Reprinted by permission of Little, Brown and Company.

Figure 9-8: From Frederic S. Mishkin, *Money, Banking, and Financial Markets.* Copyright © 1986 by Mishkin Economics Inc. Reprinted by permission of Little, Brown and Company.

Figure 9-9: Figure from *Geography, A Modern Synthesis* by Peter Haggett. Copyright © 1983 by Peter Haggett. Reprinted by permission of HarperCollins Publishers.

Figure 9-10: From Barbara Walton Spradley, *Community Health Nursing,* 2nd ed. Copyright © 1985 by Barbara Walton Spradley. Reprinted by permission of Little, Brown and Company.

Figure 9-11: Figure from *American Democracy, Institutions, Politics and Policies,* 3rd ed. edited by William J. Keefe. Copyright © 1989 by HarperCollins Publishers.

Figure 9-14: From Randall B. Dunham and Jon L. Pierce, "Figure 7.4 The Effects of the Presence of Others on Task Performance" from *Management.* Copyright © 1989 by Randall B. Dunham and Jon L. Pierce. Reprinted by permission of Scott, Foresman and Company.

Figure 9-15: From Alan L. Prasuhn, *Fundamentals of Fluid Mechanics,* © 1980, p. 36. Reprinted by permission of Prentice-

Hall, Inc., Englewood Cliffs, NJ.

Figure 9-16: From Robert L. Lineberry, *Government in America,* 3rd ed. Copyright © 1986 by Robert Lineberry. Reprinted by permission of Little, Brown and Company.

Figure 10-1: From Hugh D. Barlow, *Introduction to Criminology,* 3rd ed. Copyright © 1984 by Hugh D. Barlow. Reprinted by permission of Little, Brown and Company.

Figures 10-2 and 10-3: From Robert L. Lineberry, *Government in America,* 3rd ed. Copyright © 1986 by Robert L. Lineberry. Reprinted by permission of Little, Brown and Company.

Figure 10-4: From Elliott Currie and Jerome H. Skolnick, *America's Problems.* Copyright © 1984 by Elliott Currie and Jerome H. Skolnick. Reprinted by permission of Little, Brown and Company.

Figure 10-12: From *Focus on Human Biology* by Carl E. Rischer and Thomas A. Easton. Copyright © 1992 by HarperCollins Publishers Inc.

Chapter 11, p. 244: From Adam Smith, "Fifty Million Handguns." Copyright © 1981 by Adam Smith. Reprinted with permission of *Esquire.*

Chapter 11, p. 244: "The Need for Handgun Control" by Senator Edward Kennedy in the *Los Angeles Times,* April 5, 1981. Reprinted by permission of Senator Edward Kennedy.

Chapter 11, p. 254: From Shirley K. Bell, "Is Abortion Morally Justifiable?" *Nursing Forum,* Vol. XX, No. 3. Reprinted by permission of Nursing Forum.

Chapter 11, p. 254: "The Case for Nuclear Energy" by Roger Starr from *The New York Times,* November 8, 1981. Copyright © 1981 by The New York Times. Reprinted by permission.

Chapter 12, p. 264: From Edward M. Reingold and Wilfred J. Hansen, *Data Structures.* Copyright © 1983 by Edward M. Reingold and Wilfred J. Hansen. Reprinted by permission of Little, Brown and Company.

Chapter 12, p. 268: From Frederick A. Russ and Charles A. Kirkpatrick, *Marketing.* Copyright © 1982 by Frederick A. Russ and Charles A. Kirkpatrick. Reprinted by permission of Little, Brown and Company.

Index